Data–Exchange Standards and International Organizations:

Adoption and Diffusion

Josephine Wapakabulo Thomas
Rolls–Royce, UK

A volume in the Advances in IT Standards and Standardization Research (AITSSR) Book Series

Director of Editorial Content: Kristin Klinger
Senior Managing Editor: Jamie Snavely
Assistant Managing Editor: Michael Brehm
Publishing Assistant: Sean Woznicki
Typesetter: Sean Woznicki
Cover Design: Lisa Tosheff

Published in the United States of America by
    Information Science Reference (an imprint of IGI Global)
    701 E. Chocolate Avenue
    Hershey PA 17033
    Tel: 717-533-8845
    Fax: 717-533-8661
    E-mail: cust@igi-global.com
    Web site: http://www.igi-global.com

Library of Congress Cataloging-in-Publication Data

Thomas, Josephine Wapakabulo, 1976-
  Data-exchange standards and international organizations : adoption and diffusion / by Josephine
Wapakabulo Thomas.
      p. cm.
  Includes bibliographical references and index.
  Summary: "This book seeks to establish the factors and barriers critical to the adoption of
data-exchange standards, and ways to accelerate the adoption of these standards"--Provided by
publisher.
  ISBN 978-1-60566-832-1 (hardcover) -- ISBN 978-1-60566-833-8 (ebook) 1. Data transmission
systems--Standards. I. Title.
  TK5105.T44 2009
  004.6'2--dc22
                                    2009025622

This book is published in the IGI Global book series Advances in IT Standards and Standardization
Research (AITSSR) Book Series (ISSN: 1935-3391; eISSN: 1935-3405)

British Cataloguing in Publication Data
A Cataloguing in Publication record for this book is available from the British Library.

Advances in IT Standards and Standardization Research (AITSSR) Book Series

Kai Jakobs (Aachen University, Germany)

ISSN: 1935-3391
EISSN: 1935-3405

MISSION

IT standards and standardization are a necessary part of effectively delivering IT and IT services to organizations and individuals as well as streamlining IT processes and minimizing organizational cost. In implementing IT standards, it is necessary to take into account not only the technical aspects, but also the characteristics of the specific environment where these standards will have to function.

The **Advances in IT Standards and Standardization Research (AITSSR)** book series seeks to advance the available literature on the use and value of IT standards and standardization. This research provides insight into the use of standards for the improvement of organizational processes and development in both private and public sectors.

COVERAGE

- Analyses of standards-setting processes, products, and organization
- Descriptive theory of standardization
- Emerging roles of formal standards organizations and consortia
- Intellectual property rights
- Management of standards
- National, regional, international and corporate standards strategies
- Open Source and standardization
- Risks of standardization
- Technological innovation and standardization
- User-related issues

IGI Global is currently accepting manuscripts for publication within this series. To submit a proposal for a volume in this series, please contact our Acquisition Editors at Acquisitions@igi-global.com or visit: http://www.igi-global.com/publish/.

The Advances in IT Standards and Standardization Research (AITSSR) Book Series (ISSN 1935-3391) is published by IGI Global, 701 E. Chocolate Avenue, Hershey, PA 17033-1240, USA, www.igi-global.com. This series is composed of titles available for purchase individually; each title is edited to be contextually exclusive from any other title within the series. For pricing and ordering information please visit http://www.igi-global.com/book-series/advances-standards-standardization-research-aitssr/37142. Postmaster: Send all address changes to above address. Copyright © 2010 IGI Global. All rights, including translation in other languages reserved by the publisher. No part of this series may be reproduced or used in any form or by any means – graphics, electronic, or mechanical, including photocopying, recording, taping, or information and retrieval systems – without written permission from the publisher, except for non commercial, educational use, including classroom teaching purposes. The views expressed in this series are those of the authors, but not necessarily of IGI Global.

Titles in this Series

For a list of additional titles in this series, please visit: www.igi-global.com

Evolution and Standardization of Mobile Communications Technology
DongBack Seo (University of Groningen, The Netherlands)
Information Science Reference • copyright 2013 • 328pp • H/C (ISBN: 9781466640740)
• US $195.00 (our price)

Information Technology for Intellectual Property Protection Interdisciplinary Advancements
Hideyasu Sasaki (Ritsumeikan University, Japan)
Information Science Reference • copyright 2012 • 412pp • H/C (ISBN: 9781613501351)
• US $195.00 (our price)

Frameworks for ICT Policy Government, Social and Legal Issues
Esharenana E. Adomi (Delta State University, Nigeria)
Information Science Reference • copyright 2011 • 350pp • H/C (ISBN: 9781616920128)
• US $180.00 (our price)

Data-Exchange Standards and International Organizations Adoption and Diffusion
Josephine Wapakabulo Thomas (Rolls-Royce, UK)
Information Science Reference • copyright 2010 • 336pp • H/C (ISBN: 9781605668321)
• US $180.00 (our price)

Toward Corporate IT Standardization Management Frameworks and Solutions
Robert van Wessel (Tilburg University, Netherlands)
Information Science Reference • copyright 2010 • 305pp • H/C (ISBN: 9781615207596)
• US $180.00 (our price)

Standardization and Digital Enclosure The Privatization of Standards, Knowledge, and Policy in the Age of Global Information Technology
Timothy Schoechle (University of Colorado, USA)
Information Science Reference • copyright 2009 • 384pp • H/C (ISBN: 9781605663340)
• US $165.00 (our price)

DISSEMINATOR OF KNOWLEDGE

www.igi-global.com

701 E. Chocolate Ave., Hershey, PA 17033
Order online at www.igi-global.com or call 717-533-8845 x100
To place a standing order for titles released in this series,
contact: cust@igi-global.com
Mon-Fri 8:00 am - 5:00 pm (est) or fax 24 hours a day 717-533-8661

Table of Contents

Section 1:
Standardization and IT Standards

Section 2:
Adoption and Diffusion Case Studies

Foreword

Throughout a career in the Royal Air Force spanning almost 40 years, ranging from operational aircraft maintenance engineer and to the Chief Executive of the RAF Logistics Support Services Agency, I have been involved in the creation, maintenance and exploitation of logistics information to provide improved support to complex platforms and equipments. As the CE LSSA in 1997, I 'owned' the data collected from the RAF corporate information systems and applications that managed engineering and asset management, inventory management, technical documentation and item codification. Each of these systems and applications held data about the same ranges of equipment; some of the data items, such as product description, were the same, and some were peculiar to the application requirements. However, it was impossible to integrate the outputs from these systems to derive a coherent view of the performance of an equipment and its support environment. The benefits to be gained from resolving this issue were self evident but the technology was not available. In the absence of a suitable integration mechanism, we were obliged to resort to manual manipulation of data and graphical presentation which demanded a high degree of user interpretation and deduction of performance relationships.

In 1999, I joined LSC Group and began to understand the potential power of data standards to provide an exchange mechanism for complex engineering information between disparate systems. 1999 was also the year when the PLCS initiative was launched to extend the scope of ISO 10303, the Standard for Exchange of Product Model data, from exchange of CAD/CAM data to address the more complex performance and feedback requirements for a product and its support environment throughout the in-service phase of the product life cycle. Over the intervening seven years, I have seen PLCS develop into a highly robust information exchange standard, which has the structure to capture all of the data elements from the wide range of disparate logistics information systems and applications in an open neutral format. I have been personally involved as a defence logistics subject matter expert in the development of the various LSC Group STEP/PLCS proofs of concept and early demonstrators, and I remain excited by the emerging capability that the use of open standards offers to address the information integration challenges that I left behind in 1999.

However, on the down side, I have been less than excited by the resistance to recognise the potential benefits from the adoption of a standards based approach to information integration by both the MoD and Industry at large. There are many reasons for this, some associated with natural resistance to change, others associated with commercial and vested interests, but the main reason is lack of awareness of the potential power and availability of information standards to meet today's and tomorrow's challenges. There is also a view that the development of information standards is a specialist activity, far divorced from the realities of practical logistics engineering and conducted by 'anoraks and geeks', speaking a different language to the real world. Having had a foot in both camps over the years, I can partially sympathise with this view, but I also recognise how far the role of standards has come in providing workable solutions to the underlying issues of data integration.

Hence, I see this work by Josephine as being both timely and of crucial importance in identifying the reasons behind the resistance to adopt open standards more widely and in recommending guidelines to facilitate and accelerate the process of standards adoption. The decision to combine two established approaches into a single research methodology was innovative and courageous, requiring original thought and concept development to derive a coherent framework that could be tested and validated through case study research and direct feedback from interviews and questionnaires. This approach proved to be successful, providing Josephine with good qualitative information upon which to base her findings and recommendations, a factor which will be of increasing importance as other bodies pick up and take forward this research. I am aware that in the course of her research, Josephine has engaged with many eminent specialists in the data standards world, in industry, in academia and throughout the MoD, and she has gained their respect for her understanding of the issues, the thoroughness of her work and the positive recommendations for the way forward. This will carry great weight in the near future, and I look forward to seeing this work becoming a standard reference during the inevitable ongoing debate over the adoption of data exchange standards.

Air Commodore Ian Sloss CEng FRAeS RAF (Retd)
LSC Group

Ian Sloss joined the Royal Air Force in 1963 as an Aircraft Apprentice and was commissioned in 1969 following an Engineering Cadetship at the RAF College, Cranwell. He followed a traditional aircraft engineering management route, working on Vulcans, Tornados and Victors, and covered front line operations through to deep maintenance with staff tours in Munich and London. In 1988, he attended the Joint Services Defence College, Greenwich and in 1994 he was appointed as Commandant, No 1 Radio School and Station Commander, RAF Locking, serving as Aide de Camp to Her Majesty, The Queen. He was promoted to air commodore in 1996 and posted to RAF Wyton as Chief Executive of the Logistics Support Services Defence Agency. Since his retirement from the RAF in 1999, he has worked for LSC Group, primarily responsible for the management and development of an advanced technology team.

Preface

The evolution and advancement of company working environments, management structures, and manufacturing approaches has made the need for effective and accurate exchange of data more critical. In light of this, Product Life cycle Management (PLM) has emerged as a business strategy for creating, sharing, validating and managing a company's product related intellectual capital within and across the extended enterprise over the entire life cycle spectrum from conception to retirement (Rachuri et al., 2008). Within this extended enterprise, product data is essential to the enterprise, or as King (2002b) asserts it is the 'strategic through-life asset' of the enterprise. Poor data management and the exchange of product data that is inaccurate, incomplete or ambiguous compromises the quality of a product resulting in either an increase in the costs associated with maintaining the quality of a manufactured product over its life cycle, or expensive rework costs. This is exemplified in the manufacture of the Airbus A380. The manufacturing consortium was composed of four prime contractors from France, Germany, Spain and the United Kingdom (Airliners.net 2005), and as Rothman (2006) states, "engineers in Germany and Spain stuck with an earlier version of Paris-based Dassault Systemes SA's CATIA design software, even though the French and British offices had upgraded to CATIA 5" (p.1). As a result of this interoperability oversight Airbus had difficulties installing wiring, causing delays that significantly cut deliveries of the A380 and had costs to the business.

PRODUCT DATA EXCHANGE: CHALLENGES AND SOLUTIONS

The advent of computing technology in the 1960s revolutionised the way product data was represented and exchanged. Nevertheless, as Computer Aided Design and Manufacturing (CAx) tools proliferated into the market to meet increasingly complex and diverse PLM needs for effective data exchange, so did the formats each tool used to capture and store product data (Kemmerer, 1999). Additionally, companies often acquired varying systems without regard for the requirements of application integration or data integration, exchange and sharing. As a consequence product data was and still is created and stored in multiple, often incompatible formats, leading to interoperability problems both between and within companies (Gallaher et al., 2002). A study commissioned by NIST reported that imperfect interoperability imposes at least a billion dollars per year on the members of the US automotive supply chain (Brunnermeier & Martin, 1999). The report goes on to indicate that as much as 86% of the costs are attributed to mitigating data exchange problems related to repairing and replacing unusable data files. Ruchuri et al. (2006) offer further evidence of how big the interoperability problem really is by referencing an example where, "of 13 million engineering hours spent on (a recent aircraft program), 8 million were spent on data correction and administration" (p.16).

In response to the challenges and costs associated with product data exchange, four main solutions have been put forward. They include: 1) The manual re-entry of data, which raises potential costs from employee time sent inputting data to hidden costs associated with maintaining and storing redundant data, and rectifying error prone data. 2) The 'single' system approach, which can provide cost saving advantages by reducing diversity and cutting down, training, maintenance and acquisition costs. However, the single system approach forces suppliers to maintain redundant systems and does not eliminate interoperability problems. 3) The use of direct translations, which can achieve very high quality results and work reasonably well for some well-defined data translation. However, cooperation between vendors can tend to be limited because the development of viable translators often requires the disclosure of proprietary information about software, which vendors are understandably reluctant to share with competitors (Gallaher et al., 2002). 4) The open neutral approach which is based on the idea of developing an agreed specification or standard for data exchange that is not dependent on any proprietary computer system and is universally understood and accepted for data-exchange.

Of the four approaches, the open neutral format is often championed as the best approach to mitigate the problems associated with product data exchange. Over the years there have been a number of product data-exchange standards in use (Ravat & Nazemetz, 2003), and these standardizing activities for product data descriptions started with IGES back in the 1970s and branched out over the following years. However, IGES had major shortcomings because it was conceived as a mechanism to convey two-dimensional engineering information and was limited in its ability to transmit data from three-dimension solids (Gallaher et al., 2002). Additionally, these earlier standards tended to be bounded by their restriction to graphical and geometrical information (ProSTEP, 2004). Therefore, in order to override this problem and curb the development of a multitude of standards, work began in the mid-80s on developing a new open neutral standard known as ISO 10303 that is informally known as STEP - Standard for the Exchange of Product Data. STEP built upon the lessons learned from the previous standards and had the advantage of not just focusing on basic descriptions of what data is, but what data means and how data relate to each other (Kemmerer, 1999). A study commissioned by the US National Institute of Standards and Technology (NIST) found that STEP, has the potential to reduce mitigation and avoidance interoperability costs in the aerospace, automotive and shipbuilding industries by approximately \$928 million (2001\$) a year (Gallaher et al., 2002). Studies like these show the benefits and importance of using data-exchange standards to enable technical and business information to be shared electronically throughout an extended manufacturing enterprise (Ray & Jones, 2006).

ADOPTION OF DATA-EXCHANGE STANDARDS

Interestingly, despite the studies carried out by organizations like NIST, and the general belief that standards are a vital approach to dealing with product data exchange problems, the uptake of these standards has often fallen below expectations. Indeed, Meister (2004) points out that even though STEP is in use in companies around the world, the adoption of STEP has not been as widespread as initially expected despite the large amounts of resources that have gone into its development. Meister notes that STEP has had, at-best, mixed implementation results. Other authors such as McEwan (1995, as cited in Gallaher et al., 2002) and Rachuri et al. (2006) agree with the sentiment that the acceptance and adoption of STEP by manufacturers and software developers has been very slow. Brunnermeier and Martin (1999) list a number of issues which they believe have hampered industry's commitment to STEP, including:

- The significant investment required to develop a solution that will benefit all members of the industry;
- The technical risk associated with developing STEP translators;
- The market risk caused by competitive rivalries among the companies that develop CAD/CAM software and translators; and
- The need for an unbiased expert to negotiate, develop, and implement industry standards (p.ES-7).

This debate around the lack of involvement of software vendors in the standards process is frequently raised in STEP related literature. Generally software vendors main fear is that by providing open neutral capability through standards, their customers will find it easier to change to different system. Dreverman (2005) described this as the software vendors' fear of loosing their 'lock-in' advantage. Indeed, software vendors benefit when their customers have significant investment in legacy data, support systems and user training material they provide, and this is particularly true for vendors with a large market share who are reluctant to introcuce capabilities that will lower swticing costs (Gallaher et al. 2002).

The slow adoption of STEP is not only related to software vendor involvement. The long development timescales of standards like STEP appear to impact their adoption. Weston and Whiddett (1999) point out that time seems to be one of the major faults of standards. Dreverman (2005) made a similar discovery in his study, and goes on to explain that even though new technological developments like XML are not substitutes for STEP, they draw attention away from efforts surrounding STEP, particularly when the new standards yield benefits in a shorter time period. Other authors offer varying views on the reasons for the slow adoption of STEP. Dreverman (2005) carried out a study into the adoption of product model data standards like STEP in the process industry. Dreverman (2005) sought to establish the factors that impede or slow the adoption of these standards within the process industry. Dreverman used factor analysis and actor analysis to establish the issues surrounding three named standards. The factor analysis was based mainly around the factors identified in Diffusion of Innovation (DOI) theory, and the actor analysis described how the motives, power and actions of the various actors in the process industry affected the adoption of the standards. This study offered insight into the developmental and organizational factors that impact the adoption of these standards. Meister (2004) carried out a longitudinal study of the development and implementation of STEP over 20 years from the perspective of ISO/TC184/SC4 committee members. This study offered insight into the developmental and organizational factors that impact the adoption of data-exchange standards from the perspective of the ISO/TC184/ SC4 community. Meister (2002) conducted an additional similar study that offered a more comprehensive, empirically backed discussion into the common concerns managers need to recognise and anticipate in order to minimise the negative outcomes of using standards for manufacturing connectedness.

RESEARCH ON DATA-EXCHANGE STANDARDS ADOPTION

The literature surrounding these data-exchange standards indicates that a fairly large corpus of information is available with regards to the history, practical implementation and benefits of data-exchange standards like STEP (Kemmerer, 1999). However, there was limited empirical research that looked at the often complex and interrelated factors that influence the adoption of product data standards like STEP. The exceptions being the work done by Dreverman (2005) and Meister (2004).

A review of the wider literature surrounding the adoption of IT standards revealed that most research was based on two theories; DOI theory and a theory often termed "the Economics of Standards". Most DOI studies build on Rogers (2003) sociology model for the adoption and diffusion of technology innovations. This model captures the characteristics of the innovation, communication channels and social system as they interact over time. Rogers (2003) lists five innovation attributes that influence the adoption decision, these include: relative advantage, compatibility, complexity, trialability and obervability. In addition to classical diffusion of innovation theory, the adoption of standards has been studied from an economic perspective (Fichman & Kemerer, 1993; Katz & Shapiro, 1986). This stream of diffusion research is often labelled as "economics of standards", and focuses on an innovation's inherent economic value for potential adopters. Two main theories have been used within this economic stream. The first related theory is network effects. Network analysis is often based upon the theory of positive network effects, or network externalities, which describes a positive correlation between the number of users of an artefact and the utility of the artefact (Katz & Shapiro, 1985).

However, there is still limited empirical research that addresses the issues relating to the development, the adoption and the outcome of IT standards (Markus et al. 2003). Further testament of this was shown in a study carried out by King and Lyytinen (2003), who found that, "there have been relatively few scholarly papers on standardization informing the scholarly discussion in the IS field". King and Lyytinen (2003) go onto state that, "slightly more than 2% of the published journal articles in three top journals in the IS field (MISQ, ISR, CACM) have dealt with standards over the past 10 years. Moreover, most of this work has reported on newly established ICT standards rather than examining the events, factors and impacts related to standard setting processes" (p.2). This finding resulted in the commissioning of a special issue of MISQ on 'standard making' in 2003. What the literature revealed is that there is a requirement for further empirical research into the factors that impact the adoption of adapt-exchange standards. Therefore, the research presented in this book seeks to establish the factors and barriers critical to the adoption of data-exchange standards, and ways to accelerate the adoption of these standards using case studies and action research.

West (1999) contends that most research on innovation adoption focuses on a single innovation and who adopts that innovation. This is an innovation-centric approach. Another stream examines a single adopter, usually an organization, and the innovations it adopts. This is referred to as an adopter-centric approach. West (1999) continues his discussion by commenting that innovation-centric diffusion research tends to have a pro-adoption bias, with late adopters labelled "laggards". This bias is weaker in the study of adopting organizations, which instead demonstrates a bias towards the ability to adopt any innovation rather than any particular innovation. In order to limit the level of bias the research presented in this book seeks to offer a balanced analysis into the factors that influence the adoption and diffusion of data-exchange standards by taking both an innovation-centric and adopter-centric approach.

ORGANIZATION OF BOOK

Chapter 1

Chapter 1 gives background to the motivations behind this book, an overview of the STEP standard and the aims and objectives of the research presented in this book.

Chapter 2

This chapter presents a literature review, as a background to the research presented in this book. The initial sections of the chapter offer a brief introduction into the history of standards and an overview of standardization, and the IT standards research domain as a whole. West (2003) revealed that there is still a significant lack of direct standards related research within the IS community and went on to identify IT standards adoption as a domain that still required research. Therefore, Chapter 2 chronicles how the research presented in this book is not only filling a gap within the STEP and SC4 communities, but is also making a contribution the wider body of knowledge surrounding IT standards adoption research.

Chapter 3

This chapter builds on the literature review by assessing in more depth the models and theories that have been used to study the adoption of IT and data-exchange standards. The chapter begins by giving an overview of terminology and meanings associated with the terms 'diffusion' and 'adoption' in light of the current research. Chapter 3 introduces the novel approach of taking both an innovation-centric and adopter-centric view to address the research question, and chronicles the development of two conceptual models that capture the key factors researched.

Chapter 4

This chapter discusses the justifications for the overall research philosophy and approach subscribed to, and the multiple data collection and analysis methods used to collect sufficient data to fulfil the research aims.

Chapter 5

The unit of analysis in this innovation-centric approach is the innovation itself, which in this case is the set of ISO data-exchange standards. The chapter starts by introducing the ISO technical committee and subcommittee responsible for the development of the standards. The factors identified in the original innovation-centric model are then tested and verified against the collected data. The final sections discuss the current rate of adoption and way forward for the two chosen standards and present a revised model for the innovation-centric adoption of data-exchange standards.

Chapter 6

This chapter presents an analysis of the factors that impact the adoption of standards within the UK Ministry of Defence (MoD). The chapter starts by giving a brief overview of the MoD and the three standards that are the focus of this study. Following on from that is a detailed analysis of the factors and barriers critical to the adoption and diffusion of the three standards within the MoD. This analysis is carried out using the constructs identified in the original adopter-centric model. The concluding section presents the revised adopter-centric model.

Chapter 7

This chapter builds on the findings of Chapter 5 and 6. The innovation-centric and adopter-centric models developed in these chapters are used to create two novel 'Adoption Checklists'. The checklists are a series of questions that can be used to assess the adoptability of a data-exchange standard. The checklists have been developed so that positive answers to the series of questions indicate that a standard is more likely to be adopted. Therefore, the aim of this chapter is to chronicle the development of the checklists, which are based on the factors that have been identified as critical for the adoption and diffusion of data-exchange standards.

Chapter 8

In this chapter, the adoptability of PLCS (ISO 10303-239) is analyzed using the innovation-centric checklist developed in Chapter 7. The chapter starts by assessing each part of the checklist factors based around the four main categories of conception, standards process, standards specifications and adoption conduciveness. Following on from that, an analysis of the completed adoption checklist is carried out.

Chapter 9

This chapter presents the results of the application of the adopter-centric "Adoption Checklist" on the adoption of PLCS in the UK MoD. The chapter begins by looking at the primary adoption issues covered by the questions. Subsequently, the data obtained from a workshop based around the use of PLCS is used to give a more detailed insight into the secondary adoption issues. The final sections give an overview of the adoption of PLCS within the MoD and assess the way forward for data-exchange standards such as PLCS within the MoD.

Chapter 10

This chapter revisits the necessity for this research and summarises the whole book. This summary begins with an overview of the aims and objectives of the research, followed by a detailed account of the findings and novel contribution made. The concluding section presents recommendations for the different stakeholder groups impacted by this research and further work that can be done by practitioners and researchers involved in the development, implementation and use of data-exchange standards.

SCOPE AND DISCLAIMER

Due to this diversity of standards within IT, a broad generalisation is beyond the scope of this research. However, it is hoped that by examining standards adoption in the product data-exchange standards domain within the oil and gas and defence community, standards researchers and IT departments working in the field of product data standards will be able to use the results of these case studies as a frame of reference and guidelines to support the ongoing research, development and adoption of data-exchange standards. Finally, any comments attributable to MoD employees (as part of the interview process) reflect the thoughts of the individuals and not necessarily those of the UK MoD.

REFERENCES

Airliners.Net. (2005). *The Airbus A380 - Aircraft data.* Retrieved July 15, 2005, from http://www.airliners.net/aircraft-data/stats.main?id=29

Brunnermeier, S., & Martin, S. (1999). *Interoperability Cost Analysis of the U.S. Automotive Supply Chain.* Research Triangle Park, NC: Research Triangle Institute.

Dreverman, M. (2005). *Adoption of Product Model Data Standards In the Process Industry.* Eindhoven, The Netherlands: Eindhoven University of Technology.

Fichman, R., & Kemerer, C. (1993). Adoption of Software Engineering Process Innovations: the Case of Object Orientation. *MIT Sloan Management Review, 34* (2), 7-22.

Gallaher, M., O'connor, A., & Phelps, T. (2002). *Economic Impact Assessment of the International Standard for the Exchange of Product Model Data (Step) In Transportation Equipment Industries.* Project Number 07007.016. NC: RTI International.

Katz, M., & Shapiro, C. (1985). Network Externalities, Competition, and Compatibility. *American Economic Review , 75* (3), 424-440.

Katz, M., & Shapiro, C. (1986). Technology Adoption in the Presence of Network Externalities. *Journal of Political Economy, 94* (4), 822-841.

Kemmerer, S. (1999). *STEP: The Grand Experience.* Gaithersburg, MD: National Institute of Standards and Technology.

King, T. (2002b). Requirements for Access To Technical Data -- An Industrial Perspective. *The 18th International Codata Conference — Frontiers of Scientific and Technical Data - Book of Abstracts* (pp. 40-41). International Council for Science: Committee On Data for Science and Technology.

King, J., & Lyytinen, K. (2003). *Proceedings of MISQ Special Issue Workshop On Standard Making: A Critical Frontier for Information Systems - Call for Papers.* Retrieved November 17, 2003, from http://www.si.umich.edu/misq-stds/misq/cfp.pdf

Markus, M., Steinfield, C., & Wigand, R. (2003). The Evolution of Vertical Is Standards: Electronic Interchange Standards in the US Home Mortgage Industry. In J. King, & K. Lyytinen (Ed.), *Proceedings of MISQ Special Issue Workshop On Standard Making: A Critical Frontier for Information Systems* (pp. 80-91). Seattle: MISQ Quaterly.

Meister, D. 2. (2004). *STEP Through 20 Years: Lessons and Theoretical Implications - Working Paper Edn.* Faculty of Information Systems, Richard Ivey School of Business. London, Canada: University of Western Ontario.

Meister, D. (2002). Manufacturing Connectedness: Managerial Challenges and Solutions. In M. Warkentin (Ed.), *Business-To-Business Electronic Commerce: Challenges & Solutions* (pp. 114-131). Hershey, PA: Idea Group Publishing.

ProSTEP. (2004). *Organization / History (ISO)*. Retrieved July 16, 2004, from ProS-TEP Web site: http://www.prostep.org/en/standard-info/what-is-step/organisation-history-iso.html

Rachuri, S., Subrahmanian, E., Bouras, A., Fenves, S. J., Foufou, S., & Sriram, R. D. (2008). Information sharing and exchange in the context of product lifecycle management: Role of standards. *Computer Aided Design, 40* (7), 789-800.

Rachuri, S., Foufou, S., & Kemmerer, S. (2006). *Analysis of Standards for Lifecycle Management of Systems for US Army - A Preliminary Investigation*. Gaithersburg, MD: NISTIR 7339 National Institute of Standards and Technology.

Ravat, J., & Nazemetz, J. (2003). *Introduction to STEP*. School of Industrial Engineering and Management: Computer Assisted Technology Transfer (CATT) Research Program, Contract Number F34601-95-D-00376. OK: Oklahoma State University.

Ray, S., & Jones, A. (2006). Manufacturing Interoperability. *Journal of Intelligent Manufacturing, 17* (6), 681-688.

Rogers, E. (2003). *Diffusion of Innovations*. New York: Simon & Schuster International.

Rothman, A. (2006). *Airbus Vows Computers Will Speak Same Language After A380 Delay*. Retrieved November 16, 2008, from Bloomberg.com: http://www.bloomberg.com/apps/news?pid=20601085&sid=aSGkIYVa9IZk

West, J. (1999). Organizational Decisions for I.T. Standards Adoption: Antecedents and Consequences. *Proceedings of the 1st IEEE Conference on Standardisation and Innovation in Information Technology* (pp. 13-18). Washington, DC: IEEE.

Weston, L., & Whiddett, R. (1999). Factors Affecting the Adoption of IS Standards. In B. Hope, & P. Yoong (Ed.), *Australasian Conference on Information Systems* (pp. 1158-1169). Wellington, New Zealand: Victoria University of Wellington.

Acknowledgment

I would like to acknowledge Steve Probets and Ray Dawson, from Loughborough University, and Tim King from LSC Group, for their invaluable help, guidance and support during the course of this research and book writing. I would also like to thank LSC and Loughborough University department of Information Science for providing the sponsorship that enabled this work to be done.

Special thanks to all the interviewees who agreed to take part in the research and to those who continued to generously give of their time even after the interviews. A big thank you to Ann, Andy, Kevin and Jez from LSC, for the many interesting discussions we had that helped make this book richer. Special thanks to my Rolls-Royce colleagues for your support during the months it has taken to complete this book.

Special thanks to Kai Jakobs for proposing the idea to write this book, and to the publishing team at IGI Global, particularly Joel Gamon, who was a constant support throughout this process. I would also like to thank the reviewers for the insights they offered to enhance the content of the book.

On a personal level I would like to thank my husband Barry Thomas for his encouragement and unfailing support during this whole period, and my family in Uganda and America who have continually been a support.

Josephine Wapakabulo Thomas
March 2009

Trademarks

The following trademarked software tools are mentioned in the book and need to be acknowledged:

- ATLAS.ti© is a copyright of ATLAS.ti Scientific Software Development GmbH.
- SPSS© is a copyright of SPSS Inc.
- NUD.IST© is a copyright of QSR International Pty Ltd.
- Windows© is a copyright of the Microsoft Corporation.
- Microsoft Excel© is a copyright of the Microsoft Corporation.
- Macintosh© is a copyright of Apple Computer Inc.
- Oracle's XML Developer Kit© is a copyright of Oracle.

Chapter 1
General Introduction

INTRODUCTION

A study commissioned by the US National Institute of Standards and Technology (NIST) found that ISO 10303, the Standard for the Exchange of Product Model Data (STEP), has the potential to reduce mitigation and avoidance interoperability costs in the aerospace, automotive and shipbuilding industries by approximately $928 million (2001$) a year (Gallaher, O'connor, & Phelps, 2002). Studies like these show the benefits and importance of using data-exchange standards to enable technical and business information to be shared electronically throughout an extended manufacturing enterprise (Ray & Jones, 2006). The literature surrounding these data-exchange standards indicates that a fairly large corpus of information is available with regards to the history, practical implementation and benefits of

DOI: 10.4018/978-1-60566-832-1.ch001

data-exchange standards like STEP (Kemmerer, 1999). However, a further review of the literature shows that there is very limited empirical research into the factors that impact the adoption of data-exchange standards. This means that practitioners devoted to the ongoing development and use of standards like STEP, and academics, still lack a significant body of evidence regarding the factors and barriers critical to the adoption of these standards. The research reported in this book seeks to address this gap by developing conceptual models for data-exchange standards adoption, which are tested through a series of qualitative case studies and action research.

This chapter begins by giving an overview of the emergence and development of product data-exchange standards like STEP and the rationale behind the research presented. Following on from that is an overview of current work and research relating to the adoption of STEP. The aim, objectives and scope of this research are then stated.

PRODUCT DATA EXCHANGE

Increased competitiveness among manufacturing organizations means companies are no longer able to compete solely on the cost or functionality of their products. More emphasis is being placed on the quality, and reliability of their products and the ability to respond quickly to customer needs (Fowler, 1995). This increased competitiveness has contributed to the rise of the concept of the "extended enterprise", where companies have to work more closely with their suppliers, customers and partners in order to shorten product development life cycles and to highlight potential problems as early as possible (Al-Timimi & McKrall, 1996). Subsequently, Product Life cycle Management (PLM) has emerged as a business strategy for creating, sharing, validating and managing a company's product related intellectual capital within and across the extended enterprise over the entire life cycle spectrum from conception to retirement (Rachuri et al., 2008).

Data is intellectual capital that is created, revised, updated and used throughout the life cycle of a product, and within these collaborative and extended working environments, companies are increasingly dependent on the effective and accurate exchange of product data with their different partners (Ray & Jones, 2006). Consequently, product data is essential to the enterprise, or as King (2002b) asserts it is the 'strategic through-life asset' of the enterprise. This is largely due to the use of product data in the decision-making process. Poor data management and the exchange of product data that is inaccurate, incomplete or ambiguous compromises the quality of a product resulting in either an increase in the costs associated with maintaining the quality of a manufactured product over its life cycle, or expensive accidents. This is highlighted in the case of the Mars Climate Orbiter Crash of 1999, the loss of the $125 million spacecraft was attributed to the fact that its spacecraft and navigational teams were using different units of measure, as was noted on CNN. com, "one engineering team used metric units while another used English units for a key spacecraft operation" (CNN, 1999).

Computer-Based Product Data Exchange

The advent of computing technology in the 1960s revolutionised the way product data was represented and exchanged. According to a historical review done by PTC Inc. (PTC Express, 2000), in 1961, Ivan Sutherland developed the first mathematical equations for Computer Aided Design (CAD) in his thesis, SKETCHPAD. The PTC white paper goes on to quote Orr, a consultant, speaker and writer in engineering automation and computing technologies as proposing that Sutherland's thesis is the foundation of all of CAD as it exists today. Following from that, the evolution of CAD systems began and enterprises began to develop internal CAD and Computer Aided Manufacturing (CAM) packages. Finally, in 1984, a company called Autodesk introduced the first CAD program written strictly for the Personal Computer (PC), and work in this field has continued to grow into the Computer Aided Design and Manufacturing (CAx) industry it is today (PTC Express, 2000).

Drawings created with CAx tools represented tremendous productivity gains over paper drawings, offering improved accuracy and quality, greater speed, reduced costs of rework and the ability to perform additional analysis of models and designs before moving to production. Nevertheless, as CAx tools proliferated into the market to meet increasingly complex and diverse PLM needs for effective data exchange, so did the formats each tool used to capture and store product data (Kemmerer, 1999). What transpired was the existence of dissimilar computer-aided systems that lead to the technological legacy of 'islands of automation' or 'islands of information' that were identified during the 1970s and 1980s (Fowler, 1995). King (2002a) postulates that these islands emerged, in part at least, from the piecemeal, unplanned acquisition of computer systems without regard for the requirements of application integration or data integration, exchange and sharing. As a consequence product data was and still is created and stored in multiple, often incompatible formats, leading to interoperability problems both between and within companies (Gallaher et al., 2002).

Gallaher et al. (2002) explain that CAx interoperability problems generally fall into two categories, data exchange problems and data quality problems. They go on to point out that Original Equipment Manufacturers (OEMs) and their suppliers incur data exchange related costs when dealing with the need to:

- Maintain multiple CAx systems,
- Repair files that are translated incorrectly,
- Manually reenter data that cannot be translated;
- Scrap designs and tooling that are defective because of imperfect interoperability.

However, even when data transfers are successful, data quality issues can still lead to imperfect interoperability, and while data exchange problems are usually obvious, many data quality problems are not easily detectable (Gallaher et al., 2002). Some industries like the automotive industry have taken the initiative to deal with data quality issues. The Strategic Automotive product data Standards Industry Group (SASIG) decided to develop ISO/PAS 26183:2006 as a common set of guidelines on the aspects of product data quality. According to the ISO website (ISO, 20006), ISO/PAS 26183:2006 provides a broad range of information, divided into the following three main sections.

- Section I provides introductory and background material that frames the product data quality problem. Topics covered include the nature of product data, high-level product data quality issues, and how to use this document.
- Section II contains specific product data quality criteria for users. In this version, the content focuses primarily on CAD geometry, though other topics are also at least partially addressed. The criteria describe specific problems that can occur and suggest how to measure them and what to do when they occur.
- Section III provides information and methods that will help improve product data quality. The topics covered range from readiness for change to reward systems to supporting technologies such as tools for checking data.

Authors such as Wang (1998) and Batini and Scannapieco (2006) offer a more detailed discussion on PDQ. However, for the purpose of this book primary focus is being given to interoperability challenges associated more closely with data exchange problems.

CAx interoperability problems are further compounded by the disparity between the lifetime of computer systems and the lifetime of complex engineering assets. These complex engineering assets, like for example, aircrafts, ships, buildings and industrial plants, have a lifetime measured in decades, or longer. In contrast, as shown in Figure 1, the application software used to process the data can have a lifetime of three to five years and the operating systems may have lifetimes that are less than three years (King, 2003).

Figure 1. A comparison of the lifetime of computer systems and complex engineering assets

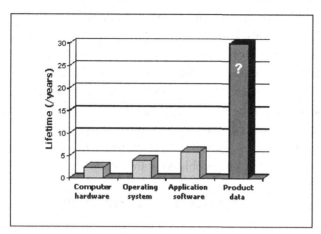

The challenge is that often each new computing system will need to access data that is created, manipulated and archived using previous systems, this will require maintaining all versions of older computer systems in order to be able to access legacy data, which would be costly.

The economic impact of ineffective interoperability can be high. Indeed, a study commissioned by NIST estimated that interoperability problems in the product development stage alone cost the U.S. automotive industry approximately $1 billion a year primarily due to the need to support multiple CAx systems and correct errors in product data exchange (Brunnermeier & Martin, 1999). In a more recent example, the lack of integrated data systems is reported to have also hampered U.S. reconstruction efforts in Iraq. According to (Rachuri, Foufou, & Kemmerer, 2006) Gen. Lance Smith, Commander U.S. Joint Forces Command, is quoted as stating, "I can't begin to tell you how much of that $18 billion was spent on just trying to get systems to talk to one another" (p.16).

The challenges of poor interoperability are not limited to different CAx systems, the lifetime of application software means that interoperability can exist be between two versions of the same CAx system. This was highlighted in the manufacture of the Airbus A380. The manufacturing consortium was composed of four prime contractors from France, Germany, Spain and the United Kingdom (Airliners.net 2005), and as Rothman (2006) states, "engineers in Germany and Spain stuck with an earlier version of Paris-based Dassault Systemes SA's CATIA design software, even though the French and British offices had upgraded to CATIA 5" (p.1). Rothman goes on to quote Charles Champion, the A380 program's one-time chief, as stating that, "That meant the German teams couldn't add their design changes for the electrical wiring back into the common three- dimensional digital mockup being produced in Toulouse" (p.1). As a result of this interoperability oversight Airbus had difficulties installing wiring, causing delays that significantly cut deliveries of the A380. In the Rothman article Champion is further quoted as stating "Attempts to have common tools failed for various reasons. It's all about legacy: When you start to use a tool, changing tools is an enormous investment. The question is always, what is the business case to change tools?" (p.1). However, Wong (2006) in his analysis of what grounded the Airbus A380 postulates that the cost of sidestepping the investment to deal with tool changes resulted in an enormous loss of about US$6.1 billion over four years for Airbus. These examples showcase the importance and need to address interoperability problems within PLM.

Addressing Product Data Exchange Problems

Rachuri et al. (2006) note that the importance of effective interoperability across the phases and functions in PLM have been recognized by a number of institutions including NIST, the US Department of Defense (DoD), the European Ministries of Defense and, more recently, by the vendor and end-user communities. In order to enable effective interoperability, a review of the literature reveals four main approaches to deal with data exchange problems (Fowler, 1995), namely:

1. **Manual re-input of data:** Manual re-input of data is carried out when the output of one computer system is physically entered into a different system. This solution raises potential costs from employee time sent inputting data to hidden costs associated with maintaining and storing redundant data, and rectifying error prone data.
2. **Adoption or imposition of a single "standard" system:** In this situation every participant within a particular supply chain use the same system. Elements of this approach have been adopted within most companies and can offer cost saving advantages by reducing diversity and cutting down, training, maintenance and acquisition costs. However, creating an infrastructure where all companies use the same computing systems is difficult to incorporate, especially when companies can be dealing with many clients at one time, each with their own "standard" system. In the end, either the customer or supplier becomes responsible for data translation, and often companies with strongest market position tend to try and set the 'standard' system, putting a load on smaller companies further down the supply chain. Ultimately, the single system approach forces suppliers to maintain redundant systems and does not eliminate interoperability problems (Rachuri et al., 2008).

Figure 2. A comparison of the number of translations required for 'point-to-point' and standards-based data exchange

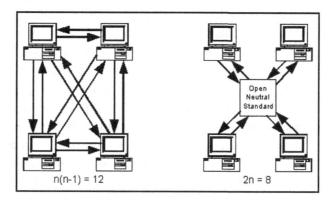

3. **Direct translation:** The drawbacks of manual re-input and system standard-ization have led to the use of point-to-point customised solutions, which are achieved by the use of system converters. Converters change one data format into another through direct translations. These translations can achieve very high quality results and work reasonably well for some well-defined data translation tasks and there are software packages available that accomplish this, but these packages can be costly and require updating with each system update. In addition, converters are "point solutions" and the number of transla-tions increases non-linearly with the number of computer systems, as shown in Figure 2. That is, n (n-1), where n is the number of computer systems. This approach requires a high degree of vendor cooperation for the development of direct translators. However, this cooperation tends to be limited because the development of viable translators often requires the disclosure of proprietary information about their software, which vendors are understandably reluctant to share with competitors (Gallaher et al., 2002).

4. **Open neutral translations:** The final approach involves the use of open neutral standards. This neutral approach is based on the idea of developing an agreed specification or standard for data exchange that is not dependent on any proprietary computer system and is universally understood and accepted for data-exchange. Standardization calls for all relevant participants within the extended enterprise to be able to import and export information using the same data formats. The use of standards has the benefit of eliminating the drawbacks of the direct translation approach, which is limited to 'point solu-tions' and high maintenance costs. The use of data-exchange standards also has the benefit of allowing systems to be added, upgraded or removed with little or no impact on remaining systems, and the number of translations is now

reduced to twice the number of computing systems, 2n, as shown in Figure 2. The use of data-exchange standards is not without its challenges, a reduction in number of translations does not guarantee error free translations, and data repair and recovery activities may still need to take place. Furthermore, Gielingh (2008) highlights the fact that additional challenges are caused by differences between the internal schemas of CAx applications. Gielingh rightly notes that the internal schema of a CAx system strongly influences its performance and functionality, and a vendor who wants to be distinctive will usually offer more functionality then a data-exchange standard permits. Consequently two vendors may claim to use the same standard, but the scope of their internal schemas may vary, causing interoperability problems. The only way to avoid this is for the vendors to strictly conform to the standard and restrict their internal schemas. This is not always an appealing option to CAx vendors and it could be argued that this might be one of the reasons some vendors are reluctant to provide software based on data-exchange standards. Issues like this ultimately have an impact on the subsequent adoption of a standard, and more detailed discussion of the challenges faced by open neutral standards and the impact on adoption of these standards are discussed in the data analysis presented in Sections I and II of this book.

DATA-EXCHANGE STANDARDS

Over the years there have been a number of product data-exchange standards in use (Ravat & Nazemetz, 2003), such as the Initial Graphics Exchange Specification (IGES), The Electronic Design Interchange Format (EDIF), Data-exchange File or Format (DXF), Standard D'Exchange et de Transfert (SET) and Verband Der Automobilindustrie-Flachen-Schnittstella (VDA-FS), full descriptions of each of these standards can be found in Appendix A. These standardizing activities for product data descriptions started with IGES back in the 1970s and branched out over the following years. However, IGES had major shortcomings because it was conceived as a mechanism to convey two-dimensional engineering information and was limited in its ability to transmit data from three-dimension solids (Gallaher et al., 2002). Additionally, these earlier standards tended to be bounded by their restriction to graphical and geometrical information (ProSTEP 2004). Therefore, in order to override this problem and curb the development of a multitude of standards, work began in the mid-80s on developing a new open neutral standard known as ISO 10303. The official title of ISO 10303 is 'Industrial automation systems and integration - Product data representation and exchange', and the standard is informally known as STEP - Standard for the Exchange of Product Data. STEP built upon the lessons learned from the previous standards and had the advantage of not just focusing on basic descriptions of what data is, but what data means and how data relate to each other (Kemmerer, 1999).

Overview of STEP

The first parts of STEP were published as an international standard in 1994 under the banner of the International Standards Organization (ISO) Technical Committee 184 (Industrial Automation Systems and Integration), and the Sub-Committee 4 (Industrial Data) also known as ISO/TC184/SC4. What emerged from the standardization effort has been a comprehensive series of documents, which provide industry with the ability to exchange and share information used to describe a product, both throughout the supply chain and throughout the entire life cycle of the product (Manson, 2002).

The architecture of STEP was built as a series of parts to provide a capability for product data exchange, sharing and archiving. The main parts of STEP are:

- Parts 1x: Description methods
- Parts 2x: Implementation methods
- Parts 3x: Conformance testing methodology and framework
- Parts 4x to 6x: Integrated generic resources
- Parts 1xx: Integrated application resources
- Parts 2xx: Application Protocols (AP)
- Parts 3xx: Abstract Test Suites (ATS) for APs
- Parts 4xx: Application Protocol Modules
- Parts 5xx: Application Integrated Constructs (AIC)
- Parts 1xxx: Application Modules (AM)

A more detailed description of STEP and the STEP architecture can be found at the ISO/TC184/SC4 website (SC4Online, 2009).

According to Part 1 of the standard, STEP enables 'the computer-interpretable representation and exchange of product data. The objective is to provide a mechanism that is capable of describing product data throughout the life cycle of a product, independent from any particular system. The nature of this description makes it suitable, not only for neutral file exchange, but also as a basis for implementing and sharing product databases and archiving' (Al-Timimi & McKrall, 1996). STEP data models are defined using the EXPRESS data modelling language, which itself is Part 11 of the standard. EXPRESS has both textual and graphical notations with the latter known as EXPRESS-G. A STEP implementation is an application that uses this standard to exchange product information, or makes it possible for other applications to do so (Loffredo, 2002). Parts 201 to 240 detail the implementable data specifications of STEP known as Application Protocols (AP). Examples of APs include:

- **AP203:** Configuration – controlled 3D design of mechanical parts and assemblies
- **AP224:** Mechanical product definitions for process planning using machining features
- **AP239:** Product life cycle support

STEP Application Protocols (AP's) are the main parts that are relevant to Cax vendors and end-users. STEP APs consist of three elements, an Application Activity Model (AAM), which provides an understanding of the scope, information requirements and usage scenarios for the exchange of product data, an Application Reference Model (ARM), which documents high level application objects and the basic relations between them, and an Application Interpreted Model (AIM), which is a set of information models containing constructs that can be shared by multiple AP's (Gielingh, 2008). Additionally, every AP defines one or several Conformance Classes, suitable for a particular kind of product or data exchange scenario.

STEP Adoption and Research Motivation

STEP is already in use within the CAD community and enables the sharing of the underlying analysis information in industries such as aerospace, automotive, shipbuilding and construction (Manson, 2002). Working alongside many of these industry groups are a number of software vendors, such as Eurostep, EPM Technology and STEPtools Inc., who specialise in developing software solutions based on STEP. Another company, LSC Group, who are co-sponsors of this research, have a team devoted to the development and implementation of STEP and they are currently engaged in a number of STEP development and implementation projects. Specific sets of projects are underway in the UK Ministry of Defence (MoD) using various STEP Application Protocols. Some examples include a series of pilots and demonstrations that are looking at the practical implementation of STEP AP239, which is informally known as PLCS.

During the development and preparation of some of the projects that were being undertaken in conjunction with LSC Group, questions began to be raised, during informal discussions, with regards to whether the standard, PLCS, would be successfully adopted or not, who would adopt the standard and would there be delays in its adoption? It was recognised that a key to answering these questions would involve analysis of the general adoption of the underlying data-exchange standard,

STEP. Indeed, Meister (2004) points out that even though STEP is in use in companies around the world, the adoption of STEP has not been as widespread as initially expected despite the large amounts of resources that have gone into its development. Meister notes that STEP has had, at-best, mixed implementation results. Other authors such as McEwan (1995, as cited in Gallaher et al., 2002) and Rachuri et al. (2006) agree with the sentiment that acceptance and adoption of STEP by manufacturers and software developers has been very slow. Gallaher et al. (2002) propose four major issues that have impeded the use of STEP down the supply chain:

1. The lack of capable STEP translators for AP203 and other formally approved STEP parts in PC-based CAD systems,
2. The lack of STEP APs providing the capabilities needed for many applications,
3. The lack of knowledge about STEP and what it provides in such companies, and
4. Customers do not necessarily advocate the use of STEP.

A further review of the literature surrounding STEP, revealed extensive studies on the history of STEP, the implementation technologies surrounding STEP, the use of STEP, and shortcomings of data-exchange standards like STEP within various industry groups (Kemmerer, 1999; Loffredo, 1998; Kauhaniemi, 2003; Zhang & Warren, 2002; Gielingh, 2008). However, there was a significant lack of studies devoted to the factors and barriers critical to the adoption of STEP. Two noted exceptions are research carried out by Dreverman (2005) and Meister (2004). Dreverman carried out a study into the adoption of product model data standards like STEP in the process industry. This study offered insight into the development and organizational factors that impact the adoption of data standards. Meister carried out a longitudinal study of the development and implementation of STEP over 20 years from the perspective of ISO/TC184/SC4 committee members.

This initial literature review highlighted the fact that there was very limited empirical research into the factors that impact the adoption of data-exchange standards like STEP. This means that academics and practitioners, such as LSC Group, who are devoted to the ongoing development and use of these data-exchange standards, still lack a significant body of evidence with regards to the factors that influence their adoption. This reaffirmed the need for a more in-depth study into the factors and barriers critical to the adoption of data-exchange standards, and led to the development of the two main research questions that acted as a basis for the research presented in this book:

- What are the factors and barriers critical to the adoption and diffusion of data-exchange standards across their target population?
- What can be done to facilitate and accelerate the adoption of data-exchange standards across their targeted population?

The next section details the aims and objectives that have been established to answer these research questions poised.

CONCLUSION

Research Aim and Objectives

This research seeks to contribute to the current limited body of knowledge available relating to the adoption of data-exchange standards. The two main aims of this research are:

1. To establish the factors and barriers that influences the adoption of data-exchange standards.
2. To develop guidelines to facilitate and accelerate the adoption of data-exchange standards.

In order to establish the factors and barriers that influence the adoption of data-exchange standards and to answer the research questions posed, the following objectives were pursued to provide guidance and direction to realise the aims of the study:

- Develop a preliminary conceptual model that identifies the factors and barriers critical to the adoption of data-exchange standards, through the study of published literature.
- Revise and refine the preliminary conceptual models by analyzing the information obtained from interviews and other data sources related to the adoption and diffusion of two ISO/TC184/SC4 standards and two military standards, and.
- Further refine and test the preliminary conceptual model against the current adoption and implementation of PLCS using a 'Standards Adoption Checklist' developed from the conceptual model.
- Present recommendations to facilitate the adoption of data-exchange standards in general and PLCS specifically, from the experience gained in the above objectives.

Research Scope and Target Audience

The main aim of this research is to establish the factors that influence the adoption and diffusion of data-exchange standards across their target populations. The purpose being to develop a model and 'Standards Adoption Checklist' that translates into frames of reference and guidelines that can be used to support the decision-making process in the development, adoption, implementation and evaluation of new and emerging standards such as PLCS. However, as Rachuri et al. (2008) point out, Product Life cycle Management (PLM) is a multi-dimensional information exchange undertaking, that requires a variety of contents be exchanged within and across a number of disciplines and functions over time. Consequently, a range of standards is needed to support PLM. A topology of the standards that can be used to support PLM first presented by Subrahmanian at al. (2005) and reported by Rachuri et al. (2006) has the following categories:

Type Zero: Standards for Implementation Languages

These languages include programming, scripting, assembly-level and other computable languages used to implement the remaining standards in the topology. Examples include Basic, FORTRAN, C, C++, Java, C#, Prolog.

Type One: Information Modeling Standards

EXPRESS and UML (Unified Modeling Language) are two examples of information modeling languages. XML Schema is also becoming popular for expressing the structure and typing constraints for data embedded in XML documents. Other semantically rich information modeling language standards include, Knowledge Interchange Format (KIF), Resource Description Framework (RDF) and Ontology Web Language (OWL).

Type Two: Content Standards–Domains of Discourse

The standards relate to information models specifically defined for particular domains using a Type One standard or an extended one. Content standards subdivide into several categories based on the specialization of the content addressed. These include:

- Product information modeling and exchange standards - Standards like STEP would come under this category.

- Information exchange standards - Examples of information exchange standards are the electronic data interchange (EDI) and the simple object access protocol (SOAP) standards.
- Product visualization standards - Product visualization standards address the issue of rendering and editing the graphics objects and creating object schema repositories. Examples include the U3D graphics standard and X3D which is an XML-enabled 3D standard for real-time communication of 3D data.
- E-business and value chain support standards - Extensions to XML have been developed to describe the business activities associated with all phases of satisfying customer demand, e.g electronic business XML (ebXML), commerce XML (cXML) and RosettaNet.
- Security standards – These standards deal with how much of the information needs to be exchanged and with whom, which is important from the point of view of information overload, intellectual property rights and security. Various organizations such as the NIST Information Technology Laboratory and the World Intellectual Property Organization (WIPO) are establishing international standards in this area.

Type Three: Architectural Frameworks Standards

In order to achieve interoperability between the standards within the PLM context, standards will need to be integrated. To integrate different types of standards, it is necessary to take into consideration the architectural frameworks for creating integrated support systems. A number of integration framework standards have been proposed, such as the Zachman Framework, the Department of Defense Architecture Framework (DoDAF) and the Federal Enterprise Architecture Framework (FEAF).

Based on the topology presented by Rachuri et al. (2006), it is important to note that this research is primarily targeted at Product information modeling and exchange standards, more particularly data-exchange standards like STEP. Therefore, the applicability of the findings presented in this book are limited to data-exchanges standards and related product data technologies. Additionally, within the wider IT community (beyond PLM), standards are required for varying degrees of interoperability between various programming languages, applications, software and hardware all working to varying numbers of standards. Furthermore, the standards community knows that often for the same application or functions there may be several applicable standards (McCaleb, 1999). Due to this diversity of standards, a broad generalisation is beyond the scope of this research. However, it is hoped that by examining standards adoption in the product data-exchange standards domain within the oil and gas and defence community, standards researchers and IT departments working in the field of product data standards will be able to use the results of these case studies as a frame of reference and guidelines to support the ongoing research, development and adoption of data-exchange standards.

REFERENCES

Airliners.Net. (2005). *The Airbus A380 - Aircraft data.* Retrieved July 15, 2005, from http://www.airliners.net/aircraft-data/stats.main?id=29

Al-Timimi, K., & Mackrell, J. (1996). *STEP: Towards Open Systems.* Michigan: Cimdata Inc.

Batini, C., & Scannapieco, M. (2006). *Data Quality: Concepts, Methodologies and Techniques* (Data-Centric Systems and Applications). New York: Springer-Verlag.

Brunnermeier, S., & Martin, S. (1999). *Interoperability Cost Analysis of the U.S. Automotive Supply Chain.* Research Triangle Park, North Carolina: Research Triangle Institute.

CNN. (1999). *NASA's metric confusion caused Mars orbiter loss.* Retrieved November 17, 2002, from CNN.com: http://edition.cnn.com/TECH/space/9909/30/mars.metric/

Dreverman, M. (2005). *Adoption of Product Model Data Standards in the Process Industry.*

Egyedi, T., & Verwater-Lukszo, Z. (2004). Coping With Flexibility: Standards in IT and the Batch Processing Industry. In F. B. Bousquet (Ed.), *Proceedings from the 9th Euras Workshop On Standardization* (pp. 105-120). Paris: Accedo Verlag.

Fowler, J. (1995). *STEP for Data Management Exchange and Sharing.* Twickenham, UK: Technology Appraisals Ltd.

Gallaher, M. O'connor, A., & Phelps, T. (2002). *Economic Impact Assessment of the International Standard for the Exchange of Product Model Data (STEP) In Transportation Equipment Industries.* Project Number 07007.016. North Carolina: RTI International.

Gielingh, W. (2008). An Assessment of the Current State of Product Data Technologies. *Computer Aided Design, 40*(7), 750–759. doi:10.1016/j.cad.2008.06.003

ISO. (20006). Retrieved March 31, 2008, from ISO/PAS 26183:2006: http://www.iso.org/iso/iso_catalogue/catalogue_tc/catalogue_detail.htm?csnumber=43436

Kauhaniemi, M. (2003). *How Step and Related B2b Standards Support Integrated Product Data Exchange In the Web Environment.* T-86.161 Special Topics in Information Technology for Production II. Helsinki, Finland: Helsinki University of Technology.

Kemmerer, S. (1999). *STEP: The Grand Experience.* Gaithersburg, MD: National Institute of Standards and Technology.

King, T. (2002b). Requirements for Access To Technical Data -- An Industrial Perspective. *The 18th International Codata Conference — Frontiers of Scientific and Technical Data - Book of Abstracts* (pp. 40-41). International Council for Science: Committee On Data for Science and Technology.

King, T. (2003). *Implementation of ISO 10303 Enabled Business Processes.* PLCS Training. Tamworth, UK: LSC Group.

Loffredo, D. (1998). *Efficient Database Implementation of Express Information Models.* Troy, MI: Rensselaer Polytechnic Institute.

Loffredo, D. (2002). *Fundamentals of STEP Implementation.* Retrieved November 13, 2002, from STEP Tools Inc. Web site: http://www.steptools.com/library/fundimpl.pdf

Männistö, T., Peltonen, H., Martio, A., & Sulonen, R. (1998). Modelling Generic Product Structures in STEP. *Computer Aided Design, 30*(14), 1111–1118. doi:10.1016/S0010-4485(98)00067-0

Mason, H. (2002). ISO 10303 – STEP a Key Standard for the Global Market. *ISO Bulletin, April* (1), 9-13.

Mccaleb, M. (1999). A Conceptual Data Model of Datum Systems. *Journal of Research of the National Institute of Standards and Technology, 104*(4), 349–400.

McEwan, I. (1995). *In STEP with suppliers: GM's perspective on product data exchange.* Retrieved December 18, 2002, from AutoFact '94, PRONews: www.scra.org/uspro//events/gm_persp.html

Meister, D. (2004). *STEP Through 20 Years: Lessons and Theoretical Implications - Working Paper Edn.* Faculty of Information Systems, Richard Ivey School of Business. London, Canada: University of Western Ontario.

ProSTEP. (2004). *Organization / History (ISO).* Retrieved July 16, 2004, from ProSTEP website: http://www.prostep.org/en/standard-info/what-is-step/organisation-history-iso.html

Rachuri, S., Foufou, S., & Kemmerer, S. (2006). *Analysis of Standards for Lifecycle Management of Systems for US Army - A Preliminary Investigation.* Gaithersburg, MD: NISTIR 7339 National Institute of Standards and Technology.

Rachuri, S., Subrahmanian, E., Bouras, A., Fenves, S. J., Foufou, S., & Sriram, R. D. (2008). Information sharing and exchange in the context of product life-cycle management: Role of standards. *Computer Aided Design, 40*(7), 789–800. doi:10.1016/j.cad.2007.06.012

Ravat, J., & Nazemetz, J. (2003). *Introduction to STEP.* School of Industrial Engineering and Management: Computer Assisted Technology Transfer (CATT) Research Program, Contract Number F34601-95-D-00376. OK: Oklahoma State University.

Ray, S., & Jones, A. (2006). Manufacturing Interoperability. *Journal of Intelligent Manufacturing, 17*(6), 681–688. doi:10.1007/s10845-006-0037-x

Rothman, A. (2006). *Airbus Vows Computers Will Speak Same Language After A380 Delay.* Retrieved November 16, 2008, from Bloomberg.com: http://www.bloomberg.com/apps/news?pid=20601085&sid=aSGkIYVa9IZk

SC4Online. (2009). *STEP Overview.* Retrieved January 18, 2009, from ISO TC184-SC4.org: http://www.tc184-sc4.org/sc4_open/sc4%20legacy%20products%20(2001-08)/step_(10303)/

Subrahmanian, E., Sudarsan, R., Fenves, S. J., Foufou, S., & Sriram, R. D. (2005). Challenges in supporting product design and manufacturing in a networked economy: A PLM perspective. *Proceedings of the International Conference on* (pp. 495-506). Lyon: Inderscience Publishers.

Wang, R. Y. (1998). A Product Perspective on Total Data Quality Management. *Communications of the ACM, 41*(2), 58–65. doi:10.1145/269012.269022

Wong, K. (2006). *What Grounded the Airbus A380?* Retrieved March 11, 2009, from Cadalyst.com: http://management.cadalyst.com/cadman/article/articleDetail.jsp?id=390124

Zhang, J., & Warren, T. (2003). *SMEs and STEP.* School of Industrial Engineering and Management: Computer Assisted Technology Transfer (Catt) Research Program, Contract Number F34601-95-D-00376. Oklahoma State University.

Section 1
Standardization and IT Standards

This section encompasses and captures developments, controversies and break-throughs engaging practitioners within standards adoption research. This section also sets out in great detail precisely what was researched and why, the overall aim being to carry the academic discussion forward through the development of conceptual models.

Chapter 2

Benefits, Classifications and Research Surrounding Standardization and IT Standards

INTRODUCTION

Standards have been in existence since the beginning of recorded history. One of the earliest indications of a standard is the beginning of written alphabets by the Egyptians and Babylonians around 4000 BC (Krechmer, 1996). Another example of early standards effort is the work done by Shih Huang-Ti, the founder of the Chinese Empire, under whose reign the Great Wall was built. He enforced one law, one weight, and one measure to rule out discord and confusion between petty states. The standards proposed by the Chinese Emperor were used only for the construction of the Great Wall and are no longer used today, but the testament of his efforts are still seen today. (Perry, 1955 as cited in Deshpande & Nazemetz, 2003a)

DOI: 10.4018/978-1-60566-832-1.ch002

The term "standard" has multiple definitions. Indeed the Oxford English dictionary offers up to thirty different definitions of the word "standard" (OED Online, 2005). However, a commonly cited definition is one offered by the International Organization for Standardization (ISO), which defines a standard as: "A document, established by consensus and approved by a recognized body, that provides, for common and repeated use, rules, guidelines, or characteristics for activities or their results, aimed at the achievement of the optimum degree of order in a given context" (ISO/IEC, 1996).

Although this definition sheds light on what a standard is, it does not give an indication of the multiple dimensions of a standard. These additional dimensions relate to issues like how a standard is developed, when a standard is developed and why a standard emerges. The remainder of this section addresses some of these dimensions by looking at the standardization process, the benefits of standardization and the classification of standards.

The Standardization Process

The standardization process, which deals with the development and utilisation of standards, is characterised by intricate interactions between stakeholders and organizations known as 'standardizers'. According to the National Standardization Strategic Framework (NSSF, 2004a), these standardizers may be formal or informal alliances of public and private sector groups which are set up to assist the standardization process and work with stakeholders to develop solutions appropriate to their needs. These stakeholder needs, which may be sourced from business, government or society, drive the standardization process. Therefore, standardization activities bring together representatives from different stakeholder groups with diverse needs. These groups include: regulators, researchers, standards developers, standards sellers, standards purchasers, trainers, consultancies, certification and accreditation bodies, testing houses as well as users of the standards themselves (NSSF, 2004a). Figure 1 in the previous chapter, which is an adaptation and extension of the NSSF 'standardization map', depicts these interactions through a macro view of the standardization process (NSSF, 2004b). Looking at the right of Figure 1 in Chapter 1 it is evident that the perceived 'outcome' of the standardization process is the realisation of socio-economic benefits.

The NSSF recognise in their supporting notes that their original map only focuses on the 'outcomes' of the standardization process, which are the socio-economic benefits, and not the 'outputs'. Therefore, the original map was adjusted and extended to indicate the 'outputs' of the standardization process, which are the 'publication of standards', and 'the adoption and use of standards'.

Figure 1. Overview of the standardization process

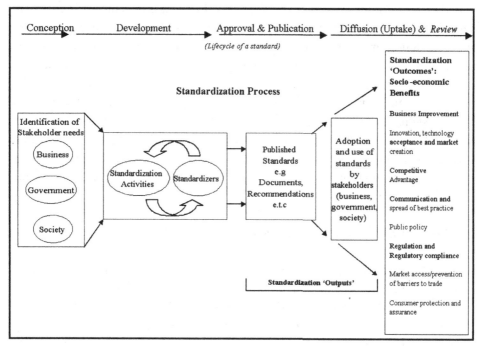

A further addition to the standardization map was the inclusion of the life cycle stages of a standard alongside the macro view of the standardization process. These life cycle stages are shown at the top of Figure 1, and this addition was made to provide both a macro and micro level view of the standardization process. The life cycle stages shown in the micro level view include:

- Conception
- Development
- Approval and Publication
- Diffusion (Uptake) and Review.

Various researcher and standard development organizations offer different breakdowns of the life cycle stages of a particular standard or standards in general. The mentioned stages were a compilation of the commonly agreed stages. There is also general consensus amongst different authors that there is overlap in the activities carried out during the different stages in the life cycle of a standard (Weiss & Spring, 2000; Deshpande & Nazemetez, 2003a).

The nature of standardization varies in different regions. For example, in the United States (US) the system of standards development is decentralised and there is a dichotomy between standards developers representing professional societies and those representing trade associations. Thus with over 600 private sector organizations involved in standards development, the US system is often described as pluralistic, sometimes fragmented, ad hoc and market-driven. In contrast, the European Community (EC) model has significant government influence and is a closed system, integrated at both national and regional levels. Participation in formal standards development activities at the regional level is limited to authorised representatives of European national standards bodies. Hence, the EC model is often considered monolithic, integrated, formalistic and policy-driven (Deshpande & Nazemetz 2003b).

The Benefits of Standardization

This link between standardization and economic performance at a macro UK economic level and at micro business level, is extensively documented but often under acknowledged (NSSF, 2004c). The NSSF estimate that, at a macro level, the effective use of standards can contribute 1% or more to GDP (Gross Domestic Product). Likewise, in Germany an extensive study initiated by DIN, the German Institute for Standardization, revealed that the benefits of standardization to the national economy amounts to more than US$ 15 billion per year, and standards contribute more to economic growth than patents and licences (DIN, 2000). In addition, some company position papers (Daimler Benz, 1998) have identified the benefits of standardization to individual companies, and Swann and Temple offer insight into the role of standards in promoting international trade (Swann, 2000).

These studies show that, at the simplest level, standards define crucial aspects of the operation, safety, reliability and quality of products, processes and services. This advances societal benefits, promotes health and safety, reassures customers and enables markets to work effectively both nationally and internationally. However, despite the contribution that the work involved in the conception, development and subsequent publication of standards makes towards the knowledge economy, there is general agreement that the publication of standards alone is not enough to create these true economic benefits (Swann, 2000). The value of standards to business and indeed the economy at large comes from the effective and efficient adoption, use and uptake (diffusion) of a standard across its target population. In other words, the effective adoption and diffusion of a standard is vital to the standardization process for economic benefits to be realised (Swann, 2000). Therefore, the focus of this research, is to look at the factors that influence the adoption and diffusion of data-exchange standards, is important in ensuring that practitioners devoted to the ongoing development and use of data-exchange standards, and academics, gain increased knowledge and understanding of these factors to ensure the benefits derived from using such standards are fully realised.

Classification of Standards

Andrew Tanenbaum is quoted as stating that, "The nice thing about standards is that there are so many to choose from" (Culshaw, 2006, pp.1). This is particularly evident when looking at the way in which standards are classified. One of the most often-cited classification schemes relates to how a standard is developed, or in other words, the origins of a standard. Using this classification, numerous standards development organizations at global (e.g. ISO, IEEE), regional (e.g. NATO, CEN), and national (e.g. BSI, DIN) levels produce what are often referred to as de-jure standards. In contrast to de-jure standards, standards are also set through the market on a de-facto basis, by a vast range of industry partners and consortia. In addition to the de-jure and de-facto classification, other authors have classified standards based on a wide range of dimensions such as, for example:

- Geographic – for example international, national or regional standards
- Industrial sector – for example, agricultural, extraction, manufacturing, and service (Deshpande & Nazemetz, 2003b)
- Function – for example product, process and control standards (Iversen, 2000)
- Conformance Requirement – for example, mandatory, regulatory or voluntary standards (Weiss, 1993; Bonino & Spring, 1999).

This list is by no means exhaustive, but gives some indication of what has sometimes been termed as the 'impenetrable maze' of what are generally called 'standards' (Jakobs, 2002).

Krechmer (2000b) offers a more holistic view of standards classification. Based on his approach, standards are classified in four ways, namely: unit and reference, similarity, compatibility, and etiquette standards. These classes relate to the waves of human progress in history, technology, communication and value systems. Krechmer (1996) contends that standards, like humans and technology, follow an evolutionary path. He goes on to explain that, "Multiple standards are created and over time winnowed down to the most desirable and culturally acceptable standards that codify the technical requirements developed during the preceding wave. Future waves build upon the previous technical work, by reference to the standards. Standards developed during one wave thus become the foundation upon which the technologies for the next wave are built".

Krechmer (1996) explains that unit and reference standards define measurable physical qualities, for example the mile and litre. In addition, reference standards of economic value (currency) are the basis of monetary systems (Krechmer, 2000b). The purpose of these standards is to achieve a sense of commonality or sameness that would have a replication effect. Equally, similarity standards define the allowed variations within a set of similar entities, for example paint colour and metal gauges. The purpose of these similarity standards is to achieve repeatability, which would enable harmonisation between like objects. The next group, which is classed as compatibility standards, define the interface between two or more mating elements that are compatible rather than similar, for example a plug and socket, or a transmitter and receiver. The purpose of these standards is to achieve inter-working. The final class, known as etiquette standards, define the initial negotiation between independent communicating processes for the purpose of establishing communications. Examples of etiquette standards include the Aloha protocol (Laynetworks, 2006), and modem handshakes. Etiquette standards are also being used to support wireless access, for example WINForum. The purpose of these standards is to achieve expandability resulting in systems having the ability to negotiate variable aspects of the physical layer process (Krechmer, 1996).

Summary

This section has detailed the importance of standardization, and emphasised the need for effective adoption and use of standards in order that the socio-economic benefits of standardization are realised. This section has also highlighted the numerous ways to classify standards, and Krechmer's (1996, 2000b) approach was analyzed in more detail because he offers valuable insight into the emergence of IT standards in relation to the historic evolution of standards in general. The next section delves deeper into the world of IT standards by giving an overview of standardization in the IT sector, the history of IT standards and research into such standards.

INFORMATION TECHNOLOGY STANDARDS

Individuals, businesses and governments throughout the world use Information Technology (IT) extensively. Indeed, the International Data Corporation predicted that information technology spending would grow to $1.1 trillion, in 2007 (Kawamoto, 2003). Consequently, in order to facilitate this extensive use of IT, systems need to be interconnected and work across applications, organizations and geographic locations (Burrows, 1999). This has resulted in a dramatic increase in network connections, a proliferation of computing devices and a varied application of IT.

These interactions highlight the critical need for a comprehensive and consistent set of standards within the IT sector (Spring et al., 1995). The definition of IT that has been adopted with regards to IT standards is similar to the definition proposed by West (2004) who states that, "we will define "IT" to refer to those information technologies (i.e. related to computers and communications) used by organizations, whether such technologies are acquired from external producers or produced internally by the organization". West (2004) goes on to explain that, "Because "IT" is most commonly used in IS journals, it is the term used in this article, but in this context it includes any communications products or services procured by organizations. In this regard, it updates the usage of the term in response to the call of Hansen (2004) to study communications technology, but excludes the consumer-oriented technologies often subsumed by the ICT classification". Therefore, the definition of IT used in this book covers both computers and communication products and services.

History and Classification of IT Standards

Standards activities in the IT sector began in the 1960s. Early standardization efforts were for programming languages like Fortran and Cobol and protocols for moving information around, such as the ASCII standard for encoding letters and symbols. As Ray (2002) points out, "these early standards typically focused on the way in which information was to be encoded (the syntax), and only peripherally described the nature of the information being standardized (the content)" (p.66). Other early standardization efforts included the development of half inch magnetic tapes and disks, which functioned as a standard medium for storage for years and insured a proper transfer of information from one computing device to another (Bonino & Spring, 1999). Further early examples of the use of standards were in optical character recognition, magnetic ink character recognition, punched cards and paper tape (Burrows 1999).

Standardization efforts have increased significantly since the 1960s, indeed the kind of information structures that are being standardized today are much more complex than even a decade ago. Computer readable forms of syntactic specifications have emerged; examples of these include the EXPRESS data modelling language and XML (eXtensible Markup Language) (Ray, 2002). In addition, the push by users for open systems environments that provide for interoperability and data exchange across different vendors, platforms, applications and software is dependent upon standardized interfaces, protocols, services and formats (Burrows, 1999). Therefore, standards in information technology can help the portability and compatibility of systems and hence the ease of exchanging information between systems (David, 1987).

The classification of IT standards, like the classification of standards in general, varies. Again the commonly used classification of de-facto and de-jure standards is found in most IT standards literature (Jakobs, 2000; Weiss, 1993). Another commonly used classification approach within the IT standards community is the concept of horizontal and vertical IT standards. Markus Steinfield and Wigand (2003) explain that horizontal IT standards are characterised by being applicable in many industries; examples of these include Windows and XML. Markus et al. (2003) go on to explain that the key movers in the development of horizontal standards are technology providers and governmental agencies. On the other hand, vertical standards are developed in order to address business problems unique to particular industries, STEP application protocols would be example of vertical standards, and other examples include CIDX, the chemical industries standards and RosettaNet, which is a not-for-profit consortium aimed at establishing standard processes for the sharing of business information. A number of other IT standards classifications have emerged. For example, in their classification matrix, Spring and Bearman (1988) classify standards according to hardware, software, behavioural standards and social standards on one dimension, and according to their information processing purpose, storage, retrieval, development and dissemination, on the other dimension. Sherif (1999) describes a classification similar to Krechmer (2000b) and classifies IT standards as reference, similarity, compatibility or flexibility standards. IT standards can also be classified in relation to the stage in the life cycle of a product and, according to this idea, standards can be classed as anticipatory, participatory or responsive standards (Baskin, Krechmer & Sherif, 1998).

Research on IT Standards

Studies into the development and implementation of standards in general, and IT standards specifically, have been carried out from a variety of perspectives. A review by West (2003, 2004) into peer-reviewed IT standards research found that such research could be classified into four main areas:

1. **Technical content:** This stream of research typically focuses on the technical implications of a standard and the goal is to enable mainly technical readers to evaluate the standard for adoption or the construction of complementary software and products. Examples of areas that are covered include system architectures (Kaletas et al., 2005), communications standards (Akgun & Parkinson, 1985) and more recently Internet-related standards (Cooper & Yen, 2005).
2. **Standards creation:** Research surrounding the creation of IT standards is subdivided into three main perspectives. The technical perspective covers

standards content, the creation of a standard and standards institutions (Lehr, 1992). From an economic perspective, a limited number of studies have been done which look at issues surrounding the economic motivations and returns of participants in the standardization process, and general questions of 'optimal' standardization and societal welfare (Weiss & Cargill, 1992; Kotinurmi et al. 2003). The organizational perspective is focused on the process and the interaction of the standardization participants and the studies are presented from a sociological, political or business strategy perspective.

3. **Standards selection/adoption:** This line of research focuses on the adoption of standards, organizational decisions for standards adoption and issues surrounding the competition between standards. A more detailed discussion of this research area is covered in later sections and Chapter Three.

4. **Standards impact (using standards):** Studies in this line of research assess the economic value or impact of standards, and measure the effect that standards adoption has on measures such as efficiency, structure, or collaboration. As was previously mentioned, the full benefits from standards are not realized by simply publishing the standards, the true socio-economic benefits are realized from the adoption and use of standards. This is further emphasized by Tornatzkky and Fleischer (1990) who point out that the adoption of an innovation is not the end of the story; there is also the question of whether it delivers the expected benefit. Therefore, studies have been done to identify the impact of standards. Like the previous research areas, studies relating to the impact of standards have been carried out at a technical (Walli, 1999), economic (Swann, 2000), and organizational perspective (Söderström, 2005).

West (2003) states that the first of these areas, technical content, is the most visible and consistent stream in IT standards research and is well covered in engineering and computer science, with many examples found in journals such as Communications of the ACM (Association of Computing Machinery), various IEEE Transactions and the Computer Standards and Interfaces Journal. However, there is still limited empirical research that addresses the remaining three areas that cover issues relating to the development, the adoption and the outcome of IT standards (Markus et al. 2003). Further testament of this was shown in a study carried out by King and Lyytinen (2003), who found that, "there have been relatively few scholarly papers on standardization informing the scholarly discussion in the IS field". King and Lyytinen (2003) go onto state that, "slightly more than 2% of the published journal articles in three top journals in the IS field (MISQ, ISR, CACM) have dealt with standards over the past 10 years. Moreover, most of this work has reported on newly established ICT standards rather than examining the events, factors and impacts related to standard setting processes" (p.2). This finding resulted in the commissioning of a special issue of MISQ on 'standard making' in 2003.

Studies, like the one carried out by King and Lyytinen (2003), show that although research into IT standards has been carried out, there is still a need for empirical research into IT standards particularly in the IS field. The term IS encompasses technology as well as the social organizational structure, culture, intellect and philosophy related to the distribution of information.

IT Standards Adoption Research

A review of the wider literature surrounding the adoption of IT standards revealed that most research was based on two theories; Diffusion of Innovation (DOI) theory and a theory often termed "the Economics of Standards". Most DOI studies build on Rogers (2003) sociology model for the adoption and diffusion of technology innovations. This model captures the characteristics of the innovation, communication channels and social system as they interact over time. Rogers (2003) lists five innovation attributes that influence the adoption decision, these include: relative advantage, compatibility, complexity, trialability and obervability. The social system characteristics can be further divided into characteristics of the individual, group, organization, decision makers, and the roles of opinion leaders and change agents such as champions. Communication channels are important to the adopting community for learning about the existence and substance of an innovation. These channels may be internal or external to the organization and may transmit either formal or informal communications (Prescot & Cogner, 1995). Mustonen-Ollila and Lyytinen (2003) go on to list 28 DOI-related attributes in their meta-analysis of over 200 information-system adoption decisions. These DOI studies show that this theory provides a rich explanation of how new innovations are adopted, and how adoption decisions are affected by perceptions of the standard itself as well as the characteristics of the adopters and their environment.

In addition to classical diffusion of innovation theory, the adoption of standards has been studied from an economic perspective (Fichman & Kemerer, 1993; Katz & Shapiro, 1986). This stream of diffusion research is often labelled as "economics of standards", and focuses on an innovation's inherent economic value for potential adopters. Two main theories have been used within this economic stream. The first related theory is network effects. Network analysis is often based upon the theory of positive network effects, or network externalities, which describes a positive correlation between the number of users of an artefact and the utility of the artefact (Katz & Shapiro, 1985). In other words, as more people adopt a particular standard, the value of that standard increases, encouraging additional adoption (Nitin & Walden, 2003). A second factor that is often classed under 'economics of standards' is switching costs. In this context, it refers to a standard specific investment that makes organizations hesitant to change a supported standard. Other theories, such as Game Theory have been used to understand the adoption of IT related standards using simulated models (Xia et al., 2003; Belleflamme, 1999; Stockheim et al., 2003). However, Fichman (2000) argues that the variety among potential scenarios is so great that no single theory of innovation adoption and diffusion is likely to emerge. Nonetheless, they do propose that innovations are most likely to be dominant when they score highly on both diffusion of innovation and economics of standards criteria (Fichman & Kemerer, 1993).

Within the STEP community, only two specific studies by Dreverman (2005) and Meister (2004) have been carried out to assess the factors that impact the adoption of ISO data-exchange standards. Dreverman carried out a study, sponsored by USPI-NL (The Dutch process and power industry association), into the adoption of three product model data standards in the process industry supply chain. The three standards studied were ISO 10303 (STEP), ISO 15926 and ISO 13584, all of which are developed by the ISO sub-committee ISO/TC184/SC4. The initial problem statement for his research was: The speed of adoption of product model data standards in process industries seems to be lower than in other industry sectors.

Consequently, Dreverman (2005) sought to establish the factors that impede or slow the adoption of these standards within the process industry. Dreverman used factor analysis and actor analysis to establish the issues surrounding the three named standards. The factor analysis was based mainly around the factors identified in DOI theory, and the actor analysis described how the motives, power and actions of the various actors in the process industry affected the adoption of the standards. This study offered insight into the developmental and organizational factors that impact the adoption of these standards.

Meister (2004) carried out a longitudinal study of the development and implementation of STEP over 20 years from the perspective of ISO/TC184/SC4 sub-committee members. Meister notes in his study that while STEP is in use in companies around the world, its adoption has not been as widespread as initially expected. As a consequence, Meister's research sought to answer two questions:

- Why were organizations not adopting STEP, even if they were participating in its development through the standards writing process?
- Why has STEP adoption been so slow, or at least is it perceived to be?

Meister answered these questions using a single-site interpretive case study approach, based on three theoretical lenses, namely:

- Economic-based literature
- Diffusion of Innovation theory
- Institutional theory.

This study offered insight into the developmental and organizational factors that impact the adoption of data-exchange standards from the perspective of the ISO/TC184/SC4 community. Meister (2002) conducted an additional similar study that offered a more comprehensive, empirically backed discussion into the common concerns managers need to recognise and anticipate in order to minimise the negative outcomes of using standards for manufacturing connectedness. Meister (2002) did offer insights into the organizational factors that may hinder the adoption of STEP. However, the study was limited to a manager's perspective and was not specific to STEP, but was a general study into standards used in manufacturing connectedness such as SGML (Standard Generalized Markup Language), ANSI X.12, EDIFACT and IGES. Nevertheless, Dreverman (2005) and Meister's (2004) research are the only two studies that have been carried out concerning the adoption of standards produced by the subcommittee ISO/TC184/SC4, which is responsible for the development of STEP, despite the fact that to date the subcommittee has published 614 standards (ISO, 2009).

This lack of published studies on the adoption of data-exchange standards validates the need for the research presented in this book, and reinforces Swann's (2000) assertion in his report for the Department of Trade and Industry in the United Kingdom, that "There is remarkably little in the literature about the factors influencing the rate of uptake (or diffusion) of standards" (p.15). This assertion by Swann is further confirmed by authors such as Bryne and Golder (2002) and Markus et al. (2003) who explicitly state that the literature surrounding IT standards adoption is limited and that there is a need for more empirical studies on IT standards adoption. Therefore, empirical studies into the adoption of IT standards, more specifically data-exchange standards such as STEP, are needed to add to the current limited research on the adoption of these IT standards within the IS field.

Summary

This section has given an overview of the history and classification of IT standards, and analyzed the four main research domains surrounding IT standards. One area that still has opportunities for additional research is IT standards adoption. The review of the literature indicated the two main theories in IT standards research. In addition, what emerged was the existence of only two studies that have analyzed the issues surrounding the adoption of standards produced by subcommittee ISO/TC184/SC4, which is responsible for the development of STEP. This lack of studies in IT standards research highlights the importance of this research in adding to the current limited body of knowledge surrounding IT standards adoption.

CONCLUSION AND VALIDATION OF RESEARCH

This chapter began by detailing the importance of having effective and efficient uptake of standards in order to realise the socio-economic benefits of the standardization process. That line of thought was then extended to show that understanding the factors that impact the adoption of standards is important in ensuring practitioners devoted to the ongoing development and use of standards, and academics, gain increased knowledge of these factors so steps can be taken to ensure these socio-economic benefits are fully realised. A brief overview of the history and classification of standards in general and IT standards specifically followed. These sections provided a richer context and background to understanding the emergence of IT standards in relation to standards in general. A more in-depth study into the literature surrounding IT standards revealed that although research on IT standards has been carried out, there was still a need for empirical research into IT standards, particularly in the IS field, and more specifically in the IT standards adoption research area. This discovery validates the aims of this research, which are to:

- Establish the factors and barriers that influence the adoption of data-exchange standards.
- Develop guidelines to facilitate and accelerate the adoption of data-exchange standards.

The purpose of fulfilling these aims is to add to the current limited body of knowledge surrounding IT standards adoption. The next chapter fulfils this objective and offers a more in-depth analysis of IT standards adoption research and presents the two models developed to capture the factors that impact the adoption of data-exchange standards.

REFERENCES

Akgun, M., & Parkinson, P. (1985). The Development of Cable Data Communications Standards. *IEEE Journal on Selected Areas in Communications, 3*(2), 273–285. doi:10.1109/JSAC.1985.1146198

Baskin, E., Krechmer, K., & Sherif, M. (1998). The Six Dimensions of Standards: Contribution Towards a Theory Of Standardization. In L. Lefebvre, & R. Mason (Ed.), *Proceedings Of 7th IAMOT Conference* (pp. 53-62). Orlando, FL: Elsevier.

Belleflamme, P. (1999). Assessing the Diffusion of EDI Standards Across Business Communities. *EURAS Yearbook of Standardization, 2*, 301–324.

Bonino, M., & Spring, M. (1999). Standards as Change Agents in the Information Technology Market. *Computer Standards & Interfaces, 20*(4-5), 279–289. doi:10.1016/S0920-5489(98)00064-6

Burrows, J. (1999). Information Technology Standards in a Changing World: The Role of the Users. *Computer Standards & Interfaces, 20*(4-5), 323–331. doi:10.1016/S0920-5489(98)00068-3

Byrne, B., & Golder, P. (2002). The Diffusion of Anticipatory Standards with Particular Reference to the ISO/IEC Information Resource Dictionary System Framework Standard. *Computer Standards & Interfaces, 24*(5), 369–379.

Cooper, M., & Yen, D. (2005). IPv6:Business Applications and Implementation Concerns. *Computer Standards & Interfaces, 28*(1), 27–41. doi:10.1016/j.csi.2004.11.001

Culshaw, S. (2006). *Towards a Truly Worldwide Web: How XML and Unicode are Making it Easier to Publish Multilingual Electronic Documents.* Retrieved January 13, 2006, from http://www.tgpconsulting.com/articles/xml.htm

Daimler Benz. (1998). *Standardization 2010.* Stuttgart, Germany: Daimler Benz Aktiengesellschaft Research and Technology.

David, P. (1987). Some New Standards for the Economics of Standardization in the Information Age. In P. Dasgupta, & P. Stoneman, *Economic Policy and Technological Performance* (pp. 206-239). New York: Cambridge University Press.

Deshpande, S., & Nazemetz, J. (2003a). *Global Harmonisation of Standards.* Oklahoma State University School of Industrial Engineering and Management, Computer Assisted Technology Transfer (Catt) Research Program. Oklahoma: Contract Number F34601-95-D-00376.

Deshpande, S., & Nazemetz, J. (2003b). *Decomposition Methodology for Making the Standards Problem Tractable.* Oklahoma State University School of Industrial Engineering and Management, Computer Assisted Technology Transfer Research Program. Oklahoma: Contract Number F34601-95-D-00376.

DIN. (2004). *Economic Benefits of Standardization*. Retrieved January 15, 2004, from Din-German Institute for Standardization, http://www.din.de/Aktuelles/Benefit.html

Dreverman, M. (2005). *Adoption of Product Model Data Standards In the Process Industry.* Eindhoven, The Netherlands: Eindhoven University of Technology.

Fichman, R. (2000). The Diffusion and Assimilation of Information Technology Innovations. In R. Zmud (Ed.), *Framing the Domains of IT Management: Projecting the Future Through the Past* (pp. 105-128). Cincinatti, OH: Pinnaflex Publishing.

Fichman, R., & Kemerer, C. (1993). Adoption of Software Engineering Process Innovations: the Case of Object Orientation. *MIT Sloan Management Review, 34*(2), 7–22.

Hansen, T. (2004). *Synchronise Work On DEXs and Reference Data Between PLCS Pilots and OASIS/PLCS.* Oslo, Norway: Det Norske Veritas As.

ISO. (2009). *ISO Website.* Retrieved February 9, 2009, from http://www.iso.org/iso/iso_technical_committee.html?commid=54158

ISO/IEC. (1996). *"Standardization and Related Activities -- General Vocabulary".* Retrieved January 15, 2004, from ISO: http://www.iso.org/iso/iso_catalogue/catalogue_ics/catalogue_detail_ics.htm?csnumber=24887

Iversen, E. (2000). *Raising Standards: Innovation and the Emerging Global Standardization Environment for ICT.* Step Working Paper Series - Number A022000. Oslo: The STEP Group.

Jakobs, K. (2000). Trying To Keep the Internet's Standards Setting Process. *Proceeding of Terena Networking Conference.* Lisbon, Portugal.

Jakobs, K. (2002). Even Desperately Needed Standards May Fail - the Case of E-Mail. *Proceedings of International Conference On the History of Computing and Networks.* Grenoble, France: IEEEXplore.

Kaletas, E., Afsarmanesh, H., Anastasiou, M., & Camarinha-Matos, L. (2005). Emerging Technologies and Standards. In L. Camarinha-Matos, H. Afsarmanesh, & M. Ollus (Eds.), *Virtual Organizations: Systems and Practices* (pp. 105-132). New York: Springer Verlag.

Katz, M., & Shapiro, C. (1985). Network Externalities, Competition, and Compatibility. *The American Economic Review, 75*(3), 424–440.

Kawamoto, D. (2003). *Gloom Lifts on IT Spending.* Retrieved November 15, 2005, from ZDNet: http://news.zdnet.co.uk/itmanagement/0,1000000308,39115536,00.htm

King, J., & Lyytinen, K. (2003). *Proceedings of MISQ Special Issue Workshop On Standard Making: A Critical Frontier for Information Systems - Call for Papers.* Retrieved November 17, 2003, from http://www.si.umich.edu/misq-stds/misq/cfp.pdf

Kotinurmi, P., Nurmilaakso, J., & Laesvuori, H. (2003). Standardization of Xml-Based E-Business Frameworks. In J. King, & K. Lyytinen (Ed.), *Proceedings of MISQ Special Issue Workshop On Standard Making: A Critical Frontier for Information Systems* (pp. 135-145). Seattle, WA: MISQ Quarterly.

Krechmer, K. (1996). Technical Sandards: Foundations of the Future. *StandardView*, *4*(1), 4–8. doi:10.1145/230871.230872

Krechmer, K. (2000b). The Fundamental Nature of Standards: Technical Perspective. *IEEE Communications Magazine*, *38*(6), 70.

LayNetworks. (2006). *Aloha Protocol.* Retrieved March 11, 2006, from LayNetworks Web site: http://www.laynetworks.com/Aloha%20protocol.htm

Lehr, W. (1992). Standardization: Understanding the Process. *Journal of the American Society for Information Science American Society for Information Science*, *43*(8), 550–555. doi:10.1002/(SICI)1097-4571(199209)43:8<550::AID-ASI5>3.0.CO;2-L

Markus, M., Steinfield, C., & Wigand, R. (2003). The Evolution of Vertical Is Standards: Electronic Interchange Standards in the US Home Mortgage Industry. In J. King, & K. Lyytinen (Ed.), *Proceedings of MISQ Special Issue Workshop On Standard Making: A Critical Frontier for Information Systems* (pp. 80-91). Seattle, WA: MISQ Quaterly.

Meister, D. (2002). Manufacturing Connectedness: Managerial Challenges and Solutions. In M. Warkentin (Ed.), *Business-To-Business Electronic Commerce: Challenges & Solutions* (pp. 114-131). Hershey, PA: Idea Group Publishing.

Meister, D. (2004). *STEP Through 20 Years: Lessons and Theoretical Implications - Working Paper Edn.* Faculty of Information Systems, Richard Ivey School of Business. London, Canada: University of Western Ontario.

Mustonen-Ollila, E., & Lyytinen, K. (2003). Why Organizations Adopt Information System Process Innovations: A Longitudinal Study Using Diffusion of Innovation Theory. *Information Systems Journal, 13*(3), 275–297. doi:10.1046/j.1365-2575.2003.00141.x

Nitin, A., & Walden, E. (2003). Monopoly Power in Standards is a Myth. In J. King, & K. Lyytinen (Ed.), *Proceedings of MISQ Special Issue Workshop On Standard Making: A Critical Frontier for Information Systems*, (pp. 49-61). Seattle, WA.

NSSF. (2004a). *National Standardization Strategic Framework - How Standardization Works the Standardization Map.* Retrieved January 17, 2004, from NSSF Web site: http://www.nssf.info/mapnotes.pdf

NSSF. (2004b). *National Standardization Strategic Framework - Standardization Map.* Retrieved January 17, 2004, from NSSF Web site: http://www.nssf.info/map.pdf

NSSF. (2004c). *National Standardization Strategic Framework – Public Discussions Document.* Retrieved January 17, 2004, from NSSF Web site: http://www.nssf.info/public_discussion.pdf

OED Online. (2005). *Oxford English Dictionary.* Retrieved July 7, 2005, from OED Website, http://www.oed.com/

Prescott, M., & Conger, S. (1995). Information Technology Innovations: A Classification By It Locus of Impact and Research Approach. *ACM SIGMIS Database, 26*(2-3), 20–41. doi:10.1145/217278.217284

Ray, S. (2002). Interoperability Standards in the Semantic Web. *Journal of Computing and Information Science in Engineering, 2*(1), 65–69. doi:10.1115/1.1480024

Rogers, E. (2003). *Diffusion of Innovations.* New York: Simon & Schuster International.

Sherif, M. (1999). Contribution Towards a theory of Standardization in Telecommunications. In K. Jakobs, & R. Williams (Ed.), *International Conference On Standardisation and Innovation In Information Technology.* Aachen, France.

Söderström, E. (2005). Connecting B2B Standards Life Cycles with Stakeholders. *Proceedings of the INTEROPE-ESA Workshop On Interoperability Standards - Implementation, Dynamics, and Impact* (pp. 223-234). Geneva: Hermes Science Publishing.

Spring, M., & Bearman, T. (1988). Information Standards: Models for Future Development. *Book Research Quarterly, 4*(3), 38–47. doi:10.1007/BF02683721

Spring, M., Grisham, C., O'Donnell, J., Skogseid, I., Snow, A., Tarr, G., et al. (1995). Improving the Standardization Process: from Courtship Dance To Lawyering: Working With Bulldogs and Turtles. In Kahin.B, & J. Abbate (Eds.), *Standards Policy for Information Infrastructure* (pp. 220-252). Cambridge, MA: MIT Press.

Stockheim, T., Schwind, M., & König, W. (2003). A Model for the Emergence and Diffusion of Software Standards. *Proceedings of the 36th Annual Hawaii International Conference on System Sciences* (p. 59). Washington, DC: IEEE Computer Society.

Swann, G. (2000). *The Economics of Standardization.* Retrieved January 21, 2004, from Report for Department of Trade and Industry, Standards and Technical Regulations Directorate: http://www.dti.gov.uk/strd/fundingo.htm#swannrep

Tornatzky, L., & Fleischer, M. (1990). *The Processes of Technological Innovation.* Lexington, KY: Lexington Books.

Walli, S. (1999). POSIX: A Case Study In A Successful Standard Or, Why We Don't Need Radical Change In the SDO Process. In K. Jakobs, & R. Williams (Ed.), *Proceedings of the 1st IEEE conference on Standardisation and Innovation in Information Technology* (pp. 183-187). Aachen, France: IEEE.

Weiss, M. B. (1993). The Standards Development Process: A View from Political Theory. *StandardView, 1*(2), 35–41. doi:10.1145/174690.174695

Weiss, M. B., & Spring, M. (2000). Selected Intellectual Property Issues in Standardization. In K. Jakobs (Ed.), *Information Technology Standards and Standardization: A Global Perspective* (pp. 63-79). Hershey, PA: IGI Publishing.

West, J. (2003). The Role of Standards in the Creation and Use of Information Systems. In J. King, & K. Lyytinen (Ed.), *Proceedings of MISQ Special Issue Workshop on Standard Making: A Critical Frontier for Information Systems* (pp. 314-325). Seattle: MIS Quaterly.

West, J. (2004). *Information Systems Standards: Seeking Compatability Between Technical, Economic and Organizational Perspectives.* San Jose State University, College of Business. San Jose, CA: San Jose State University.

Xia, M., Zhao, K., & Shaw, M. (2003). Open E-Business Standard Development and Adoption: An Integrated Perspective. In J. King, & K. Lyytinen (Ed.), *Proceedings of MISQ Special Issue Workshop On Standard Making: A Critical Research Frontier for Information Systems* (pp. 222-235). Seattle: MIS Quaterly.

Chapter 3
IT Standards Adoption and Diffusion Models

INTRODUCTION

The motivation behind this research is to identify the factors that impact the adoption of data-exchange standards, such as STEP. Research into the adoption of STEP and other standards produced by ISO/TC184/SC4, which is the ISO technical committee responsible for the development of STEP, is very limited. Currently there are only two specific empirical studies (Dreverman, 2005; Meister, 2004) that shed light on the factors associated with the adoption of ISO/TC184/SC4 (referred to as SC4 for the remainder of the chapter) standards like STEP. This means that practitioners devoted to the ongoing development and use of these standards, and academics, still lack a significant body of evidence regarding the factors and barriers critical to their adoption.

DOI: 10.4018/978-1-60566-832-1.ch003

Chapter 2 explained how research into standards adoption is important in ensuring the socio-economic benefits of standardization are fully realised. This is particularly true for IT standards, which are the cornerstone for the burgeoning IT sector. In addition, Chapter 2 gave insight into the IT standards research domain as a whole. West (2003) revealed that there is still a significant lack of direct standards related research within the IS community and went on to identify IT standards adoption as a domain that still required research. Therefore, what Chapter 2 has shown is that this research is not only filling a gap within the STEP and SC4 communities, but is also making a contribution the wider body of knowledge surrounding IT standards adoption research.

In light of this, the aim of this chapter is twofold, the first is to provide a more detailed review of the literature surrounding IT standards adoption, and the second is to develop two models that capture the factors and barriers critical to the adoption of data-exchange standards. The objective is to provide additional context and background for the research and to present evidence and support from the literature for the preliminary conceptual models that guided this research. The first section of the chapter gives an overview of the meanings and definitions associated with words like 'adoption' and 'diffusion' and correlates that with the innovation and adopter centric approaches taken in this research. The second and third sections then give a detailed background behind the development of the two models. The preliminary models developed in this chapter are viewed as a 'first cut' of the research domain as described by Miles and Hubermann (1994). The validity and relative importance of the identified factors will be assessed in Chapter Five and Six. The concluding section gives a summary of the chapter and introduces the standards and organization that will be used to test and verify these models.

ADOPTION AND DIFFUSION TERMINOLOGY

The terms adoption and diffusion are often used interchangeably in IT standards research. Some authors make a distinction between the two terms (Prescott & Cogner, 1995; Nelson & Shaw, 2003), but most authors, such as Chen (2003), tend to discuss the issues surrounding adoption and diffusion without making any clear distinction of the meanings of the two terms, leaving the readers to make assumptions about the intended meaning of the words. In light of this it was considered necessary to make a clear distinction between the meanings associated with the words 'adoption' and 'diffusion'.

The Compact Oxford English dictionary defines diffusion as 'the action or process of becoming spread over a wide area' (AskOxford.com, 2005). However, this meaning varies across different application areas. For example, within physical

Table 1. Business focused diffusion theories

Theories	Description
The trickle-down theory	Products tend to be expensive at first, and therefore only accessible to the wealthy social strata, but it is believed that in time they become less expense and are diffused to lower and lower strata. (Aghion and Bolton 1997)
Rogers' Diffusion of Innovations (DOI) theory	The adopters of any new innovation or idea can be categorized as innovators, early adopters, early majority, late majority and laggards (Rogers 2003).
Crossing the Chasm	A modification of Rogers' DOI theory applied to the technology market with a chasm added that relates to making the transition between visionaries (early adopters) and pragmatists (early majority) (Moore 1999).
Technology-driven models	These models tend to focus on software diffusion in an organization. One of the earliest and commonly referenced is the Technology Acceptance Model (TAM), which was first formulised by Davis *et al.* (1989) and Bagozzi *et al.* (1992).

sciences, diffusion relates to the spontaneous spreading of, for instance, particles, heat or momentum. Another example is in the field of anthropology, which defines diffusion as the flow of an idea or artefact from one culture to another. Further examples of different application areas include the diffusion of responsibility from a social perspective and diffusion from a business perspective (Wikipedia, 2005). The latter application area relating to business is the area that is relevant to this research. Within the business environment diffusion relates to the process by which a new idea (innovation) or new product is accepted by the market. According to the Internet encyclopaedia, Wikipedia, over the years there have been several theories that explain the mechanics of diffusion from a business perspective, examples of these are shown in Table 1.

Of the five business-focused diffusion theories, only two are relevant to this research, these include Rogers' DOI theory and the technology-driven models. The remaining three theories are beyond the scope of this research. The technology-driven models are directly relevant to identifying factors for IT standards adoption within an organization, and DOI theory is relevant because it is heavily cited in previous IT standards research. Details of each of these theories are discussed in later sections. However, the use of DOI theory does offer a starting point for a clearer definition of diffusion in the context of this research. The definition of diffusion, as prescribed by Rogers, states that: 'Diffusion is the process by which an innovation is communicated through certain channels over time among the members of a social system' (Rogers, 2003, pp.35).

The term communicated in this context can be aligned to the word adoption. Thus, in the context of this research, diffusion is seen as an aggregation of the adoption process of the members of a social system over time. However, West (1999) contends that most research on innovation adoption focuses on a single innovation and who adopts that innovation. This is an innovation-centric approach. Another stream examines a single adopter, usually an organization, and the innovations it adopts. This is referred to as an adopter-centric approach. West (1999) continues his discussion by commenting that innovation-centric diffusion research tends to have a pro-adoption bias, with late adopters labelled "laggards". This bias is weaker in the study of adopting organizations, which instead demonstrates a bias towards the ability to adopt any innovation rather than any particular innovation. In order to limit the level of bias this research seeks to offer a balanced analysis into the factors that influence the adoption and diffusion of data-exchange standards by taking both an innovation-centric and adopter-centric approach. Therefore, an important objective of this research is to make a distinction as to how the concepts of diffusion and adoption relate to these two approaches.

The innovation-centric approach focuses on the general adoption and diffusion of a standard, the adopter-centric approach examines the adoption of standards within organizations from a decision-making perspective. From an innovation-centric perspective, diffusion would be an aggregation of the adoption and implementation process of each organization within an innovations-targeted social system over time, as shown in Figure 1. Therefore, an innovation-centric study looking at the adoption and diffusion of an IT standard would tend to focus more on the innovations characteristics and the general characteristics of the organizations adopting the innovation. Details of each individual organization are generally not the focus, although generalisations may be made to establish trends across different types of organizations within a social system. For example, generalisations may be made about Original Equipment Manufacturers (OEMs), Small to Medium Enterprises (SMEs) or primary contractors and subcontractors.

According to the adopter-centric approach, diffusion would be an aggregation of the adoption and implementation decisions within an organization over time as shown in Figure 2.

Gallivan (2001) ascertains that the organizational adoption process is broken into two stages, primary adoption and then secondary adoption and assimilation (implementation). Primary adoption relates to the adoption decision by an organization to take on a new innovation, whereas secondary adoption and assimilation deals with the decisions individuals or departments make regarding an innovation their organization has decided to adopt. Secondary adoption is further broken down into processes of implementation, initiation, adaptation, acceptance, routinization and infusion (Gallivan, 2001). Therefore, at a high level, this approach will focus on the process of an organization's adoption decision and characteristics specific to the organization and departments, individuals or tasks within the organization. Most of the diffusion 'technology-driven models' deal with the issues surrounding primary and secondary adoption of technology within an organization.

Figure 1. Diagrammatic representation of innovation-centric adoption and diffusion

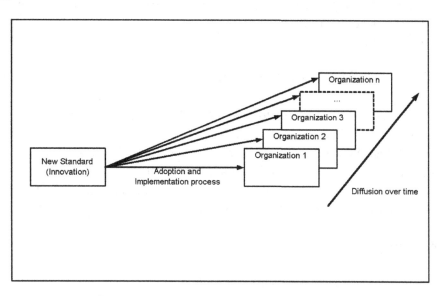

This section has shown the interrelationship between diffusion and adoption. It started by tracing the different applications of the word diffusion and, in the context of this research, diffusion can be described as aggregation of the adoption process over time. This definition was further explained in relation to the innovation and

Figure 2. Diagrammatic representation of adopter-centric adoption and diffusion

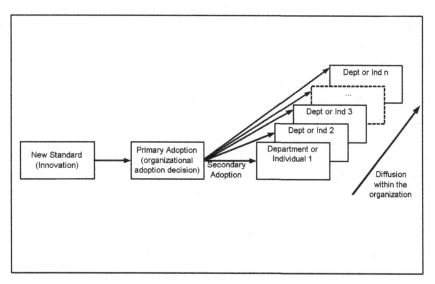

adopter centric approaches identified by West (1999) and shown in Figures 1 and 2. The following sections detail the development of these two models from the current literature surrounding IT standards adoption.

INNOVATION-CENTRIC APPROACH

The innovation-centric approach focuses on the factors and barriers that impact the adoption of an innovation across its targeted social system. In this case, the innovation being an ISO data-exchange standard produced by the SC4 subcommittee. In order to establish the factors, this section reviews the literature surrounding the innovation-centric approach and then chronicles the development of the finalised innovation-centric model that guided this research.

DOI Theory

A review of the literature surrounding the adoption of IT standards revealed that most innovation-centric research was based on Diffusion of Innovation (DOI) theory. Most DOI studies (Hovav et al.2004; Prescot & Cogner, 1995; Huff & Munro, 1985; Mustonen-Ollila & Lyytinen, 2003; Sauer & Lau, 1997; Nilkanta & Scamell, 1990) build on Rogers (2003) sociology model for the adoption and diffusion of technology innovations. This model captures the characteristics of the innovation, communication channels and social system as they interact over time. Rogers (2003) lists five innovation attributes that influence the adoption decision: relative advantage, compatibility, complexity, trialability and observability. Other researchers have either adopted or built upon these five basic attributes, but in most cases any additional attributes can be easily mapped onto one of the five attributes (Mustonen-Ollila, 1999). The social system characteristics can be further divided into characteristics of the individual, group, organization, decision makers, and the roles of opinion leaders and change agents like champions. Communication channels are important to the adopting community for learning about the existence and substance of an innovation. These channels may be internal or external to the organization and may transmit either formal or informal communications (Prescot & Cogner, 1995). Mustonen-Ollila & Lyytinen (2003) go on to list 28 DOI-related attributes in their meta-analysis of over 200 information-system adoption decisions. These studies show that DOI theory provides a rich explanation of how new innovations are adopted, and how adoption decisions are affected by perceptions of the standard itself as well as the characteristics of the adopters. The two relevant factors for the purpose of the innovation-centric approach are:

Standard (Innovation) Characteristics

An innovation may take the form of a new idea, technology, product or administrative process. In the current context, the innovation is a data-exchange standard. The standard characteristics are based on the five attributes recognized by Rogers and an additional attribute identified for data-exchange standards. An explanation of each attribute is given:

- Relative advantage is the degree to which the standard has clear advantages over others to meet the existing functionality requirement.
- Compatibility is the degree to which the standard is perceived as being consistent with the existing practices, values, skills and technological infrastructure of potential adopters.
- Complexity refers to how easy the standard is to understand, implement and use.
- Trialability refers to the ability to verify and quantify the benefits of the new standard.
- Observability is defined as the ability to observe benefits. The benefits offered by the standard are apparent by visual demonstration or logical description.
- "Characteristics of related implementation technologies" is an attribute that has been added specifically for standards similar to STEP that are implemented using different technologies. Adoption of the standard may also be influenced by the characteristics of these implementation technologies such as EXPRESS, XML and Web services. Weston and Whidett (1999) list a number of attributes that can be used to evaluate these technologies. They include: level of consensus, product availability, completeness, maturity and stability, problems and limitations and interoperability of the technology.

Characteristics of the Adopting Community

The characteristics of the adoption community relates to the innovativeness of the organizations in the adopting community or social system of a standard. Organizations that are more innovative may be more likely to consider adopting a standard at an early stage. Rogers (2003) in his adopter categorization model terms such organizations as 'innovators'. The next category, termed 'early adopters', tends to be visionaries who are more willing to take risk. The 'early majority' tend to avoid risks but are quick to adopt and implement the standard when 'early adopters' demonstrate the standard's benefits. The 'late majority' are more sceptical and are influenced because others have adopted the standard, such as when their major trading partners require to them to use the standard. The final group, termed as 'laggards', do not engage in the adoption process and tend to be more traditional. These organizations tend to lack the resources or business insight to adopt the standard, and as a consequence the organizations are not involved in adopting the standard and usually wait until they has no choice other than to adopt it. Two key factors surrounding the innovativeness of the adopting community that affect the adoption and diffusion of a standard are:

- Organization size and type: The size of an organization may influence the adoption and diffusion process. For example, the defence industry and large government agencies are traditionally said to be strong supporters of standardization efforts (Chen, 2003). Consequently, if a large organization chooses to adopt a standard, dependent SMEs (Small to Medium sized Enterprises) may be forced to adopt similar standards.
- Organization culture: The willingness of an organization to adopt a standard is also influenced by the culture of the organization. An organizations culture can be expressed in its attitudes towards change and the standard itself.

Therefore, the two factors that have emerged from DOI theory are standards characteristics and characteristics of the adopting community. The third factor identified by Rogers, communication channels, is also incorporated in the model and discussed later in this chapter.

Standards Conception and Development Process

A second group of factors have emerged from the conception and development process of a standard. In their taxonomy of the causes of standards implementation problems, Egyedi and Dahanayake (2003) identified four main categories:

- The conceptual idea of the standard
- Standards process
- Standard specification
- Implementation process

The first category in the taxonomy relates to the 'conceptual idea of a standard'. In their research, Egyedi and Dahanayake (2003) explain that the conceptual idea that underlies a standard may not work satisfactorily when implemented, for example the scalability of Java. They go on to contend that this could result in tailoring of the standard, which would jeopardise the interoperability of implementations. The second category is described as the 'standards process', which they determine as issues surrounding consensus and decision-making within a standards organization.

The third category, which is the 'standards specification', relates to the characteristics of the standard as described by DOI theory. The final category of Egyedi and Dahanayake's representation relates to the implementation process of a standard. Egyedi and Dahanayake's (2003) taxonomy is a starting point for identifying some of the key issues that impact the adoption of IT standards. This taxonomy highlights the fact that the issues surrounding the adoption of a standard start from the conception of a standard, where the conceptual ideas are formed, and continues through to the implementation process.

Within the ISO body, the development process is made up of six stages and a review process. The six stages are: Proposal stage; Preparatory stage; Committee stage; Enquiry stage; Approval stage, and Publication and review stage. A review of the standard can result in a confirmation, revision or withdrawal of the standard (ISO, 2006).

For the purpose of this research the six stages are grouped into two categories, namely: 'Conception and Development' (proposal, preparatory, committee and enquiry stages) and 'Approval and Publication'. These categories along with the review process are shown to depict the life cycle stages of an ISO standard in Figure 3. It is clear from Figure 3 that the factors that feed or point towards the adoption of the standard are 'conception and development', 'approval and publication' and 'revisions'.

Mapping this life cycle categories against Egyedi and Dahanayake's (2003) schematic representation, the three life cycle stages now represent the following:

Conception and Development Process

This relates to the first category identified by Egyedi and Dahanayake (2003), that is the 'conceptual idea of a standard'. The literature reveals other issues within this factor that may impact the adoption of data-exchange standard. Gerst et al. (2005) detail, through a case study, how standardization efforts can be triggered by a complex array of economic and political considerations. What they show is that the drivers or motivations behind the development of standard can impact the standardization process. However, it is not known if these motivations simply act as a trigger for the development of a standard or whether they have more wide reaching implications for the adoption of an IT standard. Another topic connected to the previous issue relates to the roles of the initiators of the development of a standard and whether this impacts the adoption of the standard. The development dimension of this factor covers the 'standards process' and deals with two main topics, namely:

- *The nature of the alliance body.* This topic deals with issues surrounding the nature and characteristics of the alliance body, which in the case of STEP is

Figure 3. Overview of life cycle stages of a standard

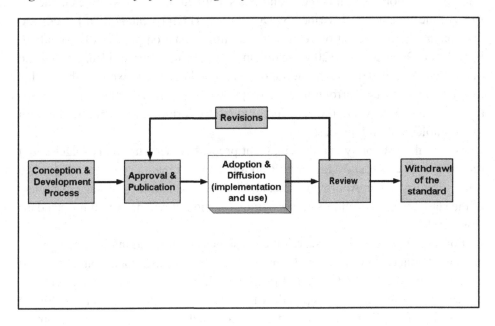

the ISO body. It also covers how issues surrounding consensus and decision making may impact the adoption of a standard. This ties in directly with some of the issues identified by Egyedi and Dahanayake (2003) and other authors (Weiss & Cargill, 1992; Nelson & Shaw, 2003) with regards to the impact of a development organization on the adoption and implementation of a standard.

- *Balance and diversity of the different stakeholder groups during the development process*. Authors, such as Jakobs (1996), have looked at the pros and cons of end-user involvement in standards development. Other authors such as de Vries et al. (2003), who have carried out in-depth analysis of the dynamics of standards setting committees, ascertain that the composition of the standards committees is an essential element of standardization. They go on to note that many standardization processes are characterized by imbalances in stakeholder representation. This research seeks to establish if these issues emerge within the development of the data-exchange standards and how they may have impacted the adoption of the standards.

Approval and Publication Process

The approval and publication process deals mainly with issues of timescales for development and reaching consensus and again deals with the 'standards process' identified by Egyedi and Dahanayake (2003). One of the most commonly debated issues within IT standards research is the perception that the standards processes of the various standards development organizations, such as ISO, are too slow to keep pace with technological innovations surrounding such areas as the Internet and other technological developments (Walli, 1999; Burrows, 1999; Sherif, 2003; Jakobs, 2002). The cause of these delays is often attributed to issues surrounding consensus and the decision-making process.

Revisions

This factor looks at revisions of the standard from two perspectives. The first looks at revisions that take place after a standard has been published and how this impacts the standard in terms of backward-compatibility issues. This is a topic that that has been touched on by Egyedi and Loeffen (2002). The second revision issue relates to revisions of the standard that take place during the development of a standard.

These three identified factors will make part of the innovation-centric adoption model shown in Figure 4 and deal mainly with issues directly surrounding the conception and development of an IT standard and how that impacts the subsequent adoption of a standard. The third category in Egyedi and Dahanayake's (2003) taxonomy, 'standard specification' is dealt with in DOI theory, and the final category, 'implementation process' is covered in the adopter-centric perspective.

Standardization Issues and Additional Factors

This next group of factors have been identified from research carried out by Krechmer (2000a) into market-driven standardization. Within his research Krechmer identified eight key areas that distinguish consortia-driven standards from standards developed by formal standards development organizations like ISO. The eight areas he identifies include: funding source, standards development process, intellectual property, national focus, brand identification, standards promotion, compatibility testing and collusion. Collusion addresses the issues surrounding illegal agreements that participants of a standards committee may make to restrain trade, and as is out of the scope of this research. In addition to that, one factor, the standards development process, has already been considered in the previous section. Therefore, the remaining six factors are considered relevant within the scope this research and have been added to the innovation-centric model as issues that require further investigation to assess if they have an impact on the adoption of a data-exchange standard. These six factors are grouped under the title 'standardization issues'.

The final group of factors is taken from research carried out by Themistocleous (2002) into the adoption of Enterprise Application Integration (EAI) technologies.

Figure 4. Innovation-centric adoption and diffusion framework

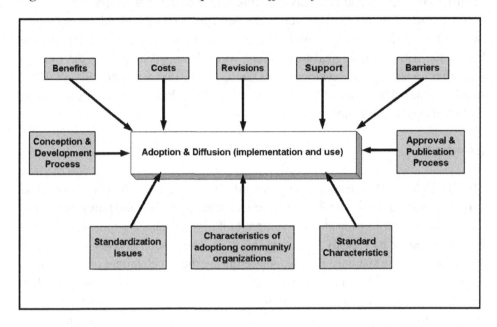

In his study, Themistocleous recognised four main areas that would be relevant to an innovation-centric approach, namely;

- Costs, which may be explicit or hidden and cover both development costs and implementation costs;
- Benefits, which may be intangible and tangible. Included in this is the issue of the Return on Investment (ROI) of a standard. What is key is ascertaining whether this has been established in any case studies;
- Barriers that may be common to the adopting community at large or be organization specific.
- Support in the form of promotion and awareness, pilots and demonstrations, sponsorship and information and communication channels identified by Rogers (2003).

Summary and Innovation-Centric Model

This section has chronicled and discussed the factors that may impact the adoption of a data-exchange standard from an innovation-centric perspective. The validity of these factors and the nature in which they may interact is not immediately obvious. Therefore, a simple conceptual model shown in Figure 4 to represent all the factors discussed in this section. The next section chronicles the development of the adopter-centric model.

ADOPTER-CENTRIC APPROACH

The adopter-centric approach focuses on the factors and barriers that impact the adoption of an innovation within an organization. This section chronicles the development of the adopter-centric model from previous theories and models.

Two-Stage Organization Adoption and Adopter-Centric Model

The adopter-centric approach looks at the diffusion of an innovation within an organization. Zaltman et al. (1973) examined innovation adoption within organizations and determined that the adoption process frequently occurs in two stages, an organization-level decision to adopt an innovation (primary adoption), followed by actual implementation, which includes individual adoption by users (secondary adoption). According to Gallivan (2001), managers identify objectives to change some aspect of their business, seek available innovations, which may fit their objectives, and then make the primary adoption decision. Gallivan goes on to explain that once the primary adoption decision has occurred, management may decide to proceed in three different paths to ensure secondary adoption: (1) they can mandate that the innovation be adopted throughout the organization at once; (2) they can provide the necessary infrastructure and support for users to adopt the innovation, while allowing it to diffuse voluntarily; or (3) they may target specific pilot projects within the firm, observe the processes and outcomes that unfold, and decide whether to implement the innovation more broadly later on.

Most technology diffusion models focus on secondary adoption. Indeed the frequently cited Technology Acceptance Model (TAM), proposed by Bagozzi et al. (1992) and Davis et al. (1989), is used to address this issue. Recent studies have extended the original TAM model. Venkatesh et al. (2003) carried out an extensive review of eight predominant IT acceptance models. The eight models they reviewed were the theory of reasoned action, the technology acceptance model (TAM), the motivational model, the theory of planned behaviour, a model combining the technology acceptance model and the theory of planned behaviour, the model of PC utilization, innovation diffusion theory, and the social cognitive theory. Venkatesh et al. (2003) went on to develop a unified model, called the Unified Theory of Acceptance and Use of Technology (UTAUT) that was empirically tested against four organizations. This model and many of the previously established models provide insight into individual acceptance of information technology, which relates more directly to secondary adoption. However, due to time and resource constraints the scope of this research was limited to primary adoption. So details of many of the technology acceptance models went beyond the scope of this research. Nonetheless, aspects relating to secondary adoption will be indirectly assessed in terms of their relation to the adoption decision. In light of this, a model was developed to assess the primary adoption decision process.

Adopter-Centric Model

A starting point for this model was the model developed by Chen (2003) when looking at the adoption of XML and Web services. Chen's model, is based on the idea of an IDEF0 diagram, IDEF standards are the 1320 series of IEEE standards (IEEE 2006). There are five elements in the IDEF0 functional model, as Whitman et al. (1997) explain, "The activity (or function) is represented by the boxes; inputs are represented by the arrows flowing into the left hand side of an activity box; outputs are represented by arrows flowing out the right hand side of an activity box; the arrows flowing into the top portion of the box represent constraints or controls on the activities; and the final element represented by arrows flowing into the bottom of the activity box are the mechanisms that carry out the activity" (p.2). This model was a starting point for Chen (2003). He identified several factors that affect the adoption and diffusion decision, namely, the stakeholders, organizational factors and IT standards characteristics. Two of the factors link to factors identified in traditional DOI theory (Rogers, 2003). However, an organization's primary adoption decision will be impacted by an additional input factor. As West (2003) points out, "Much of the technology diffusion literature focuses on the adoption decisions of individuals, either for themselves or for their employers. But for organizations, many technologies are "too big and complex to be grasped by a single person's cognitive power—or usually, to be acquired or deployed within the discretionary authority of any single organizational participant" (p.238).

West (2003) goes on to contend that a more robust and influential framework for understanding technology adoption in an organizational context has been developed by DePietro et al. (1990, as cited in Dedrick & West, 2003). Their model defines a 'context for change' consisting of three elements:

- **Technology.** The model subsumes the five innovation attributes that Rogers (2003) argues influence the likelihood of adoption.
- **Organization**. Adoption propensity is influenced by formal and informal intra-organizational mechanisms for communication and control. The resources and innovativeness of the organization also play a role.

- **Environment.** Organizational adoption of new technologies depends on having the prerequisite skills for effective deployment, so as Attewell (1992) found, the availability of external skills (such as through integrators or consultants) is essential for adoption by some organizations.

Indeed Nelson and Shaw (2003) confirm West's (2003) assertion in their study of 21 inter-organizational standards adoption and diffusion models, Nelson and Shaw also discovered that the most common set of constructs utilized in the study of inter-organizational standards diffusion is the 'organizational – technology – environmental' framework, which is often referred to as 'TOE'. These three elements are posited to interact with each other and to influence technology adoption decisions (West, 2003). Nonetheless, the TOE framework is simply a taxonomy for categorizing variables, and does not represent an integrated conceptual framework or a well-developed theory. However, the TOE framework is a key starting point for identifying key factors and the author contrasted the TOE framework with the model presented by Chen (2003). What emerged was that two features of the TOE framework, technology and organization, have been used in Chen's model. However, the environment factor has not been included and was therefore added to Chen's model and presented in the author's finalised adopter-centric model as the 'environmental characteristics', shown in Figure 5.

With the inclusion of the environmental characteristics, the 'stakeholder' input variable was abandoned, as it was not deemed relevant to the scope of this research, which is looking at a specific organizations adoption decision process. Any influence from external stakeholders is considered within the 'external driver' factor. The finalised model presented in Figure 5 has adjusted Chen's (2003) model to include environmental factors, which was lacking from Chen's original model, and offers additional features to the organizational characteristics, the decision criteria, the mechanisms and finally the outputs. Chen's model was also adjusted to capture the process of diffusion from both an innovation- and adopter-centric view. In addition, the impact individual organization decision outcomes have on the attributes of the standard and environmental characteristics are shown. The reasons and theoretical backing for these additions are explained in the following sections, which offer a description for each of the elements of the adopter-centric model developed and shown in Figure 5.

Adopter-Centric Factors

The adopter-centric factors are discussed based on four main categories taken from the model, namely:

Figure 5. Adopter-centric adoption and diffusion model

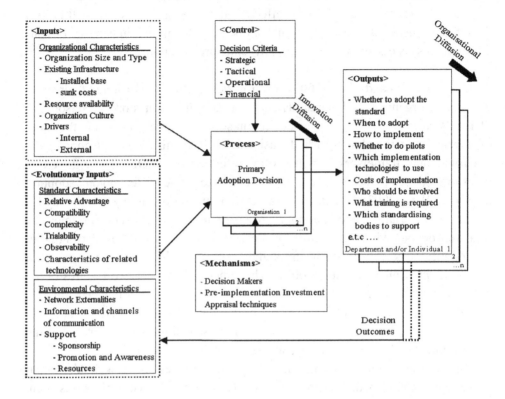

- Inputs
- Evolutionary inputs
- Control and mechanisms
- Outputs

Inputs

Organizational Characteristics: The attributes of this factor include the 'organizations size and type' and 'organization culture' which were described in the innovation-centric model section, and three additional attributes, namely:

- Existing Infrastructure: If organizations have a large installed base of existing standards they may be reluctant to adopt new standards due to familiarity of the existing standards and the prevalence of a well-established skill set. In addition, the amount of capital and equipment already invested in the existing infrastructure (sunk costs) may have to be discarded as a result of adopting the new standard, which may present a barrier. There is a perception that increased sunk costs lead to lower proliferation of the new innovation (standard) and can cause resistance to change (Hovav et al., 2004).

- Resource availability: This refers to the current resources available within the organization that may have to be deployed in the adoption and use of the new standard.
- Drivers: The drivers involved in the adoption of the standard may be internal, based on an organizational need, or internal pressure from, for example, senior management. External pressure may be as a result of the pressure from trading partners, or in the form of a mandatory standard or legal requirement.

Evolutionary Inputs

- Standard Characteristics: These attributes are identical to the attributes described in the innovation-centric model. In summary, standards that are perceived by organizations as having greater relative advantage, compatibility, trialability, observability and less complexity will be adopted more readily than other standards (Rogers, 2003). In addition, the characteristics of the related implementation technologies should be favourable to support the adoption of the standard.
- Environmental Characteristics: The environmental characteristics describe the set of factors that favour an organization's adoption of a standard by assessing the environmental conduciveness, which include:
  - ◦ Network Externalities: According to this theory the likelihood of adoption is a function of current adopters in the network. As previously mentioned, this is said to be true in relation to economies of scale where costs decrease as volume increases. In addition, as the number of adopters increases, there is an expected increase in experience, skills and supporting tools.
  - ◦ Information and channels of communication: This refers to the amount of information available to organizations regarding features of the new standard and how to gain access to the information. Information may be acquired through interpersonal communication or mass media. Availability of information has a positive effect in diffusion of innovations (Mustonen-Ollila, 1999).
  - ◦ Support: This may be in the form of sponsorship or funding, promotion and awareness and additional resources relating to the standard. This support may be offered by the standardization bodies involved in the development of the standard, such as national standard organizations,

international standard organizations, government, consortia, private alliances or individual organizations.

Control and Mechanisms

The decision criteria organizations use to adopt a standard will vary between different organizations. According to Irani et al. (1997) an organization will make a decision based on strategic, tactical, financial or operational criteria. All four categories may be relevant to an organization or they may base their decision on any combination of the different criteria. However, if the adoption of the standard is based on a mandatory or legal requirement, the importance of the different decision criteria is reduced because the decision to adopt the standard is not optional. According to Rogers (2003), the innovation decision process is a mental process through which an individual (or other decision-making unit) passes first from knowledge of an innovation, to forming an attitude toward the innovation through persuasion, to a decision to adopt or reject the innovation, to the implementation of the new innovation. Therefore, another mechanism in the decision-making process is the use of some form of pre-implementation investment appraisal techniques to persuade the decision maker(s). Common examples of these are business cases or doing some form of Return-on-Investment (ROI) analysis.

Outputs

The output of the standards adoption process represents the decisions an organization makes with regards to whether to adopt a standard or not and other implementation and project-related issues. The outcomes or consequences of these decisions will ultimately have an evolutionary impact on the attributes of the standard over time. If a group of organizations decide to adopt, implement and use a standard, there may be greater relative advantage, trialability and observability of the standard. This may be as a consequence of information gathered from some form of post-implementation appraisal and evaluation that may take place to highlight the benefits of the standard. Additionally, the compatibility of the standard may become more apparent as organizations begin to adopt and use the standard. Complexity relating to understanding, implementing and using the standard may also be reduced as more examples or case studies emerge relating to implementation and use of the standard. However, if a standard is continually rejected and not adopted it will have a negative impact on its attributes.

The results of decision outcomes will also have an impact on the environmental characteristics. If the number of organizations adopting and implementing the standard increases, this will have a positive impact on the network effects (network externalities), information and communication channels and support for the standard. Likewise if the standard is rejected or only adopted by a limited number of organizations, there may be a negative impact on the environmental characteristics, which may reduce the likelihood of the standard being adopted. In summary, over time the outcomes of the decision regarding whether to adopt a standard or not, may have an innovation (standard), organizational, and user impact that may be positive or negative, anticipated or unanticipated and perceived and/or verified.

Summary

This section has chronicled the development of an adopter-centric model. The section began by making a distinction between primary and secondary adoption. Following on from that Chen's (2003) organizational decision-making model was adjusted and revised to include the categories highlighted by main organizational IT adoption taxonomy TOE. These adjustments gave a more detailed view of the factors that impact the adoption of IT data-exchange standards from an adopter-centric perspective.

CONCLUSION

The models presented in this chapter have been developed as part of this research to capture the factors that influence the rate of adoption and diffusion of standards across their target population. Both the innovation-centric and adopter-centric model have an advantage over previous models by providing a more holistic view of the adoption issues facing a standard. In addition, taking both an innovation-centric and adopter-centric approach under one research project limits the bias of each individual approach.

The models provide a checklist of factors that need to be addressed in the adoption and diffusion of data-exchange standards from both a general innovation-centric perspective and an adopter-centric, decision-making perspective. However, the models do not provide any guidance on the validity, relevance and priority of these factors. In addition, it would seem likely that these factors may not be able to be generalised, and priorities may be different for different standards and organizations. Therefore, it was recognised that further investigations were required to verify the factors identified in the models and to understand their applicability. It was decided the investigations should be carried out based on the adoption and diffusion of four standards to be assessed as case studies. The chosen standards were:

- ISO 10303 – 224: STEP Application Protocol 224 (AP224), which defines the product definition for process planning using machining features. This is a standard that captures and communicates the information required for the process planning of mechanical machined parts, including simple assemblies (ISO, 2006a).
- ISO 15926-2: This is an international standard for the representation of oil and gas production facility lifecycle information. This representation is specified by a generic conceptual data model that is suitable as the basis for implementation in a shared database or data warehouse (ISO, 2006b).
- The NATO Codification System (NCS): The NCS is the common classification system adopted by all NATO member countries and used to support inventory management (Allied Committee135, 2005).
- DEF STAN(Defence Standard) 00-60: This is a Ministry of Defence (MoD) standard for Integrated Logistics Support (ILS) in the through-life management of defence equipment (UK MoD, 2005a).

The first standard, AP224, was chosen because it is a STEP application protocol. The next standard, ISO 15926-2, was chosen because it is one of the other standards produced by the SC4 community and, therefore, offers the opportunity to contrast two ISO/TC184/SC4 standards. The third and fourth standards are military standards that have been chosen as contrasting cases to the two ISO standards in order to determine if there are any common trends and features in the adoption of ISO data-exchange standards and military standards.

In the case of the adopter-centric model, the investigations were carried out based on the adoption of standards within the UK Ministry of Defence (MoD). The UK MoD was chosen since data-exchange standards like PLCS are promoted and used in the company, and there are very limited empirical studies that look at the adoption of standards within the defence community. Thus, the investigations into the adoption of standards within the UK MoD were carried out based on the adoption-decision process of three of the four standards named above, that is, AP224, DEF STAN00-60 and the NATO Codification System. Analysing the adoption-decision process across the three standards helps to reduce the bias recognised by West (2003), and also provides a comparative analysis of the adoption of an international standard (AP224), a regional standard (NCS) and a national military standard (DEF STAN00-60). Consequently, the results of these investigations not only fill a gap identified within the STEP and ISO/TC184/SC4 communities but also the military perspective, which will make a relevant contribution to the wider body of knowledge surrounding IT standards adoption. In addition, by taking both an innovation- and adopter-centric view, which is an approach that has not been previously identified in other research, the level of bias that has been recognised in each individual approach has been addressed. The next chapter details the research philosophy and strategy that has been adopted to verify the factors and barriers critical to the adoption of data-exchange standards.

REFERENCES

Aghion, P., & Bolton, P. (1997). A Theory of Trickle-Down Growth and Development. *The Review of Economic Studies, 64*(2), 151–172. doi:10.2307/2971707

Allied Committee 135. (2005). *The Group of National Directors on Codification.* Retrieved June 3, 2005, from http://www.nato.int/structur/ac/135/welcome.htm

Askoxford.Com. (2005). *Compact Oxford English Dictionary.* Retrieved December 6, 2005, from http://www.askoxford.com/?view=uk

Attewell, P. (1992). Technology Diffusion and Organizational Learning: The Case of Business Computing. *Organization Science, 3*(1), 1–19. doi:10.1287/orsc.3.1.1

Bagozzi, R., Davis, F., & Warshaw, P. (1992). Development and Test of a Theory of Technological Learning and Usage. *Human Relations, 45*(7), 659–686. doi:10.1177/001872679204500702

Burrows, J. (1999). Information Technology Standards in a Changing World: The Role of the Users. *Computer Standards & Interfaces, 20*(4-5), 323–331. doi:10.1016/S0920-5489(98)00068-3

Chen, M. (2003). Factors Affecting the Adoption and Diffusion of XML and Web Services Standards for E-Business Systems. *International Journal of Human-Computer Studies, 58*(3), 259–279. doi:10.1016/S1071-5819(02)00140-4

Davis, F., Bagozzi, R., & Warshaw, P. (1989). User Acceptance Of Computer Technology: A Comparison Of Two Theoretical Models. *Management Science, 35*(8), 982–1003. doi:10.1287/mnsc.35.8.982

De Vries, H., Verheul, H., & Willemse, H. (2003). Stakeholder Identification in IT Standardization Processes. In J. King, & K. Lyytinen (Ed.), *Proceedings of MISQ Special Issue Workshop on Standard Making: A Critical Frontier for Information Systems* (pp. 92-107). Seatle: MIS Quarterly.

Dreverman, M. (2005). *Adoption of Product Model Data Standards In the Process Industry.* Eindhoven, The Netherlands: Eindhoven University of Technology.

Egyedi, T., & Dahanayake, A. (2003). Difficulties Implementing Standards. In T. Egyedi, K. Jakobs, & K. Krechmer (Ed.), *Proceedings From the 3rd Conference On Standardization and Innovation In Information Technology* (pp. 75-84). Delft, The Netherlands: Tud-Tbm.

Egyedi, T., & Loeffen, A. (2002). Succession in Standardization: Grafting XML onto SGML. *Computer Standards & Interfaces*, *24*(4), 279–290. doi:10.1016/S0920-5489(02)00006-5

Gallivan, M. (2001). Organizational Adoption and Assimilation of Complex Technological Innovations: Development and Application of A New Framework. *Sigmis Database*, *32*(3), 51–85. doi:10.1145/506724.506729

Gerst, M., Bunduchi, R., & Williams, R. (2005). Social Shaping & Standardization: A Case Study from Auto Industry. *Proceedings of the 38th Hawaii International Conference On System Sciences*, Hawaii, (p. 204).

Hovav, A., Patnayakuni, R., & Schuff, D. (2004). A Model of Internet Standards Adoption: the Case of Ipv6. *Information Systems Journal*, *14*(3), 265–294. doi:10.1111/j.1365-2575.2004.00170.x

Huff, S., & Munro, M. (1985). Information Technology Assessment and Adoption: A Field Study. *MIS Quarterly*, *9*(4), 327–340. doi:10.2307/249233

Irani, Z., Ezingeard, J., & Grieve, R. (1997). Integrating the Costs of An IT/IS Infrastructure Into the Investment Decision Making Process. *The International Journal of Technological Innovation Entrepreneurship*, *17*(11-12), 637–647.

ISO. (2006a). *ISO 10303-224 Details*. Retrieved February 16, 2006, from http://www.Iso.Org/Iso/En/Cataloguedetailpage.Cataloguedetail?Csnumber=36000&Scopelist=Programme

ISO. (2006b). *ISO15926-2 Details*. Retrieved February 11, 2006, from http://www.Iso.Org/Iso/En/Cataloguedetailpage.Cataloguedetail?Csnumber=29557&Ics1=25&Ics2=40&Ics3=40

ISO. (2006c). *ISO Website*. Retrieved February 9, 2006, from http://www.iso.org/Iso/En/Isoonline.frontpage

Jakobs, K. (1996). On the Relevance of Global IT-Standardisation - Should User Companies Participate? *Proceedings of Fifth Annual Bayer International Conference*, Pittsburgh.

Jakobs, K. (2002). Even Desperately Needed Standards May Fail - the Case of E-Mail. *Proceedings of International Conference On the History of Computing and Networks.* Grenoble, France: IEEEXplore.

Krechmer, K. (2000a). Market Driven Standardization: Everyone Can Win. *Standards Engineering, 52*(4), 15–19.

Meister, D. (2004). *STEP Through 20 Years: Lessons and Theoretical Implications - Working Paper Edn.* Faculty of Information Systems, Richard Ivey School of Business. London, Canada: University of Western Ontario.

Miles, M., & Huberman, A. (1994). *Qualitative Data Analysis.* Newbury Park, CA: Sage Publications.

Moore, G. (1999). *Crossing the Chasm: Marketing and Selling Technology Products to Mainstream Customers.* Oxford, UK: Capstone Publishing Ltd.

Mustonen-Ollila, E. (1999). Methodology Choice and Adoption: Using the Diffusion of Innovations Theory (DOI) as the Theoretical Framework. In T. Käkölä (Ed.), *Proceedings of the 22nd Information Systems Research Seminar In Scandinavia (Iris22): Enterprise Architectures for Virtual Organisations.* Keuruu, Finland.

Mustonen-Ollila, E., & Lyytinen, K. (2003). Why Organizations Adopt Information System Process Innovations: A Longitudinal Study Using Diffusion of Innovation Theory. *Information Systems Journal, 13*(3), 275–297. doi:10.1046/j.1365-2575.2003.00141.x

Nelson, M., & Shaw, M. (2003). The Adoption and Diffusion of Interorganizational System Standards and Process Innovation. In J. King, & K. Lyytinen (Ed.), *Proceedings of MISQ Special Issue Workshop On Standard Making: A Critical Frontier for Information Systems,* (pp. 258-301). Seattle.

Nilakanta, S., & Scamell, R. (1990). The Effect of Information Sources and Communication Channels on the Diffusion of Innovation in a Data Base Development Environment. *Management Science, 36*(1), 24–40. doi:10.1287/mnsc.36.1.24

Prescott, M., & Conger, S. (1995). Information Technology Innovations: A Classification By It Locus of Impact and Research Approach. *ACM SIGMIS Database, 26*(2-3), 20–41. doi:10.1145/217278.217284

Rogers, E. (2003). *Diffusion of Innovations.* New York: Simon & Schuster International.

Sauer, C., & Lau, C. (1997). Trying to Adapt Systems Development Methodologies a Case-Based Exploration of Business Users' Interests. *Information Systems Journal, 7*(4), 255–275. doi:10.1046/j.1365-2575.1997.00022.x

Sherif, M. (2003). When is Standardization Slow? *International Journal of IT Standards and Standardization Research, 1*(1), 19–32.

Themistocleous, M. (2002). *Enterprise Application Integration.* Brunel, Australia: Brunel University.

Venkatesh, V., Morris, M., Davis, G., & Davis, F. (2003). User Acceptance of Information Technology: Toward A Unified View. *MIS Quarterly, 27*(3), 425–478.

Walli, S. (1999). POSIX: A Case Study In A Successful Standard Or, Why We Don't Need Radical Change In the SDO Process. In K. Jakobs, & R. Williams (Ed.), *Proceedings of the 1st IEEE conference on Standardisation and Innovation in Information Technology* (pp. 183-187). Aachen, France: IEEE.

Weiss, M., & Cargill, C. (1992). Consortia in the Standards Development Process. *Journal of the American Society for Information Science American Society for Information Science, 43*(8), 559–565. doi:10.1002/(SICI)1097-4571(199209)43:8<559::AID-ASI7>3.0.CO;2-P

West, J. (1999). Organizational Decisions for I.T. Standards Adoption: Antecedents and Consequences. *Proceedings of the 1st IEEE Conference on Standardisation and Innovation in Information Technology* (pp. 13-18). Washington, DC: IEEE.

West, J. (2003). The Role of Standards in the Creation and Use of Information Systems. In J. King, & K. Lyytinen (Ed.), *Proceedings of MISQ Special Issue Workshop on Standard Making: A Critical Frontier for Information Systems* (pp. 314-325). Seattle: MIS Quaterly.

Weston, L., & Whiddett, R. (1999). Factors Affecting the Adoption of IS Standards. In B. Hope, & P. Yoong (Ed.), *Australasian Conference on Information Systems* (pp. 1158-1169). Wellington, New Zealand: Victoria University of Wellington.

Whitman, L., Huff, B., & Presley, A. (1997). Structured Models and Dynamic Systems Analysis: The Integration of the IDEF0/IDEF3 Modeling Methods and Discrete Event Simulation. In S. Andradóttir, K. Healy, D. Withers, & B. Nelson (Ed.), *Proceedings of the Winter Simulation Conference* (pp. 518-524). Washington, DC: IEEE.

Wikipedia. (2005). Retrieved December 18, 2005, from Wikipedia - The Free Encyclopedia: http://en.wikipedia.org/wiki/main_page

Zaltman, G., Duncan, R., & Holbek, J. (1973). *Innovations and Organizations.* New York: Wiley & Sons.

Chapter 4
Research Philosophy and Strategy

INTRODUCTION

This research focuses on the development and uptake of data-exchange standards in order to gain an understanding of how such standards are adopted and diffuse across their target population. Hence, case studies and action research are used to fulfill the aims of the research, which are to:

- Establish the factors and barriers that influence the adoption of data-exchange standards
- Develop guidelines to facilitate and accelerate the adoption of data-exchange standards

DOI: 10.4018/978-1-60566-832-1.ch004

Chapter 2 highlighted both the critical need for data-exchange standards and the current limit of empirical research in the adoption of information technology standards and more specifically data-exchange standards such as STEP. These two issues were key motivations for this research. Therefore, to achieve the aims of this research, a qualitative approach was used to support the exploratory and descriptive nature of the research. This chapter discusses the justifications for the overall research philosophy and approach subscribed to, and the multiple data collection and data analysis activities used to collect sufficient data to answer the study's research questions.

RESEARCH PHILOSOPHY

Data-exchange standards are not adopted in isolation, they are implemented and used as part of an information system. The terms information system (IS) and information technology (IT) are commonly used interchangeably. However, it is important to distinguish that IS is a much wider term; as well as technology, it encompasses the social organizational structure, culture, intellect, and philosophy related to the distribution of information through the organization, whilst for IT the emphasis is only technology (Orlikowski & Bardoudi, 1991; Walsham, 1993; Themistocleous, 2002). Therefore, information systems are multi-disciplinary with different aspects relating to natural sciences, mathematics, engineering, linguistics and behavioural sciences, so there is no single framework that encompasses all the domains of knowledge needed for the study of information systems (Galliers, 1992). Nonetheless, Myers (1997) stresses that all research is based on some underlying assumptions about what constitutes valid research and which research methods are appropriate. Orlikowski and Bardoudi (1991) claim that information systems are rooted in a single theoretical perspective, but there is a wide range of philosophical assumptions regarding the underlying nature of a phenomenon under investigation. The various philosophies of research available are encompassed by the terms epistemology (what is known to be true) as opposed to doxology (what is believed to be true). Galliers (1992) therefore reflects that the purpose of science is the process of transforming things believed into things known: doxa to episteme. Several philosophical approaches are available for IS research including: positivist, critical and interpretive (Orlikowski & Baroudi, 1991). However, the main two approaches used in IS research are positivism and interpretivism.

Positivism

Evidence from IS literature suggests that the positivism approach has been the dominant epistemology in IS research (Galliers, 1992; Miles & Huberman, 1994; Walsham, 1995; Yin, 1994; Themistocleous, 2002). The positivist tradition has taken a firm hold in IS research since the late 1970s (Dickson & DeSanctis, 1990 as cited in Jackson, 2001), with Orlikowski and Bardoudi (1991) noting that 96.8% of research in the leading US IS journals conform to this theory. The positivism approach has risen from scientific tradition and therefore, it is characterised by repeatability, reductionism and refutability (Galliers, 1992). Positivist studies generally attempt to test theory, with the aim of increasing the predictive understanding of a phenomenon. They generally assume that reality is objectively given and can be described by measurable properties that are independent of the observers (researchers) and their instruments (Myers, 1997). However, Jackson (2001) notes there has been much debate on the issue of whether or not this positivist paradigm is entirely suitable for the social sciences with many authors calling for a more pluralistic attitude towards IS research methodologies. In line with this, Orlikowski and Baroudi (1991) only classify IS research as positivist if there is evidence of formal proposition, quantifiable measures of variables, hypothesis testing, and the drawing of inferences about a phenomenon from the sample to a stated population.

Interpretivism

Positivism is not the only relevant approach that can be used to understand IS. In both organization science and information systems research, interpretive research used to be the norm, at least until the late 1970s (Vreede, 1995, as cited in Jackson, 2001). Interpretive studies generally attempt to understand phenomena through the meanings people assign to them (Myers, 1997). Interpretive methods of IS research are "aimed at producing an understanding of the context of the information system, and the process whereby the information system influences and is influenced by the context" (Walsham, 1993, pp.4-5). In interpretivism, researchers tend to allow concepts (constructs) to emerge from field data rather than entering the field with pre-conceived theories (Galliers, 1992; Miles & Huberman, 1994). Interpretive researchers start out with the assumption that access to reality (given or socially constructed) is only through social constructions such as language, consciousness and shared meanings (Myers, 1997). Interpretive research does not predefine dependent and independent variables, but focuses on the full complexity of human sense making as the situation emerges (Kaplan & Maxwell, 1994).

Rationale for Choice of Philosophy

The choice between positivism and interpretivism has an impact on the empirical research strategy, since the former dictates that the researcher takes the role of an observer, whilst the latter dictates that the researcher gains knowledge by participating in the subject of the empirical study (Irani et al., 1999). Therefore, for the purpose of this research, the interpretivist philosophy has been chosen. The justification for this choice is based the fact that the aim of this research is to allow concepts to emerge from field data, using documentation, interviews and a questionnaire, with regards to the factors that affect the adoption of standards, which requires participation in the subject of study. In addition, the positivist philosophy is disqualified based on the findings of Orlikowski and Baroudi (1991), who classify IS research as positivist if there is evidence of formal proposition, hypothesis testing, and the drawing of inferences about a phenomenon from the sample to a stated population, which this research does not seek to do. Additionally, positivism cannot be used in the context of this research, since positivism assumes that knowledge consists of facts that are independent (Themistocleous, 2002). However, the literature indicates that there are many organizational, political, cultural, managerial, social and technical issues related to the adoption of data-exchange standards across a target population and within an organization, and these factors appear to be multiple, complex and interrelated.

RESEARCH APPROACH

Many different research approaches could have been adopted and used as a framework to undertake the planned research. One of the most common distinctions is between qualitative and quantitative methods. Myers (1997) lists some of the other distinctions as:

- Objective versus subjective;
- Being concerned with the discovery of general laws (nomothetic) versus being concerned with the uniqueness of each situation (idiographic);
- Aimed at prediction and control versus aimed at explanation and understanding,
- Taking an outsider (etic) versus an insider (emic) perspective.

The distinction discussed in this section is between quantitative and qualitative research.

Quantitative research methods were originally developed in the natural sciences to study natural phenomena, and qualitative research was developed in the social sciences to enable researchers to study social and cultural phenomena (Myers, 1997). In their book, 'Qualitative Data Analysis', Miles and Huberman (1994) quote quantitative researcher, Kerlinger, as saying, "There's no such thing as qualitative data. Everything is either 1 or 0" (p. 40). They go on to explain that in response to this, another researcher, Campbell, asserts, "All research ultimately has a qualitative grounding" (Miles & Huberman, 1994, pp. 40). According to Miles and Huberman (1994), this ongoing debate among qualitative and quantitative researchers is essentially unproductive. Miles and Huberman go on to argue that, like Howe (1985, 1988), "quantitative and qualitative methods are 'inextricably intertwined', not only at the level of specific data sets but also at the levels of study, design and analysis" (p.40). To support this view, Sieber (1973) offers a detailed list of reasons to combine methods. However, Firestone (1987) argues that quantitative studies 'persuade' the reader through de-emphasising individual judgement, stressing the use of established procedures, which leads to more precise and generalizable results. Firestone goes on to point out that qualitative research 'persuades' through rich depiction and strategic comparison across cases, and consequently overcomes what he terms the 'abstraction inherent in quantitative studies". In line with this, Weiss and Sirbu (1990) state, "when studying the process by which voluntary standards are developed, one is struck by the complexity and subtlety of the process" (p.111).

Therefore, a suitable research approach for the study of data-exchange standards adoption needs to acknowledge the complexity of the social processes and focus on both the context and specifics of standards adoption cases, making the qualitative approach more suitable for this research. This is in agreement with Dedrick and West's (2003) suggestion that a richer framework for understanding organizational standards adoption decisions can be developed through a qualitative study of a specific standards adoption case. However, Miles and Huberman (1994) suggest that researchers should not fall into a default mode that sees qualitative data as the only way of proceeding, and suggest considering whether a study could benefit from a quantitative aspect or component. Therefore, despite the fact that this research is based on a qualitative approach, a quantitative component in the form of a questionnaire was deemed as suitable to test some of the factors established from the four retrospective case studies.

RESEARCH STRATEGY

Galliers (1992) defines research strategy as the means of going about one's research, taking on a particular style and utilising different research methods with which to collect data. Cavaye (1996, as cited in Khalifa, 2002) suggests several research strategies that a suitable for collecting qualitative data and these are:

- Field Study - Where the researcher develops constructs (hypotheses) before entering the organization, collects the data with certain techniques, acting as an observer and does not wish to manipulate or control variables.
- Action Research - Where the researcher both observes and participates with the organization, but does not have an idea about the phenomena, and uses collected data to solve the issue of the phenomena and have control over variables.
- Application Description - Where the researcher accounts for the actual events surrounding the phenomena for display and learning purposes to the audience.
- Ethnographic Research - Where the researcher attempts to understand the meaning that practitioners attach to the phenomena and data is interpreted from the viewpoint of the practitioner.
- Case studies - Where the researcher enters the study environment (with or without theoretical constructs) for the purpose of studying a phenomenon in its real life context without intending to interfere with the phenomena.

In this research, both the case study and action research strategies were used. The research was divided into two phases in order to effectively carry out the specified aims. The case study strategy was used to revise and refine the preliminary conceptual models developed in Chapter II, by interviewing stakeholders in the adoption and diffusion of two ISO/TC184/SC4 standards and two military standards, and by analyzing the information obtained from the interviews and other data sources.

The case study strategy was chosen as the appropriate method because it offers the ability to describe relationships that exist in reality, and case study research is the most common qualitative method used in information systems (Orlikowski & Baroudi, 1991; Alavi & Carlson, 1992). Although there are numerous definitions, Yin (2002) defines the scope of a case study as an empirical inquiry that:

- Investigates a contemporary phenomenon within its real-life context, especially when,
- The boundaries between phenomenon and context are not clearly evident (Yin, 2002)

Yin (1994) suggests that there are different types of case studies, such as exploratory, descriptive and explanatory, depending on whether they are used to answer what, how and why research questions respectively. Based on this taxonomy, the case study followed in this research can be classified as exploratory. The reason for this is that the research questions are of a 'what' type. Additionally, case studies can be single or multiple and the decision to analyze one or more multiple cases is a central one to case study design (Yin, 1994). Single case studies provide 'rich' primary data of an organizational context. However, a single case study may not provide sufficient data that would justify conclusions about standards adoption and evaluation. Therefore, the use of a single case study has been abandoned in preference of multiple cases. Conducting multiple cases will enable crosschecking of findings. Eisenhardt (1989a) recommends that a research strategy that employs multiple case studies should not conduct more than ten, and no less than four cases. As such, the research will employ multiple case studies as suggested by Eisenhardt (1989a). Therefore, in order to fulfil the aims of this research, four standards have been chosen for the first phase of this research. The chosen standards for the first phase are:

1.   ISO 10303-224: Mechanical product definition for process planning using machining features.
2.   ISO 15926-2: Integration of lifecycle data for process plants including oil and gas production facilities, Part 2 - data model.
3.   The NATO Codification System.
4.   Def Stan 00-60 - Integrated Logistics Support.

A brief description of each of the standards can be found in the conclusion section of Chapter 3. The second phase of the research sought to further refine and test the preliminary conceptual models against the current adoption and implementation of PLCS, which is formally known as ISO 10303-239, using a 'Standards Adoption Checklist' developed from the case study analysis.

PLCS is a mechanism by which to ensure that support information is aligned with the evolving product definition over the entire life cycle of the product. There are a number of PLCS demonstration and implementation projects underway, and action research was viewed as the best strategy for this phase. There are various definitions of action research. However, one of the most widely cited is that of Rapoport (1970), who defines action research in the following way: "Action research aims to contribute both to the practical concerns of people in an immediate problematic situation and to the goals of social science by joint collaboration within a mutually acceptable ethical framework" (p.499). This definition draws attention to the relevance of action research for this phase due to the fact that focusing specifically on PLCS addresses some of the initial questions and concerns that were raised regarding the adoption of data-exchange standards. In addition, an active contribution was made through the development of guidelines and other practical steps, based on the finalised model, to support the uptake of PLCS.

QUALITATIVE RESEARCH PROCESS

Miles and Huberman (1994), state that an important factor in qualitative research is to establish the approach for gathering data. Many social anthropologists and phenomenologists advocate a 'loosely' structured, emergent, inductively grounded approach to gathering data, which is well suited for studies that are exploring understudied phenomena, exotic cultures, or very complex social phenomena. This approach provides the potential for a rich data set but equally posses a danger of data overload, which may require a lengthy period of time for analysis and cause a lack of comparability in multi-case research. The counter approach involves a "tighter" pre-structured design, which is relevant for researchers working with well delineated constructs where something is known conceptually about a phenomenon but not enough to house a theory. This approach provides clarity and focus, and can diffuse data overload. However, this "tighter" approach is argued to be more susceptible to bias, and it produces less case sensitive data that may be skewed or distorted to answer cross-case analytic questions. Miles and Huberman (1994) advocate a stance that is slightly off-centre leaning towards the structured end, and they quote Wolcott (1982) as stating that it is 'impossible to embark upon research without some idea of what one is looking for and foolish not to make that quest explicit'. In this study into the adoption and diffusion of data-exchange standards, the stance advocated by Miles and Huberman (1994) is the preferred approach. This is due to the fact that this research builds upon ideas developed in Diffusion of Innovation (DOI) theory, the economics of standards, organizational culture and previous studies. Hence, something is known conceptually about the phenomenon, but further empirical research is required to test and further explicate the conceptualisation.

In the light of this decision regarding data gathering, the next actions in the qualitative research process could now be carried out. Figure 1 was created during the research to act as an aid in pursuing the qualitative research process. Figure 1 is a diagrammatic representation of the qualitative research process discussed by Miles and Huberman (1994) in their book 'Qualitative Data Analysis'.

Action 1: Focusing and Bounding the Collection of Data

This action involves the following five activities:

Figure 1. The qualitative research process

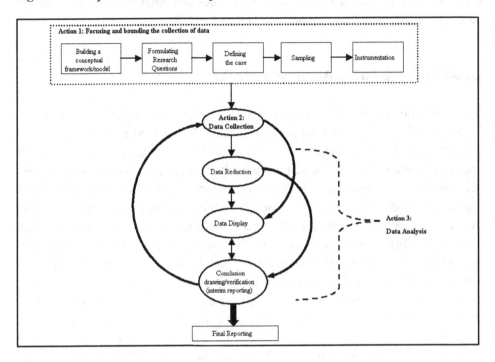

1. Building a Conceptual Framework (Model)

Initially, intellectual "bins" containing discrete events and behaviours, which have been sourced from a combination of theory, experience and the general objectives of the study, are created. Setting out these "bins", naming them, and clarifying their interrelationships lead to the development of the conceptual framework (model). Miles and Huberman (1994) describe the conceptual framework (model) as "simply the current version of the researcher's map of the territory being investigated" (p.18). The models detailed in Chapter 3 organised concepts such as inputs, outputs, processes, information feedback, boundaries and environment that were explored directly in data collection, in order to characterise important categories, dimensions and potential interrelationships within the adoption of data-exchange standards.

2. Formulating Research Questions

The two main research questions, given in Chapter One, laid the groundwork for the literature review and the development of the conceptual models. The formulation of the remaining, or second-tier research questions emerged from the conceptual models. These second-tier questions make theoretical assumptions more explicit and informed about what needed to be known 'most' or 'first'. The second-tier questions based on the two models are detailed in Appendix B-1. These second-tier questions also point towards the data gathering devices and fed directly into data collection (Miles & Huberman, 1994). In both phases of the research, interviews were used to collect data. Subsequently, the second-tier research questions acted as a starting point for the interview agenda questions.

3. Defining the Case - Bounding the Territory

This is the focus or the heart of the study, or in other words, the unit of analysis. Defining the case further assists in defining the boundaries of the study: what will and will not be studied. The case may be an individual, a group, a community or a role, and a case can contain numerous sub-cases. Nonetheless, in qualitative research a case always occurs in a specified social and physical setting. Individual cases cannot be studied devoid of a context (Miles and Huberman, 1994). The case for this research is the study of 'data-exchange standards' within the context of their adoption and diffusion across their target population and within an organization.

4. Sampling – Bounding the Collection of Data

Sampling further defines the case and involves an exercise of deciding whom to look at or talk with, where, when, about what and why, within the limits of available time and means. In other words, this identifies what activities, processes, events, times, locations and role partners need to be sampled. The conceptual models and research questions help set the foci and boundaries for sampling decisions.

Sampling both within and across cases puts flesh on the bones of general constructs and relationships. Multi-case sampling further adds confidence to findings by looking at a range of similar and contrasting cases with a mix of outcomes. Multi-case sampling was chosen for this research using reputational case selection based on consultation with Dr. Tim King, who has worked in standards development and implementation. During the discussions, a number of standards were suggested and the researcher decided to study the four case-study standards, detailed at the end of Chapter 3, in phase one and PLCS in phase two of the research.

ISO 10303-224 was selected because it was an example of a STEP Application Protocol that has been used both in the US and UK defence community. ISO 15926-2 was chosen as another ISO/TC184/SC4 standard that could give insight into the development of ISO/TC184/SC4 standards like STEP. The two defence standards were chosen to give insight into the UK defence communities response towards standards in general. In addition, Def Stan 00-60 had been mapped to PLCS, which is the standard that originally motivated this research and is to be studied in the second phase of this research. The use of multi-case sampling strengthens the precision, the validity, and the stability of the findings. However, the use of multiple case studies does not change the issue of generalizability, because generalisation is taking place from one case to the next on the basis of a match to the underlying theory, not to a larger universe (Miles & Huberman, 1994).

Ideally, researchers should stop adding cases when theoretical saturation is reached (Eisenhardt, 1989a). According to Glaser and Strauss (1967), theoretical saturation is the point at which incremental learning is minimal because the researchers are observing phenomena seen before. However, Pare (2002) points out that, "In practice, however, theoretical saturation often combines with pragmatic considerations to dictate when case collection ends. In fact, it is not uncommon for researchers to plan the number of cases in advance"(p.1). This was true for this research, and consequently due to time and resource constraints a limit of two cases were chosen for the initial innovation-centric analysis detailed in Chapter 5, and three standards for the adopter-centric analysis, detailed in Chapter 6. However, it is not certain whether theoretical saturation was reached and further investigations can be carried out to ascertain if these factors hold true for other data-exchange standards.

An additional level of sampling had to be carried out with respect to the roles of the interviewees. There are numerous different stakeholder groups involved in the development and use of a standards, these include: regulators, researchers, standards developers, standards sellers, standards purchasers, implementers, trainers, consultancies, certification and accreditation bodies, software vendors and testing houses as well as end users (adopters) of the standards themselves (NSSF, 2004a). During a series of pilot interviews, it became apparent that most people involved with standards have multiple roles within the range of stakeholder groups identified. Therefore, a reassessment was made of the stakeholder roles presented in the piloted interview agenda. The list was reduced to cover four main roles, which were established as being vital for this research on the adoption of standards. The four roles were seen as vital for this research because they covered the main groups involved in the development of a standard and the implementation and use of a data-exchange standard. The chosen roles include:

- Developers – because there are specific questions relating to the development process of a standard in relation to adoption
- End users of the standard – due to the fact that they are the actual users of the standard and may have been involved in the decision to adopt the standard
- Implementers – they may be from within an organization or external consultants and are responsible for the successful implementation of the standard within the adopting organizations

Table 1. Data gathering methods

Methods	Phase 1 - Case Studies	Phase 2 - Action Research
Interviews	√	√
Documentation	√	√
Archival Records	√	√
Direct Observation	x	√
Questionnaire	x	√

• Software vendors – this relates specifically to individuals or organizations devoted to developing software based on the data-exchange standards

In picking interviewees, a deliberate effort was made to make sure all four roles were covered for each of the five named standards, and the interviewees answered questions based on their roles. Therefore, part of the interview technique followed the 'guided interview' principles, which are described by Patton (1990) as being those where the interviewer improvises questions, adapting to the interviewee's personality and priorities, or in the case of this research the roles of the interviewees. What emerged in during the interviews was that most interviewees had multiple roles therefore, some interviewees answered questions from multiple sections of the interview agendas shown in Appendix B-2 and B-3.

5. Instrumentation

Instrumentation involves identifying the appropriate data gathering methods. Yin (1994) suggests six main data gathering methods in case study research. These include documentation, archival records, interviews, direct observations, participant observation and physical artefacts. Yin (1994) gives a detailed review of the strengths and weaknesses of the different methods. For the purpose of this research the four methods chosen include, documentation, archival records, interviews and direct observation. In addition, a questionnaire was administered during the second phase of active research of PLCS to empirically test some of the findings from the first phase. Table 1 details the breakdown of the methods used in each phase.

Yin (1994) recommends that a case study employ multiple methods of data collection. The use of variety of data collection methods enables data triangulation to take place in order to add validity and reliability to the research findings. The data gathering methods used were:

- Interviews
- Documentation and archival records
- Direct observation and questionnaire

Interviews

Interviews are the main tool for the collection of data within qualitative research (Denzin & Lincoln, 1994) and were the main data gathering method used in this research. Denzin & Lincoln explain that interviews can be structured, semi-structured and unstructured. In this research, guided semi-structured interviews were carried out with a variety of individuals based on the four roles specified in the sampling section, and a deliberate effort was made to make sure all roles were adequately represented for each standard. In addition to that, some interviewees suggested further people as potential interview candidates. In the end, five candidates were interviewed for each of the four standards in phase one, resulting in a total of twenty interviews for the first phase. In the second phase, which focused on the adoption of PLCS, a further five interviews were conducted. However, two of the interviews in the second phase were group interviews.

Of the total twenty-five interviews, twenty-one were conducted face to face and four over the phone. All interviews were recorded and transcribed and reviewed by the different interviewees, so that permission could be gained to use direct quotes from the interviews. A stipulation was given that if the interviewees so chose, neither they nor the organization they were affiliated with would be associated with any of the quotes or paraphrases of their words. Consequently, for this study the interviews served several of the purposes, as listed by Lincoln and Guba (1985):

- Obtaining here-and-now constructions of a phenomena
- Reconstructing previous events
- Obtaining projections of the future
- Verifying and corroborating data from other sources.

The first draft of the phase one interview agenda was piloted with three additional employees of the LSC Group (at that time based in Tamworth, England) who had each had at least four years experience with one of the five named standards. As a result of the pilot interviews, changes were made to the interview agenda. The interview agenda of phase two was based on the results of the first phase. Full copies of the phase one and phase two interview agendas can be found in Appendix B-2 and Appendix B-3 respectively.

Documentation and Archival Records

Yin (1994) states that documentary information is likely to be relevant to every case study. Documents of all types can help the researcher uncover meaning, develop understanding, and discover insights relevant to the research problem (Merriam, 1988). In this research, documentary information was used to help develop a chronology of the development and uptake of the named standards. Most documents and archival records were summarised and analyzed.

Direct Observation and Questionnaire

This was done in phase two during a series of workshops carried out on the practical implementation of PLCS. For 6 weeks, over 200 military and industry end-users were observed as they discussed and interacted with the PLCS-based systems. During the observations, a full log of all questions and concerns raised during the workshop was taken, and in addition, a questionnaire was administered at the end of the workshop to assess end-user attitudes to data-exchange standards.

Action 2: Data Collection

This action deals with the management issues surrounding the collection of data. This includes issues such as: purchase of analysis software; time planning; acquisition of recording equipment, and identification and notification of potential interviewees. In light of this, the following actions were taken:

- Development of a data collection agenda: This agenda took into account any possible failures of or delays that interviewees may experience, by setting up back-up plans to deal with such problems.
- Development of an interview timetable: This timetable set aside dates and times and possible durations of interviews.
- Identification of supplementary framework procedures: This is where additional confidentiality agreements were made with regards to names of organizations or specific employees. In addition recording and transcribing equipment was booked. A copy of the letter sent to all interviewees can be found in Appendix B-4.

Action 3: Data Analysis

Data analysis is broken down into three types of activities, namely: data reduction, data display, and conclusions drawing or verification. Miles and Huberman (1994) advise interweaving data collection and analysis from the start. In their view, the three analysis activities and the activity of data collection itself form an interactive cyclic process (shown in Figure 1). A researcher moves steadily among the four activities during collection of data and then shuttles among reduction, display and conclusion drawing or verification for the remainder of a study until a final report is produced. A description of each of the named activities follows.

1.   **Data reduction:** This refers to the process of selecting, focusing, simplifying, abstracting and transforming the data that appear in written-up field notes or interview transcripts. This is the part of analysis that sharpens, sorts, focuses, and discards and organizes data in such a way that final conclusions can be drawn and verified (Miles & Huberman, 1994). It can also be seen as data condensation. Examples of data reduction methods include, writing summaries, coding, teasing out themes, making clusters, making partitions and writing memos. Summaries and memos were made of the documents and archival records collected, the main form of data reduction was coding. Strauss and Corbin (1998) define coding as the analytical processes through which data are fractured, conceptualised and integrated to form theory. Coding is a significant form of data reduction because it is a powerful data labelling and data retrieval device that helps speed up analysis and is the main method of data reduction used in this research. The codes are tags or labels for assigning units of meaning to the descriptive or inferential information complied during a study. This part of analysis covers how to differentiate and combine the data that has been retrieved and the reflections one makes about this information. The code list used for this research is shown in Appendix B-5. The code was initially based on the research questions, but additions were made to include the factors that emerged from the data.

2.   **Data display:** This is an organized, compressed assembly of information that permits conclusion drawing and action. Matrices, graphs, charts and networks are all designed to assemble organized information into an immediately accessible, compact form so that the analyst can see what is happening and either draw justified conclusions or move on to the next step of analysis the display suggests may be useful. The displays chosen for this research are shown in Chapters Five, Six, Eight and Nine.

3.   **Conclusion drawing/verification:** From the start of data collection, qualitative decisions are made with regards to, the noting of regularities, patterns, explanations, possible configurations, casual flows and propositions. Miles and Huberman (1994) state that there will be numerous iterations of this process before final conclusions and recommendations for future work are published.

This aspect of qualitative analysis can be found in Chapters 5, 6, 8 and 9 of this book.

Tools Used for Data Analysis

In order for data analysis to be carried out different software applications can be used. The choice of tool for data analysis is dependent on the nature of the data, more specifically, if the data is qualitative or quantitative. In this research, both sets of data were used; consequently both qualitative and quantitative data analysis tools were used. The remainder of this section discusses the two tools that were used and the reasons for choosing the tools.

Qualitative Data Analysis Tool: ATLAS.ti

Tools for the analysis and management of qualitative data have come of age (Lewis, 1998). According to Barry (1998) the growing literature on Computer Assisted Qualitative Data Analysis Software (CAQDAS) expresses both hopes and fears. The hopes are that CAQDAS will, amongst other benefits, help automate, speed up and liven the coding process, and aid more conceptual and theoretical thinking about data. Some of the main fears are that CAQDAS will distance people from their data, and will lead to qualitative data being analyzed quantitatively (Barry, 1998).

Two of the most commonly used CAQDAS tools are ATLAS.ti and NUD.IST. Choosing between the two tools can be difficult, both NUD.IST and ATLAS.ti have been developed on the background of Grounded Theory (Koenig, 2006), and offer similar functionality (Lewis, 1998). The final choice of tool is often based on a combination of practical considerations and personal preference. Some of the practical considerations include:

- System requirements: For example, ATLAS.ti cannot run on a Macintosh operating system. However, both tools run on Windows-based personal computers.
- Document types they can handle: For example ATLAS.ti can handle ASCII text, graphics, video and audio data. On the other hand NUD.IST can only handle ASCII text.

Some of the personal and subjective considerations include ease of use and the 'interface feel'. Koenig (2006) offers a comprehensive and detailed comparison of the main features of the main CAQDAS tools including ATLAS.ti and NUD. IST. However, for the purpose of this research ATLAS.ti was chosen as the most appropriate tool. The two main reasons for this being:

- The research required the coding and analysis of twenty-five transcribed interviews, and was therefore a relatively simple and straightforward project. ATLAS.ti is generally recommended for use in simple projects (Barry, 1998).
- ATLAS.ti was visually more attractive with a well-designed interface.

Quantitative Data Analysis Tool: SPSS

A questionnaire was administered during the second phase of the research to test user attitudes towards standards. The data collected was analyzed using a series of statistical tests detailed in Chapter Nine. The analysis tool used to carryout the statistical tests was SPSS. SPSS (originally, Statistical Package for the Social Sciences) was released in its first version in 1968, and is among the most widely used programs for statistical analysis (SPSS website – www.spss.com). SPSS was chosen because it can read data from other spreadsheets and databases, and in this research, data was uploaded from a Microsoft Excel spreadsheet into SPSS. SPSS also provided a quick and simple means of carrying out the descriptive and non-parametric statistical tests used in the research.

CONCLUSION

This chapter has detailed the research philosophy, approach and strategy that has been chosen to fulfil the aims specified, and best answer the research questions posed. These methodology choices are summarised in Table 2. The justifications for each methodological were explained and the final sections of this chapter gave

Table 2. Overview of research philosophy, approach and strategies

Research Philosophy			
Interpretivism			
Research Approach			
Qualitative Research (With a quantitative element in phase 2)			
Research Strategies			
Phase 1 - Case Studies		Phase 2 - Action Research	
Innovation-centric analysis ISO 10303-224 ISO 15926-2	Adopter-centric analysis ISO 10303-224 NCS Def Stan 00-60	Innovation-centric analysis ISO 10303-239 (PLCS)	Adopter-centric analysis ISO 10303-239 (PLCS)

a detailed breakdown of the qualitative research process that has been followed in this research. The next two chapters, Chapters 5 and 6 present the findings of case studies in phase one. At the beginning of each of these chapters is a more detailed description of the methodological approach specific to each chapter.

REFERENCES

Alavi, M., & Carlson, P. (1992). A Review of MIS Research and Disciplinary Development. *Journal of Management Information Systems, 8*(4), 45–62.

Barry, C. (1998). *Choosing Qualitative Data Analysis Software: Atlas/ti and Nudist Compared.* Retrieved December 8, 2005, from Sociological Research Online: http://www.socresonline.org.uk/3/3/4.html

Cavaye, A. (1996). Case Study Research: A Multi-Faceted Research Approach for IS. *Information Systems Journal, 6*(3), 227–242. doi:10.1111/j.1365-2575.1996.tb00015.x

Dedrick, J., & West, J. (2003). Why Firms Adopt Open Source Platforms: A Grounded theory of Innovation and Standards Adoption. In J. King, & K. Lyytinen (Ed.)*: Proceedings of MISQ Special Issue Workshop on Standard Making: A Critical Frontier for Information Systems* (pp. 236-257). Seattle: MISQ Quaterly.

Denzin, N., & Lincoln, Y. (1994). *Handbook of Qualitative Research.* Thousand Oaks, CA: Sage Publications.

Eisenhardt, K. (1989a). Building Theories from Case Study Research. *Academy of Management Review, 14*(4), 532–550. doi:10.2307/258557

Firestone, W. (1987). Meaning in Method: The Rhetoric of Quantitative and Qualitative Research. *Education Researcher, 16*(7), 16–21.

Galliers, R. (1992). *Information Systems Research: Issues, Methods, and Practical Guidelines.* Oxford, UK: Blackwell Scientific Publications.

Glaser, B., & Strauss, A. (1967). *The Discovery of Grounded theory: Strategies for Qualitative Research.* Chicago: Aldine Publishing Company.

Irani, Z., Grieve, R., & Race, P. (1999). A Case Study Approach to Carrying Out Information Systems Research: A Critique. *International Journal of Computer Applications in Technology, 12*(2), 190–198. doi:10.1504/IJCAT.1999.000203

Jackson, T. (2001). *The Cost Effectiveness of Electronic Communication.* Loughborough University.

Kaplan, B., & Maxwell, J. (1994). Qualitative Research Methods for Evaluating Computer Information Systems. In J. Anderson, C. Aydin, & S. Jay (Eds.), *Evaluating Health Care Information Systems: Methods and Applications* (pp. 45-68). Thousand Oaks, CA: Sage Publications.

Khalifa, G. (2002). *Information Systems Investment Evaluation in the Public Sector.* Brunel: Brunel University.

Koenig, T. (2006). *CAQDAS Comparison.* Retrieved January 5, 2006, from Loughborough University Web site: http://www.lboro.ac.uk/research/mmethods/research/software/caqdas_comparison.html

Lewis, R. (1998). Atlas/Ti and Nud.Ist: A Comparative Review of Two Leading Qualitative Data Analysis Packages. *Cultural Anthropology Methods, 10*(3), 41–47.

Lincoln, Y., & Guba, E. (1985). *Naturalistic Inquiry.* Newbury Park, CA: Sage Publications.

Merriam, S. (1988). *Case Study Research In Education: A Qualitative Approach.* San Francisco: Jossey-Bass Inc.

Miles, M., & Huberman, A. (1994). *Qualitative Data Analysis.* Newbury Park, CA: Sage Publications.

Myers, M. (1997). Qualitative Research in Information Systems. *MIS Quarterly, 21*(2), 241–242. doi:10.2307/249422

NSSF. (2004a). *National Standardization Strategic Framework - How Standardization Works the Standardization Map.* Retrieved January 17, 2004, from NSSF Web site: http://www.nssf.info/mapnotes.pdf

Orlikowski, W., & Baroudi, J. (1991). Studying Information Technology in Organizations: Research Approaches and Assumptions. *Information Systems Research, 2*(1), 1–28. doi:10.1287/isre.2.1.1

Pare, G. (2002). Enhancing the Rigor of Qualitative Research: Application of a Case Methodology to Build Theories of IT Implementation. *Qualitative Report, 7*(4).

Patton, M. Q. (1990). *Qualitative Evaluation and Research Methods.* Newbury Park, CA: Sage.

Patton, M. Q. (2002). *Qualitative Evaluation and Research Methods.* Newbury Park, CA: Sage.

Rapoport, R. (1970). Three Dilemmas in Action Research. *Human Relations, 23*(4), 499–513. doi:10.1177/001872677002300601

Strauss, A., & Corbin, J. (1998). *Basics of Qualitative Research: Techniques and Procedures for Developing Grounded theory.* Newbury Park, CA: Sage Publications.

Themistocleous, M. (2002). *Enterprise Application Integration.* Brunel: Brunel University.

Vreede, G. (1995). *Facilitating Organisational Change: The Participative Application of Dynamic Modelling.* Delft, The Netherlands: Delft University of Technology.

Walsham, G. (1993). *Interpreting Information Systems in Organizations.* Chichester, UK: Wiley & Sons.

Weiss, M., & Sirbu, M. (1990). Technological Choice in Voluntary Standards Committees: An Empirical Analysis. *Economics of Innovation and New Technology, 1*(1), 111–134. doi:10.1080/10438599000000007

Wolcott, H. (1982). Differing Styles of On-Site Research, Or, "If It Isn't Ethnography, What Is It? *The Review Journal of Philosophy and Social Science, 7*(1-2), 154–169.

Yin, R. (1994). *Case Study Research: Design and Methods.* Newbury Park, CA: Sage Publications.

Yin, R. (2002). *Case Study Research: Design and Methods.* Newbury Park, CA: Sage Publications.

Section 2
Adoption and Diffusion Case Studies

This section presents the empirical data collected from two case studies that were carried out to validate the innovation-centric and adopter-centric conceptual models that were developed. The innovation-centric case study focuses the adoption and diffusion of two standards developed by the ISO technical committee and subcommittee responsible for the development of the data-exchange standards. The adopter-centric case study focuses on the adoption and diffusion of three standards within the UK Ministry of Defence. All case study information presented in this section is based on data collected and analysed between October 2002 and July 2006.

Chapter 5
Innovation–Centric Perspective:
ISO Technical Committee 184 Sub–Committee 4

INTRODUCTION

The standardization process and the success and failure of standards takes place in complex socio-technical settings that are shaped by a variety of factors and a multitude of actors (Gerst et al., 2005). The research reported in this book seeks to establish these factors in relation to the adoption and diffusion of data-exchange standards. Chapter 2 identified that there was a need to investigate the factors and barriers critical to the adoption of data-exchange standards to fill gaps within both the ISO/TC184/SC4 community and the research community for IT-standards adoption. Chapter 3 then introduced the novel approach of taking both an innovation-centric and adopter-centric view to address the research question, and chronicled the development of two conceptual models that capture the key factors to be researched. Following

DOI: 10.4018/978-1-60566-832-1.ch005

on from that, Chapter 4 went on to discuss the justifications for the interpretivist philosophy, qualitative approach and case study research strategy subscribed to for this phase of the research. Consequently, the aim of this chapter is to verify and examine the validity of the factors identified in the original innovation-centric model. The remainder of this introduction section gives an overview of the data collection and analysis processes that has been used in this chapter, and gives a brief overview of the ISO sub-committee responsible for the development of the two case study standards and concludes with a brief introduction to the chosen standards.

Data Collection and Analysis Process

Yin (1994) suggests that there are numerous data gathering methods in case study research. The main methods used in this part of the research, and the purpose for the chosen methods is detailed below:

- Interviews: This was the primary data collection tool used in this part of the research. Five interviews were carried out for each of the two standards. The interviews were carried out with developers, implementers, software vendors and end-users related to each standard from August 2004 to January 2005.
- Documentation: Documents and archival records were used to verify and add information regarding different issues raised during the development and adoption process.

In addition to these data sources the interviewees were asked to rate the importance of different factors during the interview using the five-point interview scale: very important, quite important, fairly important, slightly important and 'not important at all'. The results of this feedback are included in the discussions for each factor.

Silverstein (1988) ascertains that the key issue when dealing with multiple cases is the need to reconcile the tension between the particular and the universal. This involves reconciling an individual case's uniqueness with the need for more general understanding of more generic processes that occur across cases. This leads to the debate regarding the use of a variable (factor) or case-orientated approach when displaying multiple case data. Miles and Huberman (1994) point out that, "The variable approach is good for finding probabilistic relationships among variables in large populations, but it is poor in handling the real complexities of causation or dealing with multiple sub-samples, its findings are often very general or 'vacuous'. Case-orientated analysis is good at finding specific, concrete, historically grounded patterns common to small sets of cases, but its findings often remain particularistic, while pretending to great generality" (p.174). This confirms Ragin's (1987) view that each approach has plusses and minuses. In light of this authors such as Eisenhardt (1989b) recommend a mixed strategy. Consequently, Miles and Huberman (1994) have developed a series of tables, checklist matrices and causal networks that facilitate the mixed approach in a way that will, as Ragin (1987) puts it, "allow analysis of parts in a way that does not obscure wholes.... and compare wholes as configurations of parts" (p.83). Hence, the results of the data analysis in this chapter were displayed using the display techniques prescribed by Miles and Huberman (1994) in order to show the importance, validity and interrelationships amongst the various factors. The main technique used was causal network diagrams including some tables. The causal diagrams are presented as a series of models under each of the main factors. In the concluding section, a finalised model is presented, which represents an aggregation of the models of each main factor.

The final product from cross-case analysis may be concepts, a conceptual framework, propositions or possibly mid-range theory (Eisenhardt, 1989) or themes (Gallivan, 2001). In this research, the two chosen products are a revised conceptual model and themes, which are verified against the extant literature. Therefore, in addition to the causal diagrams and tables, themes were developed that are presented in this chapter. The development of themes is in keeping with work done by Gallivan (2001) on the adoption of technologies within organizations.

ISO Technical Committee 184 Sub-Committee 4

ISO Technical Committee 184 - Industrial-Automation Systems and Integration, is responsible for the development of the ISO data-exchange standards that have been chosen for this analysis. According to the ISO/TC184 (2005) website Business plan, the overall objective of the technical committee and its subcommittees is "To ensure timely availability of a consistent and coherent set of globally relevant standards for manufacturing systems and their integration within and across enterprises, including support for supply chain management and e-business, and meet current and planned industry requirements according to ISO vision and policy" (p.8). Major international companies from automotive, aeronautics, space and defence, electrical device, energy as well as IT companies, research institutes, trade associations, consortia, and academia participate in the development of ISO/TC184 standards. The work of ISO/TC 184 is divided among four sub-committees:

- **TC184/SC 1** - Physical device control;
- **TC184/SC 2** - Robots for industrial environments;
- **TC184/SC 4** - Industrial data,
- **TC184/SC 5** - Architecture, communications and integration frameworks.

The many companies involved in the various sub-committees are not direct members of the committees; national delegations are nominated from "mirror committees" formed by the national standardization bodies. For example, the British Standards Institute through committee AMT/4 develops the UK position on SC4 standards. Therefore, decision-making in ISO is based on the principle of 'one nation-one vote' (Witte, 2004), and according to the ISO website (2006a), the total number of published ISO standards related to TC184 and its sub-committees is 614.

The sub-committee relevant to this research is ISO/TC184/SC 4 (referred to as SC4 for the remainder of the chapter). The mission of SC4 is to develop and promulgate standards for the representation of scientific, technical and industrial data, to develop methods for assessing conformance to these standards, and to provide technical support to other organizations seeking to deploy such standards in industry (ISO/TC184/SC4, 2004). SC4 operates through a series of interdependent working groups and a quality committee. The committee's work is published through a series of multi-part standards in six areas of industrial product that are:

- **ISO 10303:** STEP - Standard for product data representation and exchange
- **ISO 13584:** PLIB - Parts library
- **ISO 15531:** MANDATE- Industrial manufacturing management data exchange
- **ISO 15926-2:** Integration of life-cycle data for oil and gas production facilities
- **ISO 18629:** PSL - Process specification language
- **ISO 18876:** IIDEAS - Integration of industrial data for exchange, access, and sharing

Details of each standard are available on the ISO/TC184/SC4 website (2004).

Two SC4 standards were chosen as case studies for the innovation-centric analysis. The first standard is ISO 10303-244 - a mechanical product definition for process planning using machining features (which will be informally referred to as AP224 for the remainder of this chapter). AP224 was chosen due to the fact that, like STEP-AP239 (PLCS), AP224 is being adopted within the UK MoD. ISO 15926-2, which is the data model part of ISO 15926-2, was chosen to bring a comparison of development and adoption of an SC4 standard within the oil and gas community.

This section has detailed the data analysis process that was followed for this part of the research and introduced the two case study standards. The remainder of the chapter gives a detailed analysis of each of the innovation-centric factors identified in the original model and chronicles the development of the revised model and themes.

Table 1. Drivers behind the development of the case study standards

	ISO 10303-224	ISO 15926-2
Drivers (motivations) behind development	To enable the RAMP process to facilitate the exchange of data between the US Navy and partner organizations	To facilitate the integration of data to support the life cycle activities and processes of production facilities
Nature of motivation	Economic	Economic
Impact on adoption	+ Indirect	+ Indirect
Importance of factor	Very important	Very important

CONCEPTION

This section assesses if the conception phase of a data-exchange standard has an impact on the adoption and diffusion of the standard. The term conception as it related to this research refers to three factors:

- The drivers behind development
- The initiators of development
- The conceptual idea and scope of the standard.

The first two factors are analyzed in this section, and the final factor emerges from within the analysis of other factors.

Driver Behind Development of the Standards

Standardization efforts are triggered by a complex array of economic and political considerations (Gerst et al., 2005). Table 1 summaries the main drivers behind the development of the two standards, the nature of these drivers and the impact these drivers had on the adoption of the standards. In the case of AP224 the driver behind development of the standard was to support and underpin the Rapid Acquisition of Manufactured Parts (RAMP) process within the US Navy. RAMP is based on the premise of applying just in time manufacturing to spares provisioning. There is a cost associated with part manufacture and storage and this cost exists whether or not the parts are required in service (LSC, 2002). In the case of ISO 15926-2 the motivation behind development is best explained by one of the key original members of the development team as being, *"to reduce data transcription costs of data handlers from the construction phase into the commission and operation phase"*.

The drivers behind the development of both standards had an underlying emphasis on the sharing, integration and interoperability of information relating to products and processes, and the drivers were predominately economic. The economic drivers were to reduce costs and save money by standardising descriptions and definitions of equipment and process data, in order to create efficiencies by which this data is collected, exchanged, shared and stored. For example, in the case of ISO 15926-2, original members of the development team explained in the interview that, *"The economic driver was significant because... if you are talking about an offshore platform which is 80 million pounds, then you can save millions of pounds, say typically 5 million down to 1 million of the cost of handing over the engineering information, and that is enough to be a motivation"*. The importance of these economic imperatives was captured by another developer who noted that, *"drivers [motivations] are critical and have to be economic, you develop standards for money, there is an economic driver and the driver is [that] there is benefit in doing things the same way"*.

None of the interviewees indicated that the drivers or motivations behind the development of the standard directly impacted the adoption of the standard. However, they did indicate that these drivers are critical to the entire standardization process and consequently all relevant interviewees described this factor as very important. Their views are summarised in a comment made by one ISO 15926-2 developer that *"The drivers [motivations] for creating the whole process were very clear and without those drivers I do not think anything would have happened"*. These drivers are a summary of the main perceived benefits of the standards, and as one interviewee noted, *"the benefits are the first driver."* What this shows is that these drivers are the trigger for the standardization efforts and motivated the initiators of development of the standard to embark on the development process. Therefore the resultant theme is:

Theme 1: The drivers behind the development of the standards were mainly economic and a direct reflection of the perceived benefits of the standard and, in turn, they triggered the standardization efforts by motivating the initiators to embark on the development process.

This mirrors an assertion made by Bonino and Spring (1999) that standards are generally considered to arise from purely economic motives or a desire for technical superiority. However, Bonino and Spring (1999) do go on to point out that standards can emerge in the realm of strategic decision-making where an organization views standards as a process of staking out a position in the market in advance of the technology. This feature was not identified in the development of the two case study standards. Nonetheless, what is important about this factor in relation to the adoption of the standards is captured by David and Shurmer (1996) who postulate that when the perceived mutual gain from a universal standard is low, the speed of standardization decreases. Hence, though the drivers behind the development of the

Table 2. Initiators of the development of the case study standards

	ISO 10303-224	ISO 15926-2
Initiators of development	South Carolina Research Association (SCRA) for the US Navy	Main Europeans oil and gas companies
Stakeholder role of initiator	Standard developers and implementer	Standard developers and end-users
Impact on development	The military provided most of the funding for development of the standard and tools for the standard	Encouraged contractors and software vendors to get involved in the development process. Provided funding
Impact on adoption	- Direct	+ Indirect
Importance of factor	Very important	Very important

standard do not directly impact adoption, they have an underlying influence on the overall development and adoption of a standard.

Initiators of Development of the Standards

The standardization arena is characterized by a complex web of interests (Gerst et al., 2005). Consequently, there are numerous stakeholders involved in the life cycle of a standard (NSSF, 2004a).

Table 2 details the main initiators of the development of the case study standards, and their impact on the development and adoption of the standards. In the case of AP224, South Carolina Research Association (SCRA) initiated the development of the standard to support the RAMP process. Though the South Carolina Research Association could be viewed as eventual implementers of the standard, they were central in the development of the standard, and used the requirements of the US Navy to initiate the development process. The close involvement of the US Navy meant that they were the main funder of the development of the standard, which had a positive impact on the development process funding and the resources available to develop the standard. Therefore, the resultant theme is:

Theme 2: The involvement of end-users in the conception of a standard can have a direct positive impact on the development of the standard, specifically through the funding arrangements.

However, the head AP224 developer pointed out that developing a standard, and tools for a standard, that has it roots in the defence environment, causes challenges when you try and sell products. He explained that, *"the big problem is, once you have developed for the defence community, [it] is not advantageous to eventually try and go out and sell your product on the market place, I do not know why that is.... so from the point view of us doing this development under our customer [the Navy] then trying to go and resell it ... that was not successful"*. Therefore, the resultant theme is:

Theme 3: Developing ISO standards from within a predominately defence background can have a direct negative impact on the subsequent adoption of the standard.

This theme confirms a discovery made by Meister (2004) during an interview at a SC4 committee annual meeting. Meister reports that the interviewee found that it was difficult to promote STEP in his country because of the significant involvement by military organizations in the development process. However, as part of his study, Meister (2004) put this finding to STEP experts who disagreed with this view and argued that STEP's military uses have been a positive factor. Nonetheless, the results expressed in Theme 3 seem to suggest otherwise and give another example of military involvement having a negative influence on the adoption of a STEP standard. A further review of the literature revealed no additional information regarding the impact of developing ISO standards from within a predominately defence background. Therefore, the finding presented in Theme 3 offers new insights into the impact initiators of the development of a standard can have on the subsequent adoption of a standard, and provides an opportunity for further research, which is detailed in chapter Ten.

In the case of ISO 15926-2, the initiators of the development of the standard were predominately the main oil companies in Norway, the UK and the Netherlands and they had a positive impact on development by providing funding. In addition, these main oil companies had a direct positive impact on the balance and diversity of the development team. One of the interviewees explained that, *"If the oil companies were not driving this nothing would happen. The contractors are there because the oil companies are there, and the software vendors are there because they see a large market place with all their customers."* What this shows is that, with their position at the head of the supply chain, having the oil companies initiate development encouraged contractors and organizations further down the supply chain to get involved in the development of the standard. The impact the balance and diversity of the development team has on adoption is discussed in detail in a later section. Therefore, the resultant theme is:

Theme 4: Having initiating organizations that are at the head of a supply chain has a direct positive impact on the balance and diversity of the development team.

What has emerged is that for both standards, the initiators of development had a direct positive impact on funding and in the case of ISO 15926-2 an additional direct positive impact on the balance and diversity of the development team. In relation to the adoption of the standards, this factor was described as very important because having end-users involved in the initiation of a standard indicates that there is a ready market for the standard, which has a direct positive impact on adoption.

Summary

This section has shown that issues surrounding the conception of a standard impact the adoption and diffusion of a standard. What has emerged is that perceived benefits of the standard underpin the drivers behind development, and these drivers motivated the initiators of development, who in turn had a direct impact on the development, funding and adoption of the standard. These key themes are summarised in Figure 1. Unless otherwise stated, the arrows indicate that 'X impacted Y' in the direction of the arrow.

DEVELOPMENT PROCESS

The two data-exchange standards that are being analyzed are ISO standards. This section aims to establish if any of the issues surrounding the development of these ISO standards has impacted their adoption. The section starts by giving an overview of the history of the development of the standards followed by a look at how the following three factors impact the adoption of a standard:

- Development process timescales
- Balance and diversity of development team
- Revision process

ISO 10303-224 and ISO 15926-2 Development Process History: ISO versus Consortia Development

The history of the development of the two standards varies. AP224 was developed solely through the ISO process. However, the development of ISO 15926-2 was initially through a series of consortia, followed by the ISO process. An overview of the development history of both standards is described in this section.

Figure 1. The impact of the conception stage on the adoption and diffusion of the standards

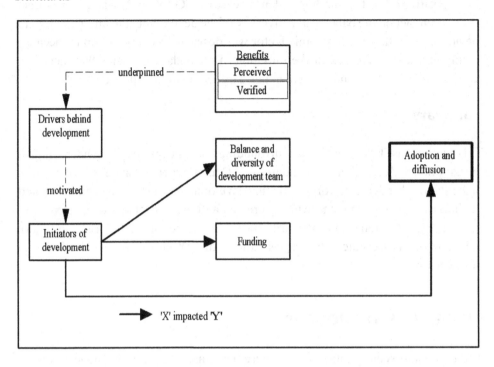

ISO 10303-224 Development History

The South Carolina Research Institute (SCRA) had a contract with the US Navy to develop software to support the RAMP process, and as early as November 1986 the RAMP Conceptual Design had been confirmed (RAMP virtual enterprise 2005). Within the scope of the RAMP mission, the South Carolina Research Institute recognized that some of the issues dividing customer and manufacturing communities included the availability, completeness and usefulness of technical data packages (RAMP Virtual Enterprise, 2005). To overcome these shortcomings, the South Carolina Research Institute pioneered and promoted the development of AP224 as a CAD-independent format, which is easily distributed, complete and included the necessary data to manufacture the modelled part. AP224 was first registered as a proposed new project within ISO/TC184/SC4 in October 1993. The head of AP224 development team explained that the project was carried out in two phases, which he detailed as follows, *"in the first phase we went to our customers, basically the Navy, and we did requirements gathering and asked them 'What do you want?'. Once we had that then we went to ISO and started participating [soliciting] requirements from additional countries so that we could indeed get international support"*.

AP224 was formally published as an ISO standard in December 1999. Since then the standard has had one completed formal review that was published as edition two in April 2001. AP224 is currently under review again, and as a consequence edition two of AP224 was withdrawn as a international standard in December 2005. The proposed publication date of edition three is April 2007 (ISO, 2006a).

ISO 15926-2 Development History

Over the years, the technical work of an oil and gas consortium called POSC Caesar was more and more related to the STEP standard and influenced by similar work in European standardisation consortiums such as PISTEP in UK and USPI in the Netherlands. In 1993 the three consortiums POSC Caesar, PISTEP and USPI_NL, in addition to a European Commission funded project, Processbase, and some French companies, came together under the umbrella of the virtual organization EPISTLE (European Process Industries STEP Technical Liaison Executive) to develop the EPISTLE data model. The EPISTLE data modelling team adopted the Shell Generic Entity Framework as the EPISTLE core model v1. Subsequent versions of the EPISTLE core model were developed over the following years. Then in September 1997, POSC Caesar initiated the New Work Item for ISO 15926-2 based on the EPISTLE core model. The EPISTLE data modelling team continued development of the data model as the EPISTLE core model, to make it publicly available, with different versions being submitted at various ISO stages of ISO 15926-2. The finalised version of ISO 15926-2 was formally published by ISO in December 2003, which is EPISTLE core model v4.5.1. Therefore, ISO 15926-2 has its roots in the Shell Generic Entity Framework, and is regarded as the formal standardization of the EPISTLE core model.

ISO versus Consortia Development

AP224 had straightforward development through the ISO process, but ISO 15926-2 had a more chequered history. The development of ISO 15926-2, first by consortia and then by the ISO process, touches on the debate within the IT standards community regarding the contrast between IT standards development through consortia as opposed to development through traditional bodies like ISO. Traditional standards development organizations (SDOs), like ISO, operate in an open, voluntary public fashion, observe a form of due process and make decisions through consensus. Standards development processes based on due process and the consensus principles are often criticized for being ineffective and time-consuming (Sherif, 2003; Belleflamme, 2002; Jakobs et al., 1996). For example, the time taken to develop an IEEE standard used to be an average of seven years, and the development time for an ISO standard has been known to exceed seven years (Spring et al., 1995). This time delay was expressed by the head of ISO 15926-2 development team who noted that, *"we had a good enough [standard] at the end of 1997 but the Board, including myself, decided we should go for ISO adoption and then we, in a way, started from scratch again because then we had to get involved with the Netherlands and UK and then we had to get new ideas on how to move on. So we had a detour and, after 2 to 3 years, we ended up with something very close to what we had at the end of 1997 I think. This ISO process caused delays."* Nonetheless, some of the other developers recognised the fact that having an ISO standard brought some brand identification benefits, and this is discussed in more detail later in this chapter.

Consortia were a vendor solution to the problem of long delays and ambiguous compromises in the SDOs formal standards process (Weiss & Cargill, 1992). No accepted definition, as yet, exists for the term 'standards consortium', and in practice, it can cover a variety of alliances. Authors such as Updegrove (1995), Weiss and Cargill (1992) and Hawkins (1999) provide classifications for different types of consortia. Egyedi (2003) offers a definition of a consortia that is relevant to this research, explaining that, "a consortium is an alliance of companies and organizations financed by membership fees, the aims of which include developing publicly available, multi-party industry standards or technical specifications" (p.1). From the point of view of the formal standards bodies, the challenge is that standards developing consortia are rivals (CEN/ISSS, 2000 as cited in Egyedi, 2003). Egyedi (2003) explains that this rivalry is mainly due to the fact that consortia can produce specifications quicker than the formal bodies because they do need not bother with a lengthy democratic and open process that demands consensus decision-making and a well-balanced representation of interest groups. However, as was pointed out in informal correspondence[1] with a standards 'expert', certain large consortia like OASIS (Organization for the Advancement of Structured Information Standards) do observe due process, and require a very broad level of consensus from their members. Consequently, the distinctions between SDOs and consortia are increasingly blurred.

Nonetheless, there are authors who question whether the improved speed of publication seen in many consortia is reached at a cost and at the expense of the quality and soundness of the standards (Oksala et al., 1996; Wegberg, 2004). However, as Cargill (1999) explains, "The message from the market is clear – IT standards developing organizations are no longer just the preserve of the ISO/National Body regime. The challenge that faces the discipline of standardization is healing the divide, not accentuating it" (p.9). The way to heal the divide between the two communities is best captured in an award-wining paper written by Lowell (1999) who proposes the use of the ancient Chinese statement of 'yin and yang'. Lowell explains that, "the yin and yang symbolize the dynamic balance in the world, including the standards world.... Despite the many changes that have occurred in recent years, there is still balance between the contemplative yin (the formal standards process) and the dynamic yang (the consortia standards development process)". However, Lowell does go on to caution that, "unless more can be done to expedite the formal standards development process, the union and harmony between the standards yin and yang will likely not last" (p.10). In the light of this, Bilalis and Herbert (2003) advocate closer contacts between both parties, and Kotinurmi *et al.* (2003) postulate that a hybrid system of committee and market outperforms each individual approach. Indeed, van Wegberg (2004) confirms this and explains that there are cases where firms form a consortium to develop a technology that they subsequently submit to an official SDO. This was demonstrated in the case of the development of ISO 15926-2, and two of the developers described this approach as their ideal model for standards development, and one developer stated that, "*my model for how standards get developed is that consortia do the work, and ISO provides a process through which you take things*". The interviewees went on to explain that consortia can be used as a vehicle to deal with mistakes before you go to ISO, and as a means of verification before you go public.

Development Process Timescales: Impact on Adoption

Weston and Whiddett (1999) point out that time seems to be one of the major faults of standards. As was mentioned in earlier sections, the process in use today for developing voluntary consensus standards, like ISO standards, is often criticized for its slowness and inefficiency (Weiss, 1993). The ISO development timescales for both standards took six years. One of the original ISO 15926-2 developers interviewed explained that at the beginning everyone naively thought the ISO process would take about three years. The developer went on to explain that this was very unrealistic and noted that, "*the reality is that you can have any amount of delay, almost anyone can delay a standard going through, whether intentionally or unintentionally and it is a deeply frustrating process*". This development timescale factor was described as a 'fairly important' factor by the interviewees because it impacted three other main factors:

1. End-User Involvement in the Standards Process

One interviewee explained, "*it was taking longer and people's interest diminished... the view was [that the standard] was taking too long and it is never going to work and [end-users] dropped out*". The resultant theme is therefore:

Theme 5: The long development timescales have a direct negative impact on end-user involvement in the standards process, resulting in a direct negative impact on the adoption of the standard.

2. Software Vendors Involvement in the Standards Process

Software vendors became disheartened and left the development process. The price was then paid when the process came to the adoption and implementation phase because as one AP224 developer explained, *"now we are paying that price, [software vendors] got out because [the standards] were not being developed fast enough and it is hard to get [software vendors] back in"*. Therefore the resultant theme is:

Theme 6: The long development timescales have a direct negative impact on software vendor involvement in the standards process, resulting in a direct negative impact on the adoption of the standard.

The details of the impact of end-user and software vendor involvement on the adoption of the standards are discussed in detail in later sections. Nonetheless, as a consequence of some stakeholders, like end-users and software vendors, pulling out of the development process, the funding levels were impacted, which again resulted in longer development times, so it is recursive problem.

3. Relative Advantage of the Standard

The relative advantage of a standard is also impacted by the development timescales, which has a subsequent impact on adoption. As one interviewee stated, *"the other concern is that [development] takes a long time and [during that development time] you get new technology, so [the standard] is old before it is finished"*. The notion of a standard being 'old before it is finished' impacts relative advantage because there will be new products that can compete and out perform the published standard. The resultant theme is therefore:

Theme 7: The long development timescales have a direct negative impact on the relative advantage of the standards due to the fear that the standards are lagging behind current technological advancements.

Dreverman (2005) made a similar discovery in his study, and goes on to explain that even though these new technological developments are not substitutes for STEP, they draw attention away from efforts surrounding STEP, particularly when the new standards yield benefits in a shorter time period. This concern has also been raised by others authors who recognise that the time for getting IT products to market in a rapidly changing environment is short (Burrows, 1999). If standards are slow in development, they may be too late for implementation in products". Therefore the concern that standards may be old before they are published is very valid, and this is particularly true for anticipatory standards like ISO 15926-2 and AP224. Cargill (1994) describes an anticipatory standard as ones that standardize a technology in advance of its availability as a product in any viable commercial form. Byrne and Golder (2002) point out that anticipatory standards have to be developed quickly and need to have an example installation if they are to guide future technology, otherwise, sub-optimal standards become prevalent. This concern was also expressed in the ISO/TC184 (2005) website Business Plan as one of the factors affecting completion of the technical committee's work program. The concern raised in the ISO/TC184 publication reads as follows: 'Late publication of standards that are incompatible with the demands of the advanced manufacturing applications or no longer meet industrial requirements' (p.11).

Development Process Timescales: Reasons for Delays

The data from interviews and published documents of the two standards indicate five main reasons for these delays, these are:

- Development participants commitment
- Development team dynamics
- Time taken to reach consensus
- Research nature of the development process
- Bureaucracy of ISO

1. Development Participants Commitment

Representatives to standard development groups are often 'volunteers' rather than having dedicated paid positions, which militates against the rapid development of standards (Weston & Whiddett, 1999). As a consequence of being volunteers, many participants in standards development teams work on a part-time basis, and this was true of ISO 15926-2 participants from the UK and Netherlands. However, one ISO 15926-2 developer indicated that this part-time approach was not the way things were organised in Norway, where people worked full time in standardization efforts. Nevertheless, the part-time approach used by some developers caused huge time delays and resulted in large unexpected development costs for the organizations that were paying monthly salaries for people to be involved in the development process full time. One solution offered by the Norwegian developer was to run these development programs as dedicated projects in order to counter these problems. De Vries et al. (2004) agree with this view and advocate that standardization projects should not only be managed through project management but also through process management.

2. Development Team Dynamics

The first issue relating to development team dynamics was leadership and diplomacy. As on developer noted, *"It was taking a lot of effort by some individuals to keep the diplomacy between the different types of organization, the different types of people in those organizations and the different nations"*. This confirms findings by Spring et al. (1995) who, in a survey of fifty-four IT standards committee members, found that the success of any given standardization effort is tightly coupled with the quality of the leadership provided. These leaders and committee members need to posses good political, diplomacy, and negotiating skills (Weiss 1993).

The second issue related to conflict resolution. As Spring et al. (1995) explain, "the single most important problem that must be addressed by the chairperson is the resolution of conflicts which may be technical, political, or personal in nature" (p.10). This was true in the development of both standards and most interviewees described the main conflict as being between the idealists and pragmatics. In the view of one of the AP224 developers, the idealists were more driven by academic rather than business orientation and went on to explain that, *"[idealists] are purist they get to the 80% development and they still want to carry on, and we know that the extra 20% of purism takes 80% of the money and 80% of the time"*. Other idealists were described by one AP224 interviewee as being too hung-up with trying to make the standards look *"pretty"*, but Cargill (1998) explains that the participants in standardization activities need to realise that they are not there to protect the standardization process, but they are there to get standards out. Cargill goes on to argue that perfect standards two years late are worthless. Both the issues surrounding 'development team dynamics' were impacted by the balance and diversity of the development team and led to significant time delays.

3. Time Taken to Reach Consensus

Consensus and due process are widely considered as the fundamental cornerstones of International Telecommunication Union's (ITU) and ISO's processes, it ensures that everyone who might potentially be affected by a standard has the right to participate in the process on equal terms (Jakobs, 2000). This indicates that a large group of stakeholders is able to be involved in the consensus process. Some of the interviewees noted that it took a large amount of time to reach consensus among the different members of the development team across the different countries. This confirms assertions made by authors, such as Söderström (2004) and Weiss and Cargill (1992), that consensus in large groups can be more complex and take time to reach. One interviewee pointed out that as a result of this large open group, the development team were continually going over the same issues, and he went on to explain that, " *the data model would tend to change depending on who turned up to the meetings* ". The interviewee went on to explain that, *"we elected to move to a fixed team and it was initially eight people and I was one of those eight, and they were given responsibility for the data model ... people outside that group would review the results of those eight, but those eight took the decision"*. This approach was also adopted in the development of a mortgage industry standard known as MISMO. Interviewees in a study by Markus et al. (2003) referred to this approach as the 'same ten people phenomenon', where much of the work was done by a rather small group of regular members who come to all meetings, and provided the continuity necessary to keep the process moving forward.

4. Research Nature of Development

The long development times were also attributed to the research nature of the development. In many cases, co-normative or pre-normative research is needed in order to make trustworthy standards (De Vries et al., 2004). As one interviewee explained, *"the research aspect has certainly been true for the STEP standard and ISO 15926-2. There is daily research going on because we did not have the answer when we started so this has been more of a research project"*. In addition, another interviewee went on to explain that, *"you are having to do collaborative research ... and that is the real reason why standards like STEP and ISO15926 take so long to develop"*. There were two main reasons given by the interviewees for the research nature of the development of these standards. Firstly, the standards were being developed around a technology that was not mature. One interviewee explained that, "normally when you develop standards it is around something that is well established, for example a screw size. So historically you develop standards when the technology is mature and that is not true today. What we are doing is research based standards development". However, this statement does not give a complete picture, an additional factor in this is the extent to which the debate is mathematically resolvable. For instance, the screw size works because we can agree to do the sizes to the nearest 0.25 of an inch for example. Therefore, in STEP, the application protocols that deal with geometry are easy to standardize because for example, a circle is always going to be a circle. However, difficulty comes when determining aspects like whether a 'task' is a 'process' or an 'activity'.

The second main reason is based around the conceptual idea and scope of the standard. Due to the wide scope of these standards, development of conceptual models to capture all data relating to the life cycle of a product can be a challenge. One of the ISO 15926-2 developers pointed out that dealing with the whole oil and gas industry, where different organization use different terminology and individuals have different worldview points, was genuinely difficult as all these world view-points needed placing into a model. The interviewee went on to explain that, *"we got quite deeply into the theory of classification and ontology and it was not until three years ago that we realised what we were doing ... people have been playing with this problem for the best part of two centuries."* The challenge of dealing with ontologies and semantics is a problem that is commonly acknowledged in the IT-standards world. As Jain and Zhao (2003) state, "while the standardization of the common syntax and the common mechanisms for web services can be considered in relatively healthy shape, the standardization of the common semantics is lagging far behind" (p.214).

The research nature of the development of a standard is an issue that has not been discussed in relation to the development timescales of ISO data-exchange standards. Most literature and studies attribute long development timescales to the bureaucracy of the ISO process and time taken to reach consensus. Therefore this finding has given a new perspective on the issues that cause long development timescales.

5. Bureaucracy of ISO

Discussion about the bureaucracy of ISO is prevalent (Jakobs, 1996; Weiss, 1993). Some of the developers interviewed noted that the bureaucracy of ISO is a barrier and causes time delays. However, one of the main ISO 15926-2 developers argued that, *"it is difficult to know how you could do the [ISO development process] differently when you are talking about getting so many nations involved...the bureaucracy of getting 15 or 18 nations involved and voting is going take a while.... I am not sure I could ever recommend a great change to that bureaucracy, I think one just has to work with it for the publication process".*

This section has detailed the impact of the development process timescales has on the adoption and diffusion of the case studies' standards. The section began by giving an overview of the development history of both standards and discussed the benefits of having a hybrid of market and committee standards development. Indeed, the benefit of this hybrid approach was attributed as one of the main reasons for the successful adoption of STEP AP214 in the automobile supply chain. Dreverman (2005) reports that the standard was first developed in separate project teams before going to ISO, thereby avoiding the slow ISO process. This section went on to detail the impact of development delays and the main causes of these

Figure 2. The impact of the development process on the adoption and diffusion of the standards

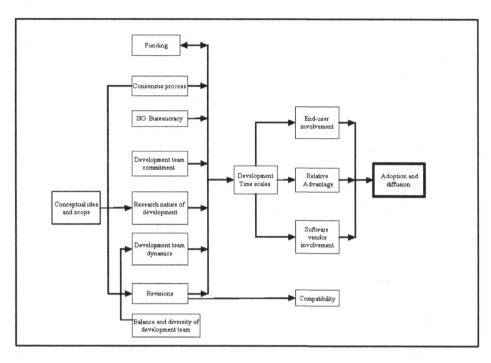

delays. The interrelationship of these different factors are summarised in Figure 2. As a final note it must be pointed out that in recent times procedures like the ISO's Fast Track have been adopted, and bodies, such as the European Telecommunications Standards Institute, have even been funded in an attempt to deliver adequate standards specifications in a timely fashion (Jakobs, 1996).

Balance and Diversity of Development Teams: End-User and Software Vendor Involvement

The composition of standard committees is an essential element of standardization processes (De Vries et al., 2003). The developers of the two ISO standards agreed with this view and described that factor as quite important. The interviewees involved with the development of both standards, when directly asked in the interview, agreed that there was a good balance and diversity of stakeholders in relation to skills and representative organizations from the different stakeholder groups. For AP224, one interviewee explained that, *"There was a balance in participation and we had representation in the US, supporting our client and huge representation internationally to give international support"*. One of the main reasons for this is that the very nature of an ISO standard dictates that there has to be representation from across the globe, which was true for ISO 15926-2 as well. There are numerous stakeholders involved in a standards development process. However, the main discussion in remainder of this section is devoted to two main groups within the development process, namely end-users and software vendors. The impact of other stakeholder groups, like for example government, national standards bodies and researchers, is not analyzed in detail in this research but there is an opportunity for further work to be done.

End-User Involvement in the Standards Process

The importance of end-user involvement in the standards process was a perennial discussion point, and the interviewees described this as a very important factor. From the end-user perspective, being involved was critical, as one interviewee put it, *"the incentive for getting involved in developing the standard is to ensure that the standard actually meets your requirements"*. This interviewee went on to say it is good to, *"put yourself in the position of being an early adopter, although you have to be careful about that"*. However, it was stated that, *"There is being on the leading edge and being on the 'bleeding' edge. That is a hard judgement"*. Therefore, in order for firms to have an appreciable impact on the shape of ISO standards they have to be involved in the development process as early as possible (Witte, 2004). This shows that, from the end-user vantage point, involvement is key and does have a positive impact on overall adoption if the organization believes that they are getting a standard that meets their requirements. Therefore the resultant theme is:

Theme 8: End-users were involved in the development process in order to ensure the standards met their requirements, which has a direct positive impact on the adoption of the standard.

This theme is confirmed by De Vries et al. (2003) who ascertain that, "involvement of users and other stakeholder groups may contribute to the quality of the resulting standards and may enhance stakeholder preparedness to use these standards"(p.95). Therefore, end-users have an important role in IT standardization, and Jakobs et al. (1997) point out that end-users are the only ones in a position to contribute meaningful real-world requirements to the standards process, and they advocate that end-user voices need to be heard and strengthened, but not at all costs, especially where there is potential for contradicting requirements. However, it seems the representation of users in IT standardization is often inadequate (De Vries et al., 2003). A research project carried out by De Vries et al. (2003) found 27 different barriers to end-user participation. These included includes issues like lack of knowledge, time and money of potential participants, lack of transparency in committee structures and standards development procedures, standardization officers' and conveners' behaviour, and committee culture.

The counter argument with regards to end-user involvement postulates that having large end-user participation, results in larger development teams, which can have a negative impact on development process, as was described in previous sections of this chapter. Jakobs et al. (1996) confirm this view in their study of standards setting working groups in the field of electronic communications. In their study they report that some of the respondents to their interviews expressed concern that having more people involved in the development process would mean more overheads, more hidden agendas, and perhaps a dilution of expertise. Nonetheless, standards organizations are looking at different ways in which end-user participation can be enhanced (Burrows, 1999), and Jakobs (1996) suggests that standards organizations should look at how the exchange of views and dissemination of information enabled by e-mail and Internet services could facilitate greater end-user participation in standards setting.

Software Vendor Involvement in the Standards Process

The interviewees cited having software vendor involvement in the standards process as a very important factor that impacts the adoption of data-exchange standards. One of the interviewees pointed out that, *"Publication of an ISO standards does not make it a standard. It is the implementation and use of the standard that does that"*. This is why software vendors are a vital part to the standards process. As one ISO 15926-2 interviewee explained, *"We had involvement from software vendors, tool providers, and indeed, it is essential to get those people involved because actually, for this standard, in the end it will be transparent to the end-users. They will never know that they have a standard. It will just work, and it will work because the tool vendors have been conforming to the standards"*. Even though software vendor involvement was critical, there were challenges at times, because as one interviewee pointed out, *"the software vendors have a natural tendency to want you to be dependent on their products."* Consequently some developers describe how development meetings could sometimes end up feeling like a software vendors marketing platform. This points to observations by Dido and Gold (1993, as cited in Warner, 2003) that corporate loyalty can supersede the objectivity of the standards process.

One of the developers involved with ISO 15926-2 explained how one consortium would not allow software vendors to be involved initially because they saw software vendors as only providing a service, and as a consequence they had an arm's length relationship with the vendors. This confirms De Vries et al.'s (2004) view that, "in formal standardization, all stakeholders have legitimacy, because all are welcome to be represented in standards setting. In practice this may be slightly different as certain committees might prefer some stakeholders not to join". However, other consortium members emphasised that they always had the software vendors and various people involved because they saw development of the standard as more collaborative. Therefore the resultant theme is:

Theme 9: Having software vendor involvement in the standards process was seen as critical to ensure the successful adoption of the standards.

This confirms Söderström's (2004) view that having software vendors involved with standards means that they can take specifications and incorporate them into software that end-users can buy and use. However, Meister (2004) points out that Software vendors are seen by some in the STEP community as reluctant, at best, integrators of STEP into their products. Some of the reasons interviewees in this research gave for this reluctance were:

- **The desire for a compelling business case**

One AP224 developer explained this by stating that, *"The CAD vendors are basically saying you need to show us the cost benefit for developing software around STEP, and that is still very hard to do ... [Software vendors] do not want to develop anything around STEP standards without a business case".*

- **Perceptions of standardization**

Some software vendors were reluctant because, as one interviewee explained, the vendors consider use of standards as a negative influence on the proprietary value of their data and tools and they see standardization as a means by which they lose control over their data, which they equated as losing control over their jobs.

The two points raised by the interviewees confirms the view postulated by Gallaher et al. (2002) that vendors will add STEP capabilities to their software tools only if they believe doing this will generate additional revenue or increase market share. The software vendors main fear is that by providing open neutral capability through standards, their customers will find it easier to change to different system. Dreverman (2005) described this as the software vendors' fear of loosing their 'lock-in' advantage. Indeed, software vendors benefit when their customers have significant investment in legacy data, support systems and user training material they provide, and this is particularly true for vendors with a large market share who are reluctant to introcuce capabilities that will lower swticing costs (Gallaher et al.

2002). Therefore, even if software vendors are willing to be data standard compliant, they will only invest if there is clear market demand and business benefit (Gielingh, 2008). More research is required to investigate methods that can be used to establish a compelling business case for the use of data-exchange standards like STEP. Therefore, recommendations for future work relating to this are detailed in Chapter Ten.

Summary Development Team Balance

In summary, the importance of the involvement of end-users and software vendors in the standards process is best summarised by Byrne and Golder (2002) who state that successful anticipatory standards have come from organizations where the users and providers of the standards have been closely integrated and involved from the start. The impact of end-user and software vendor involvement on the adoption of a standard is captured in Figure 2.

Revisions

Revisions of standards specifications takes place prior to publication and post-publication. In the case prior to publication, some issues emerged within the development of ISO 15926-2. One interviewee who worked for the main organization involved in the development process explained that, *"we took out snapshots around 1997... and we have used variants of that ever since... the latest version of ISO 15926-2 is significantly different from what we have, so [lately] we have not got engaged [in ISO 15926-2] significantly"*. Therefore what has happened is that organizations are implementing different versions of the standard and pulling out of the process. This resulted in compatibility challenges. In addition, creating these different versions had an impact on the timescales of the development process, as was pointed out by one developer, *"There has been a lot of different versions so we have been through at least five or six different versions of the data model and that has also been very demanding ... We have learned a lot during each revision but it has cost a lot of money and time"*.

In the case of post publication revisions, this is only relevant to AP224 at this point. The second edition of AP224 was published in April 2001, and the projected publication date of the edition three is June 2006. The head of the development team explained that they made a conscious decision to avoid compatibility issues during revisions but the downside was that they had a standard that was very similar to the original version, despite of a lot of effort going into the revision process. Consequently, some of the stakeholders involved in the standard argued whether these revisions were necessary. As one interviewee put it, *"What real benefits have we had from the different editions other than a lot of work and a rewrite of everything?".* However, one of the interviewees pointed out that the revisions were a key bargaining tool, *"[doing revisions] has been important. As an example, people wanted to vote down certain standards but we persuaded them not to do that because the new requirements they wanted we could put in later editions and that enabled us to keep moving on. That was an important negotiating process."* Nonetheless, the main issue surrounding the revisions was compatibility. Therefore the resultant theme is,

Theme 10: The pre- and post-publication revisions raised compatibility issues and concerns for the standards, which have a direct negative impact on the effective adoption of the standards. However, the revisions were key negotiating points during the development process.

Egyedi and Loeffen (2002) explain that succession in standardization is often a problem, and the advantages of improvements must be weighed against those of compatibility. Part of the ongoing debate raised by Egyedi and Loeffen (2002) is the dilemma between 'continuity in standards development' versus 'incompatible standards revisions'. This is due to the fact that compatibility preserves earlier investments, but that may not be of significant value if the standard is not up-to-date with current advancements. In the case of these two standards, this was a definite problem. The focus of the developers was to ensure compatibility with previous versions but not at the expense of working with up-to-date technologies. This is explained in more detail in later sections of this chapter.

Development Process Summary

This section has assessed the impact of a wide variety of development process factors on the adoption and diffusion of the data-exchange standards. The section started by contrasting ISO and consortia development processes. The next section looked at the impact of development process timescales on the adoption of a standard and the reasons for these delays. The following section looked at the impact of end-user and software vendor involvement on standards adoption. The final section discussed the impact the revisions of a standard have on its adoption. A representation of all of the relationships described in the themes is summarised in Figure 2.

STANDARD CHARACTERISTICS

The standard characteristics factor has been divided into two issues, the five Diffusion of Innovation (DOI) theory characteristics presented by Rogers (2003) and the characteristics of the related implementation technologies.

Rogers DOI Characteristics

Rogers' (2003) five DOI innovation attributes are:

- Complexity
- Compatibility
- Relative Advantage
- Trialability, and
- Observability.

All five attributes impacted the adoption of both standards and therefore confirm Rogers' (2003) assertion that standards will be adopted more readily than other standards when they are perceived by organizations as having greater relative advantage, compatibility, trialability, observability and less complexity.

Complexity

The first and main characteristic is complexity, and most of the interviewees described this factor as very important. The term complexity covers two spheres, complexity in relation to understanding and complexity in relation to implementation. In terms of understanding there was general agreement that both standards were difficult to understand, one ISO 15926-2 interviewee noted, "*There was concern expressed by people who thought it was just getting too complicated, too messy and too difficult*". Nonetheless, the developers felt that understanding is only key to the software vendors and implementers, "*I believe that not everyone needs to understand the standard, when we have it up and running*". This confirms the belief held by many of the interviewees that complexity is not an issue for the end-user because the standard will be hidden from them within the tools developed by the software-vendors. However, this complexity can have an impact on the understanding and selling of a standard within an organization, as is noted in the next Chapter. Hence, this complexity puts a greater demand on the IT and software vendors, but this points again to the importance of software vendor involvement in the standards development process to develop tools to implement and use the standards.

One interviewee noted that complexity was something that could not be avoided, he explained that, "*We have a complex world, complexity is inevitable so the key is the implementation and you will need clever people*". Indeed the main source of complexity was attributed to the conceptual idea and scope of the standard. One ISO 15926-2 developer explained that, if dealing with a large industry group with numerous stakeholders and data, *"simplification does not work, so the common denominator is usually the more complex picture"*. This confirms Jakobs (2002) assertion that 'official' standards bodies (like for example, ISO) have a strong tendency for 'all-embracing', over-arching solutions that solve all problems at once. Jakobs goes on to explain that this sometimes leads to extremely complex specifications, that even large companies can be hesitant to implement, because of their complexity and because they tend to solve problems that nobody has ever encountered. Inevitably the main impact of this complexity is in the implementation stage as this complexity puts more pressure on the implementers. Therefore the resultant theme is:

Theme 11: The conceptual idea and scope of the standards resulted in complex data models that were difficult to understand and challenging to implement, and this has a direct negative impact on the adoption of the standards.

This is confirmed by Meister (2004) who argues that scope and requisite details of STEP have made it a complex standard and not its fundamental design or development. Complexity is one of the main factors that have emerged within IT standards adoption research (Rogers, 2003; Mustonen-Ollila & Lyytinen, 2003; Dreverman, 2005). De Vries et al. (1999), also argue that some consultants may have a special stake in creating complicated standards as this increases their work in assisting companies to implement these standards. De Vries et al.'s claim is not verified in the research, but presents an opportunity for future investigation, as detailed in Chapter Ten.

Compatibility

Compatibility was also described by the interviewees as a very important factor and was discussed in relation to two issues. Firstly, compatibility was discussed in relation to the compatibility of the standard with previous versions of the standard, which was discussed in the previous sections. The second issue relates to compatibility of the standard with related implementation technologies like XML, UML and OWL, which is discussed in more detail in following sections. Nonetheless, like complexity, compatibility is one of the main issues that has emerged from within IT standards research as impacting the adoption of standards. For example, Dedrick and West (2003) found compatibility a key issue in the adoption of Linux.

Relative Advantage

Relative advantage was considered by the interviewees as a 'quite important' factor, but was not very important because generally, both case study standards had no dominant competing standards. AP224 was developed for a specific purpose and there was no alternative when it was first conceived. However, ISO 15926-2 did experience some competition in the early days from STEP-AP221 ("Functional data and schematic representation for process plants"). In later years, the work between ISO 15926-2 and AP221 has been harmonised through EPISTLE and consequently is not currently an issue. Nevertheless, as was pointed out in previous sections, there is a danger that the relative advantage of a standard is diminished when the development timescales take too long.

Trialability

Trialability refers to the degree to which an innovation may be experimented with on a limited basis (Rogers, 2003). Most interviewees described this as a very important factor that had a positive impact on the adoption process. The main activities used to carry this out included pilots, demonstrations and workshops. However, some interviewees pointed out that carrying out pilots and demonstrations prior to the publication of the standard falsely raises expectations when the timescales do not match the promises that have been made. One ISO 15926-2 developer explained that, *"I think the biggest problem with doing those sorts of things is that they raised expectations prematurely... if you have heard that [the standard] is going to be available in three years, three times and it has not, then you kind of lose faith."* Nonetheless, there was added benefit from the pre-publication pilots and demonstrations as they provided an opportunity for feedback on the adjustments that needed to be made to the standards.

The idea of doing pilots and demonstrations was met with a negative reaction by some of the interviewees. There was a difference of opinion with regards to the need for them as some interviewees felt that benefits of the standards should be self-evident and advertising them through these pilots and demonstrations was an indication of a deficiency of the standards. Indeed one interviewee went as far as to call the demonstrations *"pseudo demonstrations"* that do not actually show true examples of the standard's working. Nevertheless, there was unanimous agreement that the best ways forward with regards to trialability was to test the standards in real, live pilots. In addition, the use of workshops was seen as a key tool to overcome some of the misgivings about demonstrations. As one ISO 15926-2 interviewee explained, *"I think the ... ongoing workshops did not over sell what was going to happen"*. Therefore, the resultant theme is:

Theme 12: The use of pilots, demonstrations and workshops generally has a positive impact on the adoption of the standards. However, there was a danger where expectations are raised falsely when timescales did not match up to predicted publication dates.

This is confirmed by Byrne and Golder (2002) who ascertain that anticipatory standards should have an example installation, which can be used to guide possible implementers and help in the diffusion of a standard.

Observability

This is where results of an innovation are visible to others (Rogers, 2003). This involves the documentation of case studies of real implementations and use of the standard where post-implementation Return on Investment (ROI) is carried out for organizations to see what benefits of the standard have been achieved. Most of the interviewees described this as a very important factor and there have been some case studies undertaken with AP224 in the RAMP project and ISO 15926-2 to show the benefits of the standards. The main benefit that interviewees described was the fact that these activities raise awareness. The second benefit of these activities is that they help to fill a credibility gap that was mentioned by one of the ISO 15926-2 developers who explained that, *"there is a big gap between 'here is the standard' and 'here is how you can use it.' And the cost of actually using the standard is very high because of that gap. The cost of bridging the gap seems to be excessive in comparison to the benefits that people can justify. There is what I would call a credibility gap"*. The use of case studies and success stories can fill that gap, which would be beneficial for uptake. Therefore the resultant theme is:

Theme 13: The use of case studies and successes stories, which present real verified benefits of the standard, has a direct positive impact on adoption

Studies done by Rogers (2003) and others (Dreverman, 2005; Meister, 2004) show that this is a critical factor to support the adoption of an innovation. Nonetheless, interviewees revealed that there were two main challenges involved in establishing the observability of a standard, these were:

1. Accessing Information about the Implementation and Use of the Standard

One of the AP224 implementers explained that, *"there are some [AP224] implementations being done. They are company implementations and they are keeping it within the company, so you are really not sure what is going on. They are not being informative of their work. That makes it very hard*". Therefore, information about implementation of the standards is not being effectively communicated.

2. Management of the Information

The second challenge is in relation to who will manage and host this pool of information so that it can be easily accessed. Some of the interviewees raised concern about how these stories will be successfully managed and monitored and who would host them because, being international standards, one cannot keep track of who is using the standards. One interviewee suggested that maybe there needs to be a stronger user community so people can be more aware about what is happening in relation to the standard.

Both these challenges point to a key issue relating to communication and information channels and this was one of the key issues that Rogers (2003) and others (West 1999; Mustonen-Ollila & Lyytinen, 2003) have found as an important factor in the adoption and diffusion of innovations. Therefore the emergent theme is:

Theme 14: Poor communication channels among developers, existing adopters and potential adopters have negatively impacted the adoption of the standards.

The voluntary flow of information between existing and potential adopters is important for creating positive expectations. The general availability of information about the standard has a positive impact on the diffusion of an innovation (Nilakanta & Scamell, 1990). However, as has been shown in the case studies, the amount of information available regarding a standard can vary between environments of different stakeholder groups (Kwon & Zmud, 1987).

Related Implementation Technologies

Data-exchange standards, such as AP224 and ISO 15926-2, are not only implemented using the prescribed data modelling languages, a series of related technologies are also used to implement the standards. This section seeks to establish what impact these implementation technologies have on the adoption of the standard. AP224, being a STEP standard, was developed using the EXPRESS data modelling language. One of the interviewees declared that, *"EXPRESS is dead"*. However, no other interviewees agreed with this view. In fact, one interviewee from a leading oil company explained that *"EXPRESS is a good data modelling language, and we are actually looking at using it for our corporate data modelling."* So EXPRESS is still considered a valuable data modelling language. In the case of ISO 15926-2, the data modelling language used is a language called Gellish. Gellish is an artificial language that enables systems to interpret the meaning of the content of a file and then process it. Gellish language is a subset of natural languages and is defined in the public domain STEPlib database (Dreverman, 2005).

Most interviewees agreed that data modelling languages like EXPRESS and Gellish were useful and pointed out that there is still a need for EXPRESS and Gellish as foundations for the development of these data-exchange standards. However, the implementation and inevitably the uptake of these data-exchange standards are closely tied to links with mainstream technologies like XML, internet technologies and other technologies such as OWL that are gaining momentum with the rise of the semantic web.

Parts of STEP have been developed to create interfaces between XML and UML technologies. Indeed Lubell and Frechette (2002) believe that he STEP community moved toward XML in order to capitalize on XML's popularity and flexibility, which would in turn accelerate STEP's adoption and deployment. Similar to this, the head of ISO 15926-2 development said in the interview that a key to the uptake of the standard is a move to technologies like XML and OWL, which he believed would make interfacing simpler and bring the benefits of the current wide user-base of these technologies to the uptake of ISO 15926-2. Indeed, one AP224 developer explained that in his experience in order to engage senior management in organizations he had to use buzz words like XML for them to get interested. Therefore, the resultant theme is:

Theme 15: The use of current technologies such as XML, UML and OWL has a direct positive impact on the adoption of standards.

This theme relates to issues that have emerged within the economics of standards relating to network effects. Network effects describe a positive correlation between the number of users of a standard and its utility (Farrell and Saloner 1985, Katz and Shapiro 1985). Due to the large user-base of technologies like XML, there is a large influx of tools, knowledge and skills relating to the technologies and, as a consequence, an organization will gain benefits from using popular standards such as XML. As Gosain (2003) points out, as one product gets ahead, it becomes progressively more attractive to the other adopters. Therefore, positive networks have influenced developers in both the STEP and ISO 15926-2 communities to move towards technologies such as XML, UML and other Internet standards, and even new and emerging standards like OWL, as this will increase the adoptability of the standards.

Figure 3. The impact of standards characteristics on the adoption and diffusion of the standards

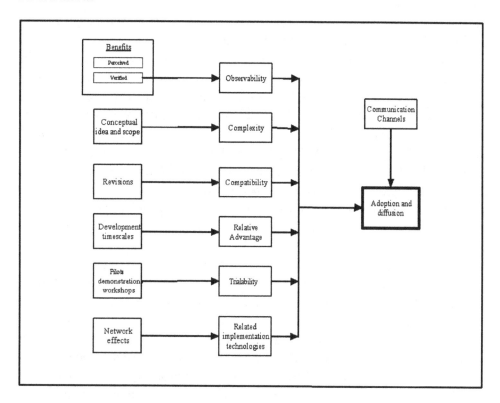

Standards Characteristics Summary

This section has looked at the impact of the standard characteristics on the adoption and diffusion of a standard. The key emergent themes are summarised in Figure 3, developed by the author.

STANDARDIZATION ISSUES

The standardization issues described here are some of the factors identified by Krechmer (2000a) as distinguishing characteristics of formal standards bodies and consortia. This section seeks to establish if any of these factors have directly impacted the adoption of the case study standards.

Funding

Funding for the development of a standard is used mainly to meet the costs associated with the development of a standard. All interviewees agreed that the main cost of development was manpower and travel expenses. One estimate suggests that the development cost for a 'major international telecommunications standard' may amount to some 1,000 person-years of experience, twenty person-years of actual effort, plus $3 million (Office of Technology Assessment, 1991). So, as the head of AP224 development pointed out, funding is critical for the successful development of these standards. In the case of AP224, most funding was obtained from the US Navy. However, this did pose a challenge because, as the head of development explained, the US and UK have deployed large numbers of troops in response to various different global security issues, which means that funding within the defence community has been diverted to these security issues. As a consequence, projects dependent on money from defence ministries have suffered a sudden lack of funding.

In the case of ISO 15926-2, most of the funding came from organizations that were members of the consortia. Again here there was a challenge because some of the organizations expected the larger companies, at the head of the supply chain to provide all the funding for development of the standard. One of the interviewees from one of the main oil companies explained, *"It has been rather hard for people outside those three main oil companies to take the initiative, because their managers would say well why are we funding this if Shell is involved, why can't they fund it. There's a natural expectation that the top of the food chain will be the ones that fund it all"*.

Another interesting note that emerged was a situation that was described in the development of ISO 15926-2, where one interviewee explained that at one point one of the consortia had too much funding and therefore pulled out of the development process. The interviewee went on to state that, *"actually having too much money is a barrier to developing truly common standards"*. This was an interesting point, although all developers involved in AP224 said they had never seen a situation like that before, and said funding tends to be tight. Nevertheless, organizations coming and going due to excess funding points to a bigger issue relating to power and politics that emerge in development team dynamics.

In the end, there was no evidence of a direct link between funding and adoption, and subsequently the interviewees described this factor as 'not important' in relation to the adoption of the standards. Where there was an impact was when funding levels fluctuated and impacted the development timescales. Several commentators have suggested that the rate of diffusion of standards' use depends, in part, on how standards institutions like ISO price their standards (Swann, 2000). Indeed, Meister (2004) found that some members of the SC4 community viewed this cost or fee for the standards an impediment to a standards adoption. When this question was posed to the interviewees the general agreement was that, though this cost or fee was at times an irritation, there was no evidence of it being a barrier in the adoption of the standards. One interviewee went on to explain that the cost of standards in relation to the multi-million projects they were being assigned to was minimal. In addition to that, most of the organizations dealing with these standards had acquired licences to various standards bodies, which enables them to easily access the standards.

Intellectual Property Rights (IPR)

IPR in standardization is a topic that over the years has gained attention from the standards community (Bilalis & Herbert, 2003; Blind & Thumm, 2004; Oksala et al., 1996). In the case of the two standards, the IPR issue was not seen as an important factor in relation to adoption. However, in the case of ISO 15926-2, one of the developers commented that it was a perennial discussion point; some developers wanted to have IPR and some developers thought that the notion of having IPRs for international standards took away from the purpose of these standards. One ISO 15926-2 developer commented, *"Immediately you start to say there is intellectual property, barriers come down all over the place"*. This had an impact on development timescales, which is in keeping with an assertion made by Weiss and Spring (2000) that the "lack of a defined IP protection policy may delay a standard, because each case must be negotiated separately" (p.13).

The conflicts of interest relating to IPR varied among different stakeholders involved in the development of the standards. This confirms a proposition put forward by Van Wegberg (2004b) that if innovators differ in the extent of IPR protection of their innovations, and they differ in how important IPR revenues are for them, then bargaining difficulties may fragment a standardization process. One developer, who represented a software company, felt that patents should not go beyond an organizations' proprietary code and made a point to promote this ethos within the organization he represented.

There have also been emergent IPR issues in relation to the reference data libraries associated with ISO 15926-2. As one interviewee pointed out, *"I think there has been a bit of problem with the reference data libraries where people have wanted to keep parts of the reference data libraries private in order to get commercial gain and that has caused upset and problems"*. Nevertheless, a number of the interviewees pointed out that having a key element, like reference data libraries, available in the public domain was central to successful uptake. So there is a potential here for an IPR issue that could impact the adoption of the standard if some potential end-user organizations are put off from adopting the standard if they have to access key parts of the standard commercially. Therefore, the resultant theme is:

Theme 16: The constant debates and conflicts surrounding IPR has a negative impact on the development timescales, and poses a potential to negatively impact the adoption of the standard if key elements of the standard are not placed in the public domain.

This theme confirms Blind and Iversen's (2004) assertion that there is a tension in the relationship between IPR and standards, which may cause a broad scope of conflict. Blind and Iversen (2004) go on to explain that this tension emerges because IPR involve a more proprietary aspect and standards more of a public domain aspect. Consequently they made a series of recommendations in dealing with IPR issues in the standards process, including measures to encourage SDOs like ISO to set up some means of dispute resolution during development to help resolve royalty disagreements, since this will be quicker and cheaper than resorting to the courts (Blind & Iversen, 2004). Nevertheless, this issue of IPR is a very complex legal issue that still needs to be addressed, mainly when it concerns the international arena (Bousquet, 2004).

Brand Identification

International standardization organizations such as ISO, ITU and International Electrotechnical Commission (IEC) have become well known 'brands' (Krechmer, 2000a). The impact of this brand identification on the adoption of the standards was seen as very important by all interviewees. Although there were differing views with regards to the nature of the impact, most of the interviewees agreed that the ISO brand has a positive impact on the adoption of the standards. As one ISO 15926-2 interviewee noted, *"I think, it is essential it is an ISO standard. In the end, the commercial [consortia] side was fine to start with but some people would not have bought into it if there was not an intent to be an ISO standard"*. One of the reasons why some of the organizations were favourable to ISO standards is because as one interviewee pointed out, *"The fact that it is an ISO standard has a positive effect on the adoption, because many companies are jaundiced about throwing away IT... and if you can say that work is being based on these standards, people perceive it has longer technological life"*.

Nonetheless, not everyone favoured the ISO brand. In the oil and gas community, one of the interviewees stated that, *"there is a very different point of view on ISO in the subsurface community - the geologists and geophysicists and these kind of people, they do not believe in ISO"*. In addition, on a practical level, what was found was that second- and third-tier organizations did not care whether it was an ISO standard or not. They followed the lead of the head of the supply chain. Some of the developers involved in ISO 15926-2 mentioned that brand identification was *also negative when dealing with some US organizations. As one of the interviewees explained, "Brand identification with ISO, tends to be rather negative, which is why I think some of the American commercial organizations have more brand value particularly to the American market."* Therefore, the resultant theme is:

Theme 17: Brand identification impacts the adoption of standard in both a positive and negative way.

This confirms Krechmer's (2000a) view that telling users that a product conforms to ISO or ITU standards has more impact than saying that a product conforms to a certain specifications. Nevertheless, certain consortia like W3C (The World Wide Web Consortium) have significant brand value for Internet standards.

Tied to the branding debate is the issue of marketing standards. All interviewees, when asked to suggest ways to facilitate the uptake of standards, mentioned marketing of standards as a key tool, for example one of the interviewees mentioned, *"I think that marketing the standard effectively is important".* However another interviewee went on to caution that, *"If you are trying to sell a standard you are wasting your time, if you are trying to sell some business functionality then people take interest. I think there is a psychology of some people who try and sell a standard, and sometimes you have to, but ultimately it is the commercial imperative".* Therefore, the emergent theme is:

Theme 18: Effective marketing of the standards has a direct positive impact on the adoption of the standards.

Most interviewees agreed with this but there was disagreement with regards to who should market the standards. One of the software vendors involved in the implementation of AP224 asked, *"Why aren't the ISO body marketing themselves? Why aren't [ISO] selling the standard? Why don't [ISO] have their own marketing, 'go the ISO way'? ...Why aren't there adverts? You need to get someone from the ISO community to sell [the standard], so an ISO body instead of a commercial organization sells them the standard".* This touches on Krechmer's (2000a) argument that SDOs like ISO should treat their brands as a more strategic asset. However, as Krechmer (2000a) goes on to point out, "many SDOs seem to operate otherwise, and these, and many other faulty brand management practices, seem to offer evidence that SDOs have focused on internal standardization issues rather than the perceptions of their customers - a significant error in the emerging, market-driven standards world" (p.1).

Cargill (1999) agrees with this view and opens the debate to a wider scope to include the contrast between SDO and consortium marketing, and makes the following statement: "In a consortium, however, there is a precondition that SDOs do not enjoy – basically, the members of the consortium are usually like minded and usually wish for action to occur …Members can see a correlation between activity and market share and market activity. And in the broadest sense of the term "marketing" [the standard] is valid…The SDOs have forgotten why people value standards. As an example, there was a new ANSI constitution (composed of ten items) that was promulgated in 1995. Approximately 50% of the text in the constitution was devoted to making sure that ANSI was regarded as the leader in standardization, nationally and internationally. About four percent of the words were devoted to teaching people about standards, and about six percent were focused on the public good. The focus is not on satisfying a user need or responding to a requirement… Rather, it is about the continuation of a power structure that the users are abandoning because it no longer fills a need in the IT arena" (p.8-9).

The counter argument relating to having SDOs like ISO market the standards was expressed by one of the developers who stated that, "*the people who have interest in marketing these things are the people who build the software and expect to sell it and they should be marketing the solutions not methods*". In other words, some of the developers felt marketing should solely be in the hand of the software vendors. This is due to the fact that, unlike consortia that can pool a small portion of their funds to promote their standards, gaining such funding from an SDO requires a new funding request to the organizations that fund the SDO. As Krechmer (2000a) points out, such a process is likely to be to slow and cumbersome, and for this reason, formal standards from an SDO are rarely promoted by the SDO. Indeed promotion of SDO standards only occurs by virtue of the products that are sold that identify the SDO standards brand (Krechmer, 2000a).

Standardization Issues Summary

This section has looked at how common standardization issues, like funding, IPR and brand identification, impact the adoption of data-exchange standards. A summary of the key themes is diagrammatically represented in Figure 4.

CHARACTERISTICS OF THE ADOPTING COMMUNITY: INNOVATIVENESS

The characteristics of the adoption community points to the innovativeness of the organizations in the adopting community or social system of a standard, and this factor was described as very important by the interviewees. Innovativeness refers to the degree to which an individual or other unit of adoption is relatively earlier in

Figure 4. The impact of standardization issues on the adoption and diffusion of the standards

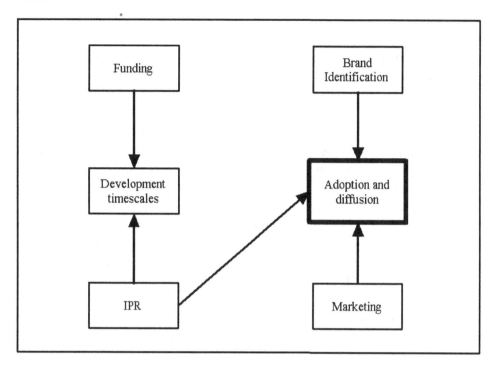

adopting new ideas than other members of a social system (Rogers, 2003).

The 'innovators' relates to firms that have a tendency to be venturesome and take on increased risk by being the first to take on board a new innovation or standard. The next category, termed "early adopters", help to trigger the critical mass when they adopt an innovation, and Rogers points out that adopters further down the supply chain tend to look to early adopters for advice and information about an innovation. The "early majority" tend to avoid risks but are quick to adopt and implement the innovation when "early adopters" demonstrate the benefits. The "late majority" are more sceptical and are influenced because others have adopted the standard, for example if their major trading partners require to them to use the standards. The final group termed "laggards" are the last to engage in the adoption process and tend to be more traditional. They may be forced to adopt an innovation or they do not have the necessary resources or business foresight to adopt an innovation any earlier (Chen, 2003).

Some potential adopters within a standards adopting community are more innovative than others, and can be identified as such by their characteristics (Fichman,

1992). The main distinguishing characteristics that impacted the innovativeness and subsequent adoption of the standards were:

- Organization size
- Organization type
- Organization culture

Organization Size

What emerged from the data was that larger organizations tended to fall in the innovators and early adopter categories for both standards. This is in agreement with Söderström's (2004) assertion that SDOs focus on large, international companies since these traditionally have readily adopted standards and related technology. This is because many of these large organizations can afford to be involved in the conception and development of standards. The SMEs (small to medium enterprises) were generally part of the late majority and this is partly tied to the position of the organization in the supply chain. Chen (2003) found similar results in the adoption of XML and Web services, SMEs were part of the late majority mainly because their major trading partners require them to use the same standards. Another reason for lack of SME involvement is a lack of resources to actively engage in the standards process. De Vries *et al.* (2004) contend that for certain standards even a large multinational can be a weak stakeholder because of lack of resources.

Organization Type

One of the interviewees stated that oil and gas industries tend to have a positive stand towards standards in general and this view was summarised in a comment made by one of the ISO 15926-2 developers that, "*In the oil and gas industry there is a push for having a standard*". The defence community also has a positive attitude towards standards as is shown in Chapter Six. This shows that organizations from industry groups like oil and gas and defence have a positive position towards the adoption of standards and they therefore tend to fall in the innovators and early adopter categories. In general, software vendors were part of the early majority and late majority. Some software vendors came and went during the development process, and only reengaged after publication and the standard had reached a level of maturity, this was particularly true in the case of AP224. A number of software vendors got involved at the start for ISO 15926-2 development because of the potential market they saw available, and this had a positive impact. This points again to the advantage of having end-users and software vendors involved in the standards process as soon as possible.

Organization Culture

This refers to specifics about an organization's attitude towards change and towards standards. Even though there is evidence that large organizations in certain industries have positive attitudes towards standards, this may vary if they are still traditionally based and they may wait to see if a standard is implemented before coming on board. An example was given by one of the ISO 15926-2 developers: "*The Shearwater project was implemented roughly around version two [of ISO 15926-2]...we were able to save, and this was documented - three million pounds against an expenditure of one million to set up the system - and that was in an 18-month period. You can't get more solid than that [in terms of verified benefits]. Now the really interesting thing is once we had done that and this was in 1996 or 1997 why weren't people queuing up to do the same thing on other projects? The answer is conservatism, if you have got a two billion pound project and somebody says they have got this new whiz bang piece of technology that could save you some money, but it is not really been tried and tested, what is your answer going to be? Are you going to try it or not? The answer often is no. They will stick with what they know*". This shows that even large multinational organizations that are traditionally described as having positive attitudes towards standards may still emerge as laggards due to issues like conservatism, which is tied to attitudes towards change. Other issues relate to attitudes towards a specific standard, which was shown in previous sections concerning brand identification.

Characteristics of the Adopting Community Summary

This section has sought to highlight how the innovativeness of the adoption community or social system related to a standard can impact its adoption. However, this section has sought to only point to some of the common trends in different industry groups, the specific innovativeness of an organization and the impact of that on the adoption of a standard is covered in more detail in Chapter 6, which looks at the adoption of standards within the UK MoD. Nonetheless, the resultant theme is:

Theme 19: The innovativeness of organizations in the adopting community impacts the adoption and diffusion of the standards - there was a positive impact when the large organizations in the oil and gas, and defence communities were involved - but issues surrounding organizational type, size and culture can negatively impact the adoption of the standards.

Table 3. Barriers to the adoption of ISO 10303-224

Barriers	Related factor
Resistance from software vendors to come on board- lack of tools (2)	Software vendor involvement
Not sharing of the results of implementations (3)	Communication channels
2nd and 3rd tiers could not afford it	Innovativeness: size
Lack of end-user acceptance of the need for the standards (4)	Innovativeness: culture
How companies have traditionally worked (2)	Innovativeness: culture
STEP community is academic focused and not credible from a commercial point of view (3)	Balance, diversity and dynamics of development team and Complexity

KEY FACTORS: BARRIERS AND FACILITATORS OF ADOPTION

The sections above have chronicled the impact of the factors identified in the original model on the adoption and diffusion of the standards. To help identify key factors, all the interviewees who were involved in the development of the two standards were asked to state their three main barriers to adoption of their respective standards. These were tabled against the main factors and used to assess the current rate of uptake of the standards.

Key Barriers and Rate of Uptake: ISO 10303-224

Each of the interviewees was asked to identify the three main barriers to the adoption of the standards they were involved in. In the case of the AP224 the three main barriers of each of the interviewees were identified and shown in Table 3. The numbers in brackets indicate where there was more than one respondent out of the five interviewed who identified a specific barrier.

All the identified main barriers can be linked to factors that have been addressed in previous sections. Three of the main factors related to innovativeness of the adopting community in relation to organizational size and culture. Some of the interviewees felt that the STEP standards community was too academic and therefore not able to relate to the commercial world, which in their view resulted in complex standards that are difficult to implement. This ties in with the discussion in previous sections, where some of the developers felt that the academics were purists looking to develop perfect standards, which in their view added complexity to the standard and increased development timescales. The next issue was in relation to communication channels to make people aware of the benefits, which would encourage adoption of the standard. The final issue related to software vendor involvement in the standards process, which all interviewees mentioned as a key barrier.

All the interviewees who had been involved in the development of AP224 described the uptake as fair. The main issue that was attributed to this was summarised by the head of development of the standard in this way, *"We obviously were hoping to have much more vendor involvement than we currently have. From that point of view, I would say we do not quite have the vendors we would have liked to get onboard. That has been a disappointment"*. The cause for this slow uptake by vendors is discussed in earlier sections, but a potential contributing factor to poor software vendor involvement could be related to the work on Abstract Test Suites within STEP. As was pointed out in email correspondence with standards developer[2], the sub-committee ISO/TC184/SC4 identified a related requirement to create an abstract test suite for each application protocol. However, eventually, standards developers overturned this requirement because funders of standards development were not willing to see the test suite as being part of the development activity but rather a natural progression once industry had identified a requirement to implement the standard. Without doubt, such test suites have the potential to encourage software vendors as to increased ease of implementation of the standard". However, as King rightly notes, if vendors are not going to step up to the plate to implement a standard, then the test suites incur additional and eventually fruitless cost as part of the development of the standard. A potential solution to this challenge would be the creation of an implementers forum where vendors can identify firm intentions with respect to implementation and create a community that has the interest to develop test cases.

Nonetheless, there is general agreement that there will be continued adoption of the standard. The concerns were just the speediness of adoption, and engaging more software vendors to enable the availability of more tools. In addition, the interviewees recommended other incentives such as more publications of success stories, marketing, education and an aggressive implementation program with usage guides as further ways to facilitate the uptake of the standard. Another practical way things are being taken forward is the provision of a suite of manufacturing APs, which incorporates AP224 and will further facilitate uptake of the standard.

Key Barriers and Rate of Uptake: ISO 15926-2

The developers interviewed with ISO 15926-2 were asked to name the three main barriers and what emerged is summarised in Table 4. This table was derived from the responses of five interviewees, and again the number in brackets indicates how many interviewees mentioned a specific factor. Complexity was a key factor that emerged with regards to the adoption of ISO 15926-2. Unlike AP224, software vendor involvement was not seen as a barrier with the adoption of ISO 15926-2 because there have been vendors who have stayed with the project from the start.

Table 4. Barriers to the adoption of ISO 15926-2

Barrier	Related factor
Understanding - cost of implementation (3)	Complexity
Finding the financial/commercial imperatives for adoption by organizations -compelling business case (3)	Observability (pre-implementation)
Available implementing technology (how to you use SQL Server and Oracle to implement)	Related technologies
Cost of change	Innovativeness: culture
Quantification of benefits	Observability (post-implementation)
Time taken to develop the standard (3)	Development timescales
Completion of a globally managed reference data library (3)	Completeness of the entire standard

There was debate about the observability of the standard prior to implementation in order to develop a compelling business case.

Then there were issues relating to post-implementation observability because as one interviewee pointed out, "*it is not easy to actually quantify the benefits*". This is made it increasingly difficult since data-exchange standards like ISO 15926-2 are an integral part of a system that impacts many other systems and processes. One interviewee proposed that the focus should be on what it enables, not quantified savings and benefits. Innovativeness relating to organizational culture is key again, and as was previously mentioned, this issue will be covered in more detail in Chapter Six because change management is very much organization specific. The time taken to develop the standard was seen as something that impacted the adoption, as was detailed in earlier sections.

The final barrier emerged within discussion regarding the adoption of ISO 15926-2, and this relates to reference data library. A number of interviewees expressed this as the key issue that will impact the successful uptake of the standard. One interviewee described it as "*the main iceberg under the water*", in the same vain as the Titanic, where progress is being made but the real problem is not immediately obvious. A number of interviewees explained the importance of the reference data library, one developer noted that, "*The reference data library is the bit that is probably most interesting to most people... It is what makes the data model useable, because the data model is relatively abstract*". Another developer went on to explain that, "*The reality is, until the software gets more sophisticated you invariably have to invent things on a project specific basis. Now we should have a system where they get put back into one common managed system, like a global reference library*". The resultant theme is therefore:

Theme 20: Not having completeness of the entire standard had a negative impact on the adoption of the standard.

This was the case for a standard known as the Information Resource Dictionary System (IRDS) that was studied by Byrne and Golder (2002). In their study, Byrne and Golder (2002) explain that this was true for the Services Interface standard which contained a list of general services and data structures which an IRDS must support to conform to the standard. However, Byrne and Golder (2002) point out that it was not until 1993 that products could claim to conform to the Services Interface standard and the IRDS Standard, and this three-year gap between the Framework and the Services Interface did not help in the diffusion of the standard. Therefore, having completeness of an entire standard is critical to the effective adoption and diffusion of that standard. The general rate of uptake at the time was generally described as fair because the interviews were carried out a short time after the standard was published. However, there was general optimism that there would be uptake of the standard, and indeed the list below is a summary of the key projects currently underway, provided by the head of the ISO 15926-2 development:

- The Norwegian Oil Industry Association has two projects implementing this standard.
- The Norwegian Ministry of Defence is implementing it for some war vessels.
- The UK Ministry of Defence is sponsoring EMSA for evaluating it in connection with the STEP-standards for the ship building industry.
- Shell UK has decided to use the standard for their refineries.
- In the United States, the FIATECH organization has decided to use ISO 15926-2 for intelligent data sheets.
- Major research in Norway has provided results that will be used in the development of the Tyrihans field by Statoil.

The main factor behind successful deployment is tied to the involvement of software vendors in the development of the standard and subsequent availability of tools and skills for the adoption of the standard.

FINALISED INNOVATION-CENTRIC MODEL AND CONCLUSIONS

This chapter has aimed to show the interactions of the key factors that affect the adoption of data-exchange standards from an innovation-centric viewpoint, based on

Figure 5. Innovation-centric adoption model

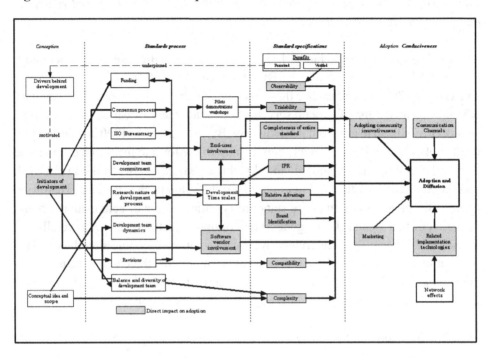

Figure 6. High-level view of main innovation-centric factors

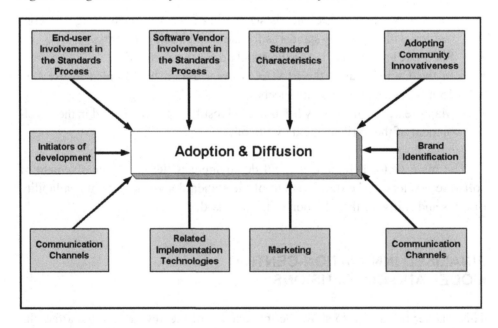

case studies of two SC4 standards. The revised model shown in Figure 5 is a summation of all the factors that impact the adoption and diffusions of data-exchange standards. The factors are categorised under four main sections: conception, standards process, standard specifications and adoption conduciveness. A high level view of the main factors within each of the four sections that directly impact the adoption and diffusion of a standard is shown in Figure 6.

What has emerged in the innovation-centric analysis is that most of the findings have confirmed existing literature. Therefore, one of the main contributions of this work is that the issues surrounding standards adoption from an innovation-centric view have been grounded in a different context, namely ISO data-exchange standards community. Nonetheless, there are some aspects where new insights have been given in relation to defence community involvement in the development of a standard, and the impact of the research nature of standards development on the development timescales of a standard. In summary, the main novel contributions of this section of the research are:

- Grounding of the issues surrounding primary standards adoption in a new context, the ISO data-exchange standards community, specifically SC4 community.

Table 5. Innovation-centric themes

Themes
Theme 1: The drivers behind the development of the standards were mainly economic and a direct reflection of the perceived benefits of the standard and, in turn, they triggered the standardization efforts by motivating the initiators to embark on the development process.
Theme 2: The involvement of end-users in the conception of a standard can have a direct positive impact on the development of the standard, specifically through the funding arrangements.
Theme 3: Developing ISO standards from within a predominately defence background can have a direct negative impact on the subsequent adoption of the standard.
Theme 4: Having initiating organizations that are at the head of a supply chain has a direct positive impact on the balance and diversity of the development team.
Theme 5: The long development timescales have a direct negative impact on end-user involvement in the standards process, resulting in a direct negative impact on the adoption of the standard.
Theme 6: The long development timescales have a direct negative impact on software vendor involvement in the standards process, resulting in a direct negative impact on the adoption of the standard.
Theme 7: The long development timescales have a direct negative impact on the relative advantage of the standards due to the fear that the standards are lagging behind current technological advancements.
Theme 8: End-users were involved in the development process in order to ensure the standards met their requirements, which has a direct positive impact on the adoption of the standard.
Theme 9: Having software vendor involvement in the standards process is seen as critical to ensure the successful adoption of the standards.
Theme 10: The pre- and post-publication revisions raised compatibility issues and concerns for the standards, which have a direct negative impact on the effective adoption of the standards. However, the revisions were key negotiating points during the development process.

Table 6. Innovation-centric themes

Themes
Theme 11: The conceptual idea and scope of the standards resulted in complex data models that were difficult to understand and challenging to implement, and this has a direct negative impact on the adoption of the standards.
Theme 12: The use of pilots, demonstrations and workshops generally has a positive impact on the adoption of the standards. However, there was a danger where expectations are raised falsely when timescales did not match up to predicted publication dates.
Theme 13: The use of case studies and successes stories, which present real verified benefits of the standard, has a direct positive impact on adoption.
Theme 14: Poor communication channels among developers, existing adopters and potential adopters have negatively impacted the adoption of the standards.
Theme 15: The use of current technologies such as XML, UML and OWL has a direct positive impact on the adoption of standards.
Theme 16: The constant debates and conflicts surrounding IPR has a negative impact on the development timescales, and poses a potential to negatively impact the adoption of the standard if key elements of the standard are not placed in the public domain.
Theme 17: Brand identification impacts the adoption of standard in both a positive and negative way.
Theme 18: Effective marketing of the standards has a direct positive impact on the adoption of the standards.
Them 19: The innovativeness of organizations in the adopting community impacts the adoption and diffusion of the standards - there was a positive impact when the large organizations in the oil and gas, and defence communities were involved - but issues surrounding organizational type, size and culture can negatively impact the adoption of standards.
Theme 20: Not having completeness of the entire standard has a negative impact on the adoption of the standard.

- Development of an innovation-centric adoption model that takes a holistic approach, which covers a wide range of factors and their interrelationships within a specific case. Most studies will focus on a specific factor and the issues surrounding that factor, but this chapter has offered a macro view to show the interactions and interrelationships of the wide range of different factors.
- The development of a list of themes that can be used by managers and practitioners as a frame of reference to support the data-exchange standards adoption and diffusion process. The themes are shown in Table 5 and Table 6.

These novel contributions attest to the importance and necessity of this research to the standards development community and the standard adoption research community. The next chapter looks at the main factors that impact the adoption of a standard from an adopter-centric viewpoint.

REFERENCES

Belleflamme, P. (2002). Coordination on Formal Vs. De Facto Standards: A Dynamic Approach. *European Journal of Political Economy, 18*(1), 153–176. doi:10.1016/S0176-2680(01)00073-8

Bilalis, Z., & Herbert, D. (2003). Standardisation From A European Point Of View. *International Journal of IT Standards and Standardization Research, 1*(1), 46–49.

Blind, K., & Iversen, E. (2004). The Interrelationship Between IPR and Standardization: Patterns and Policies. In F. Bousquet, Y. Buntzly, H. Coenen, & K. Jakobs (Ed.), *Proceedings from the 9th EURAS Workshop on Standardization* (pp. 227-248). Paris: Accedo Verlag.

Blind, K., & Thumm, N. (2004). Intellectual Property Protection and Standardization. *International Journal of IT Standards and Standardization Research, 2*(2), 61–75.

Bonino, M., & Spring, M. (1999). Standards as Change Agents in the Information Technology Market. *Computer Standards & Interfaces, 20*(4-5), 279–289. doi:10.1016/S0920-5489(98)00064-6

Bousquet, F. (2004). Role and Best Practices of "Technical Officers" in Standards Setting Organizations. In F. Bousquet, Y. Buntzly, H. H. Coenen, & K. Jakobs (Ed.), *Proceedings from the 9th EURAS Workshop on Standardization* (pp. 157-170). Paris: Accedo Verlag.

Burrows, J. (1999). Information Technology Standards in a Changing World: The Role of the Users. *Computer Standards & Interfaces, 20*(4-5), 323–331. doi:10.1016/S0920-5489(98)00068-3

Byrne, B., & Golder, P. (2002). The Diffusion of Anticipatory Standards with Particular Reference to the ISO/IEC Information Resource Dictionary System Framework Standard. *Computer Standards & Interfaces, 24*(5), 369–379.

Cargill, C. (1994). Evolution and Revolution in Open Systems. *StandardView, 2*(1), 3–13. doi:10.1145/224145.224146

Cargill, C. (1998). Standardization: Art or Discipline? *IEEE Micro, 18*(3), 18–24. doi:10.1109/40.683097

Cargill, C. (1999). Consortia and the Evolution of Information Technology Standardization. In K. Jakobs, & R. Williams (Ed.), *Proceedings of the 1st IEEE Conference on Standardisation and Innovation in Information Technology* (pp. 37-42). Aachen: IEEE.

Chen, M. (2003). Factors Affecting the Adoption and Diffusion of XML and Web Services Standards for E-Business Systems. *International Journal of Human-Computer Studies, 58*(3), 259–279. doi:10.1016/S1071-5819(02)00140-4

David, P., & Shurmer, M. (1996). Formal Standards-Setting for Global Telecommunications and Information Services. Towards an Institutional Regime Transformation? *Telecommunications Policy, 20*(10), 789–815. doi:10.1016/S0308-5961(96)00060-2

De Vries, H., Feilzer, A., & Verheul, H. (2004). Removing Barriers for Participation in Formal Standardization. In F. Bousquet, Y. Buntzly, H. Coenen, & K. Jakobs (Ed.), *Proceedings from the 9th EURAS Workshop on Standardization* (pp. 171-176). Paris: Accedo Verlag.

Dedrick, J., & West, J. (2003). Why Firms Adopt Open Source Platforms: A Grounded theory of Innovation and Standards Adoption. In J. King, & K. Lyytinen (Ed.)*: Proceedings of MISQ Special Issue Workshop on Standard Making: A Critical Frontier for Information Systems* (pp. 236-257). Seattle: MISQ Quaterly.

Dreverman, M. (2005). *Adoption of Product Model Data Standards In the Process Industry.* Eindhoven: Eindhoven University of Technology.

Egyedi, T. (2003). Consortium Problem Redefined: Negotiating 'Democracy' In the Actor Network On Standardization. *International Journal of IT Standards and Standardization Research, 1*(2), 22–38.

Egyedi, T., & Loeffen, A. (2002). Succession in Standardization: Grafting XML onto SGML. *Computer Standards & Interfaces, 24*(4), 279–290. doi:10.1016/S0920-5489(02)00006-5

Eisenhardt, K. (1989b). Making Fast Strategic Decisions In High-Velocity Environments. *Academy of Management Journal, 32*(3), 543–576. doi:10.2307/256434

Farrell, J., & Saloner, G. (1985). Standardization, Compatibility, and Innovation. *The Rand Journal of Economics, 16*(1), 70–83. doi:10.2307/2555589

Fichman, R. (1992). Information Technology Diffusion: A Review of Empirical Research. In J. Degross, J. Becker, & J. Elam (Ed.), *Proceedings of the Thirteenth International Conference on Information Systems* (pp. 195-206). Minneapolis, MN: University of Minnesota.

Gallaher, M. O'connor, A., & Phelps, T. (2002). *Economic Impact Assessment of the International Standard for the Exchange of Product Model Data (Step) In Transportation Equipment Industries.* Project Number 07007.016. North Carolina: RTI International.

Gallivan, M. (2001). Organizational Adoption and Assimilation of Complex Technological Innovations: Development and Application of A New Framework. *Sigmis Database, 32*(3), 51–85. doi:10.1145/506724.506729

Gerst, M., Bunduchi, R., & Williams, R. (2005). Social Shaping & Standardization: A Case Study from Auto Industry. *Proceedings of the 38th Hawaii International Conference On System Sciences*, Hawaii, (p. 204).

Gielingh, W. (2008). An Assessment of the Current State of Product Data Technologies. *Computer Aided Design, 40*(7), 750–759. doi:10.1016/j.cad.2008.06.003

Gosain, S. (2003). Realizing the Vision for Web Services: Strategies for Dealing with Imperfect Standards. In J. a. King (Ed.), *Proceedings of MISQ Special Issue Workshop On Standard Making: A Critical Frontier for Information Systems* (pp. 10-29). Seattle: MISQ Quaterly.

Group, L. S. C. (2002). *RAMP White Paper - Driving Down the Cost of Spares Provisioning Issue 2.* Bath: Warship Support Agency.

Hawkins, R. (1999). The Rise of Consortia in the Information and Communication Technology Industries: Emerging Implications for Policy. *Telecommunications Policy, 23*(2), 159–173. doi:10.1016/S0308-5961(98)00085-8

ISO. (2006a). *ISO 10303-224 Details.* Retrieved February 16, 2006, from http://www.iso.org/iso/en/cataloguedetailpage.cataloguedetail?csnumber=36000&scopelist=programme

ISO/TC184. (2005). *ISO/TC184 Business Plan.* Retrieved December 5, 2005, from http://Isotc.Iso.Org/Livelink/Livelink/Fetch/2000/2122/687806/Iso_Tc_184__Industrial_Automation_Systems_and_Integration_.Pdf?Nodeid=1001423&Vernum=0

ISO/TC184/SC4. (2004). *TC184/SC4 - Setting the Standards for Industrial Data.* Retrieved November 16, 2004, from http://www.Tc184-Sc4.org/

Jain, H., & Zhao, H. (2003). A Conceptual Model for Comparative Analysis of Standardization of Vertical Industry Languages. In J. King, & K. Lyytinen (Ed.), *Proceedings of MISQ Special Issue Workshop On Standard Making: A Critical Frontier for Information Systems* (pp. 210-221). Seattle: MISQ Quaterly.

Jakobs, K. (1996). On the Relevance of Global IT-Standardisation - Should User Companies Participate? *Proceedings of Fifth Annual Bayer International Conference,* Pittsburgh, PA.

Jakobs, K. (2000). Trying To Keep the Internet's Standards Setting Process. *Proceeding of Terena Networking Conference,* Lisbon, Portugal.

Jakobs, K. (2002). Even Desperately Needed Standards May Fail - the Case of E-Mail. *Proceedings of International Conference On the History of Computing and Networks.* Grenoble, France: IEEEXplore.

Jakobs, K., Procter, R., & Williams, R. (1996). Users and Standardisation -- Worlds Apart? the Example of Electronicmail. *StandardView, 4*(4), 183–191. doi:10.1145/243492.243495

Jakobs, K., Procter, R., & Williams, R. (1997). Competitive Advantage Through Participation In Standards Setting? *Fifth International Conference On Factory 2000 - the Technology Exploitation Process* (pp. 370-375). Washington, DC: IEEE Press.

Katz, M., & Shapiro, C. (1985). Network Externalities, Competition, and Compatibility. *The American Economic Review, 75*(3), 424–440.

Kotinurmi, P., Nurmilaakso, J., & Laesvuori, H. (2003). Standardization of Xml-Based E-Business Frameworks. In J. King, & K. Lyytinen (Ed.), *Proceedings of MISQ Special Issue Workshop On Standard Making: A Critical Frontier for Information Systems* (pp. 135-145). Seattle: MISQ Quarterly.

Krechmer, K. (2000a). Market Driven Standardization: Everyone Can Win. *Standards Engineering, 52*(4), 15–19.

Kwon, T. H., & Zmud, R. W. (1987). Unifying the Fragmented Models of Information Systems Implementation. In B. J.R., & R. Hirschheim (Eds.), *Critical Issues In Information Systems Research* (pp. 227-251). New York: John Wiley & Sons.

Lowell, S. (1999). The Yin and Yang of Standards Development. *ASTM Standardization, 27*(12), 30–35.

Lubell, J., & Frechette, S. (2002). XML Representation of STEP Schemas and Data. *Journal of Computing and Information Science in Engineering, 2*(1), 69–71. doi:10.1115/1.1476682

Meister, D. 2. (2004). *STEP Through 20 Years: Lessons and Theoretical Implications - Working Paper Edn.* Faculty of Information Systems, Richard Ivey School of Business. London, Canada: University of Western Ontario.

Miles, M., & Huberman, A. (1994). *Qualitative Data Analysis.* Newbury Park, CA: Sage Publications.

Mustonen-Ollila, E., & Lyytinen, K. (2003). Why Organizations Adopt Information System Process Innovations: A Longitudinal Study Using Diffusion of Innovation Theory. *Information Systems Journal, 13*(3), 275–297. doi:10.1046/j.1365-2575.2003.00141.x

Nilakanta, S., & Scamell, R. (1990). The Effect of Information Sources and Communication Channels on the Diffusion of Innovation in a Data Base Development Environment. *Management Science, 36*(1), 24–40. doi:10.1287/mnsc.36.1.24

NSSF. (2004a). *National Standardization Strategic Framework - How Standardization Works the Standardization Map.* Retrieved January 17, 2004, from NSSF Web site: http://www.nssf.info/mapnotes.pdf

Office of Technology Assessment. (1991). *Global Standards: Building Blocks for the Futur.* OTA-TCT-512. Washington, DC: U.S. Congress Government Printing office.

Oksala, S., Rutkowski, A., & Spring, M., & O'donnell, J. (1996). The Structure of IT Standardization. *StandardView, 4*(1), 9–22. doi:10.1145/230871.230873

Ragin, C. (1987). *The Comparative Method: Moving Beyond Qualitative and Quantitative Strategies.* Berkeley, CA: University of California Press.

Rogers, E. (2003). *Diffusion of Innovations.* New York: Simon & Schuster International.

Sherif, M. (2003). When is Standardization Slow? *International Journal of IT Standards and Standardization Research, 1*(1), 19–32.

Silverstein, A. (1988). An Aristitelian Resolution of the Ideographic Versus Nomothetic Tension. *The American Psychologist, 43*(6), 425–430. doi:10.1037/0003-066X.43.6.425

Söderström, E. (2004). Pros and Cons About Standards from Multiple Stakeholder Perspectives. In F. Bousquet, Y. Buntzly, H. Coenen, & K. Jakobs (Ed.), *Proceedings from the 9th EURAS Workshop on Standardization* (pp. 132-143). Paris: Accedo Verlag.

Spring, M., & Grisham, C. O'donnell, J., Skogseid, I., Snow, A., Tarr, G., et al. (1995). Improving the Standardization Process: from Courtship Dance To Lawyering: Working With Bulldogs and Turtles. In B. Kahin, & J. Abbate (Eds.), *Standards Policy for Information Infrastructure* (pp. 220-252). Cambridge, MA: MIT Press.

Swann, G. (2000). *The Economics of Standardization.* Retrieved January 21, 2004, from Report for Department of Trade and Industry, Standards and Technical Regulations Directorate: http://www.dti.gov.uk/strd/fundingo.htm#swannrep

Updegrove, A. (1995). Consortia and the Role of the Government In Standard Setting. In B. Kahin, & J. Abbate (Eds.), *Standards Policy for Information Infrastructure* (pp. 321-348). Cambridge, MA: MIT Press.

Van Wegberg, M. (2004a). Standardization and Competing Consortia: The Trade-off Between Speed and Compatibility. *International Journal of IT Standards and Standardization Research, 2*(2), 19–33.

Van Wegberg, M. (2004b). Intellectual Property Rights and Competitively Fragmented Standardization Processes: A Review of the Literature. In F. Bousquet, Y. Buntzly, H. Coenen, & K. Jakobs (Ed.), *Proceedings from the 9th EURAS Workshop on Standardization* (pp. 214-226). Paris: Accedo Verlag.

Virtual Enterprise, R. A. M. P. (2005). *Product Data Tools AP224.* Retrieved September 8, 2005, from RAMP Virtual Enterprise Web site: http://ramp.isg-scra.org/ap224_desc.html

Warner, A. (2003). Block Alliances In formal Standard Setting Environments. *International Journal of IT Standards and Standardization Research, 1*(1), 1–18.

Weiss, M., & Cargill, C. (1992). Consortia in the Standards Development Process. *Journal of the American Society for Information Science American Society for Information Science, 43*(8), 559–565. doi:10.1002/(SICI)1097-4571(199209)43:8<559::AID-ASI7>3.0.CO;2-P

Weiss, M. B. (1993). The Standards Development Process: A View from Political Theory. *StandardView, 1*(2), 35–41. doi:10.1145/174690.174695

Weiss, M. B., & Spring, M. (2000). Selected Intellectual Property Issues in Standardization. In K. Jakobs (Ed.), *Information Technology Standards and Standardization: A Global Perspective* (pp. 63-79). Hershey, PA: IGI Publishing.

West, J. (1999). Organizational Decisions for I.T. Standards Adoption: Antecedents and Consequences. *Proceedings of the 1st IEEE Conference on Standardisation and Innovation in Information Technology* (pp. 13-18). Washington, DC: IEEE.

Weston, L., & Whiddett, R. (1999). Factors Affecting the Adoption of IS Standards. In B. Hope, & P. Yoong (Ed.), *Australasian Conference on Information Systems* (pp. 1158-1169). Wellington, New Zealand: Victoria University of Wellington.

Witte, J. (2004). A "Single European Voice" In International Standardization? American Perceptions, European Realities. In F. Bousquet, Y. Buntzly, H. Coenen, & K. Jakobs (Ed.), *Proceedings from the 9th EURAS Workshop On Standardization* (pp. 2-23). Paris: Accedo Verlag.

Yin, R. (1994). *Case Study Research: Design and Methods.* Newbury Park, CA: Sage Publications.

ENDNOTES

[1] Email correspondence with Kai Jakobs, editor-in chief of International Journal of IT Standards & Standardization Research.

[2] Email correspondence with Dr. T.M. King, executive consultant LSC Group.

Chapter 6

Adopter–Centric Perspective:
The United Kingdom Ministry of Defence

INTRODUCTION

The focus of this research is to identify the factors and barriers critical to the adoption of data-exchange standards. Chapter Five identified these factors from an innovation-centric viewpoint, and the purpose of this chapter is to establish the factors that are relevant from an adopter-centric approach. This approach focuses on the adoption of an innovation, in this case standards, within an organization. The chosen organization for this research is the UK Ministry of Defence (MoD). However, in order to limit some of bias of adopter-centric studies identified by West (1999), this chapter not only focuses on the adoption of an ISO data-exchange standard within the MoD, but also looks at the adoption of a regional and UK national defence standard. It is hoped that by comparing the adoption of an ISO standard with a regional standard

DOI: 10.4018/978-1-60566-832-1.ch006

and national standard, a better distinction can be made between the factors that are unique to the adoption of an ISO data-exchange standard, and those that are common to the adoption of any standard or innovation within the MoD.

Data Collection and Analysis Process

There are numerous data gathering methods in case study research (Yin, 1994). The main methods used in this part of the research, and the purposes for the chosen methods are detailed below:

- Interviews: This was the primary data collection tool used in this part of the research. Five interviews were carried out for each of the three standards. The interviews were carried out with developers, implementers, software vendors and end-users related to ISO 10303-224 (AP224) and DEF STAN 00-60. However, only implementers and end-users were interviewed for NATO Codification System (NCS). This is because development of NCS was completed before the standard came into use in the UK, and no software vendors were available for interview. However the implementers worked closely with software that has been developed for the NCS. The interviews were carried out from August 2004 to January 2005.
- Documentation: Documents and archival records were used to verify and add information regarding different issues raised during both primary and secondary adoption.

The analysis of data from multiple case studies can be carried out using a variable (factor) or case-orientated approach. In order to draw on the benefits of both approaches, a number of authors (Eisenhardt, 1989b; Gladwin, 1989) have proposed using a mixed or integrated approach. In light of this, Miles and Huberman (1994) developed and recommended a series of displays using tables, checklist matrices, and causal diagrams, which help facilitate an integrated approach, and these display tools were used extensively in Chapter Five. However, in this chapter data analysis will be carried out using a mixed approach. Hence, in the first section, a variable (factor) approach is used to test and verify the validity of the primary adoption factors identified in the adopter-centric model presented in Chapter Three. Following this, a case approach is used to establish the secondary adoption issues surrounding the diffusion or uptake of the three standards within the MoD. Throughout the chapter, key themes that emerge are presented and discussed in relation to the current literature surrounding the different factors. This is consistent with the approach recommended by Eisenhardt (1989a) and Pare (2002), to test themes against the existing literature. The concluding section presents the revised adopter-centric model. The remainder of this section gives a brief overview of the UK MoD and the three case study standards.

Overview of the UK Ministry of Defence

From 1946 to 1964 there were five Departments of State involved in defence in the UK. In the following years from 1964 to 1971, these five departments amalgamated to form the UK MoD, and the role of the MoD has continued to be been reviewed on several occasions, most recently with the Defence Industrial Strategy (UK MoD, 2005b)/ Few commercial organizations or government departments in the UK can compare with the sheer size and sophistication of the MoD, with an annual budget exceeding thirty billion pounds and over 300,000 service and civilian personnel (UK MoD, 2005c). The MoD also works closely with a vast number of prime and sub-contractors or industry partners to achieve its goals. In addition, UK forces are operating world wide with a range of allies and partners, such as NATO, the UN and a variety of 'coalitions of the willing' across the world (UK MoD, 2002a).

Sections of the MoD are devoted to all three services, namely the Army, Navy and Air force, and others are linked predominately to specific service areas. In addition to this, sections of the MoD are focused on the front line command, personnel, procurement and logistics. Procurement and logistics are handled by two main agencies, the Defence Procurement Agency and the Defence Logistics Organization. Both agencies are made up of what are known as Integrated Project Teams (IPTs). According to MoD notes (UK MoD, 2006a), IPTs are, "Responsible for managing an equipment project from concept to disposal, bringing together all stakeholders and involving industry (except during competition phases) under a team leader able to balance trade-offs between performance, cost and time within boundaries set by the approving authority. IPTs provide a whole-life perspective, together with clearly defined customer-supplier relationships". Some IPTs are jointly managed by both agencies, other IPTs are linked to a specific agency, but all IPTs are a key and integral part of the running of the MoD. A complete overview of the structure and breakdown of the MoD can be found on the MoD website (UK MoD, 2006a).

Standardization within the MoD

According to the MoD Support Solutions Envelope, standardization is the key to ensuring the interoperability, quality, safety, reliability, maintainability, effectiveness and efficiency of the equipment used by the Armed Forces (UK MoD SSE, 2005a). More specifically the MoD needs information standards to exchange/share information internally and externally between prime and sub-contractors within the UK, and across the rest of the world, throughout the life cycle of a product. Therefore the MoD AMS (Acquisition Management Systems) standardization authoritative encourages the application of 'smart standardization' principles at all stages of the acquisition life cycle of a product, that is: concept, assessment, demonstration, manufacture, in-service and disposal (UK MoD AMS, 2003). Consequently, the choices of standards to be used in the various missions or projects within the MoD are selected against a standardization hierarchy summarised as follows:

1. **European:** European Committee for Standardization (CEN), European Committee for Electrotechnical Standardization (CENELEC), European Telecommunications Standards Institute (ETSI)
2. **International:** International Organization for Standardization (ISO), International Electrotechnical Commission (IEC), International Telecommunication Union (ITU)
3. **National:** British Standards Institution (BSI)
4. **Commercial standards widely recognised by Industry:** E.g. - Rules of the International Civil Aviation Organization (ICAO) agreed through the European, Commercial standards e.g. AECMA, ANSI, API, ASTM, IEEE
5. **International Military Alliances:** E.g. - NATO Standardization Agreements such as the NATO Codification Agreement and Allied Publications (APs), Five Nation Agreements.
6. **UK MOD Defence Standards:** E.g. - DEF STAN 00-60
7. UK MOD Departmental Standards and Specifications
8. **Other nations' military standards:** E.g. - USA DoD Mil Specs and Standards
9. **Recognized Industry/Partnership/Consortium Standards:** E.g. - PANAVIA, AIRBUS

As is shown in the hierarchy, UK Government policy is that civil standards are used wherever possible in preference to military standards. This national policy resonates with that at NATO level, which states "NATO standards will only be developed when the requirements are not covered by existing international, civil or military standards" (UK MoD, 2002b). In light of this MoD policy and the European Commission's Public Procurement Directive, European standards are the first choice of standards in the MoD followed by international, national, commercial and finally military standards (Stirling, 2001).

The standards selection hierarchy shown in Table 1 was developed to offer guidance to standards users in the MOD and, according to AMS documentation (UK MoD AMS, 2003), each mission or project must use standards that best meet the requirements of the project in accordance with MoD policy. Therefore, a wide variety of standards are used throughout the MoD to supports its business. As a consequence, it was decided that to fully appreciate the factors and barriers critical to the adoption of standards within the MoD, the case study would be carried out based on the adoption of an international data-exchange standard, a regional military standard and a UK national defence standard.

Introduction to Case Study Standards

This study looks at the adoption and diffusion of three standards within the MoD. The three chosen standards are:

ISO 10303-224 – RAMP Project

The main STEP project currently running within the MoD is the RAMP (Rapid Acquisition of Manufactured Parts) project, which is based on the ISO 10303-224 – "Mechanical parts definition for process planning using machining features" (informally referred to as AP224 for the remainder of the chapter). The RAMP process was originally conceived to enable the US DoD to overcome difficulties in obtaining small batches of spare parts, particularly those nearing obsolescence.

The principle of RAMP is that a reduction in the cost of carrying a large spares inventory can be achieved by the storage of electronic definitions of spare parts as opposed to the manufactured items themselves. Components can then be rapidly manufactured on demand, from the electronic STEP descriptions. Therefore, RAMP is a form of "just-in-time (JIT) manufacturing", and the fundamental difference between RAMP and other leading JIT technologies is that the use of AP224 means that it is a more widely applicable process that is not constrained to any particular computer hardware, software or vendor specific implementation (LSC Group, 2002). Therefore, the UK Navy saw the use of RAMP, which is based on an international standard and used in the US Navy, as an opportunity to deal with these issues. Consequently, in 1998 the UK Navy mechanical RAMP pilot project was conducted to prove that the system worked in the UK operational environment.

Following on from that, in 2001, a second study was carried out by a large prime contractor to further test the extent of RAMP applicability across a wider range of products. These two projects concluded that RAMP using AP224 could significantly reduce lead times involved in the procurement of mechanical spares and consequently, cost savings could be realised by an elimination or reduction of stockholding (LSC Group, 2002). In December 2003, a prime contactor involved in the 2001 study embarked on the implementation of the UK's first production application of RAMP within an MoD Integrated Project Team.

NATO Codification System (NCS)

The NCS provides NATO countries with a uniform and common system for the identification, classification, and stock numbering of items of supply (UK NCB, 2002). It is based on the US Federal Catalogue System, and the foundation for this system within NATO rests in two NATO Standardization Agreements (STANAGs).

- STANAG 3150, "Uniform System of Supply Classification," which adopts the US system of classifying supplies as the standard within the NATO Alliance.
- STANAG 3151, "Uniform System of Item Identification," which adopts other basic standards for identification of supply items and sets the governing structure in place for the NCS.

Allied Committee 135 - "NATO Group of National Directors on Codification", governs the NCS. This committee is composed of a representative from each NATO member nation and is committed to increasing the effectiveness and efficiency of defence logistics interoperability between participating nations. The system provides NATO allies with a common identification language for use within national activities and between member countries. Non-NATO countries that are "sponsored" members of the NCS also benefit from the system. Countries that participate in the NCS follow common standards and techniques to assign a single NATO Stock Number (NSN) to each item of supply in their defence inventory. The national codification bureau within each country is responsible for the management and assignment of NSNs for parts manufactured in that country. The assignment of an NSN fixes the identity of each distinctive item of supply. All NSNs are uniform in composition, length, and structure, and each is represented by a 13-digit number. The UK National Codification Bureau (UKNCB) is the custodian of the UK MOD's Item of Supply Information System (ISIS), which contains over 5 million NATO Stock Number records that identify and describe items of equipment used by the UK Armed Forces (UK NCB, 2002).

UK Defence Standard 00-60 – DEF STAN 00-60

The cost of in-service support of defence equipment is generally equal to, or more than, the cost of its procurement (UK MoD, 2005a). Therefore, this cost is a significant factor in procurement decisions and needs to be managed in a disciplined way. According to DEF STAN 00-60 Part 1, "Integrated Logistic Support (ILS) is the accepted discipline for managing that cost, for enabling support considerations to influence the design, including maintainability or selection of equipment, and for delivering and monitoring a consistent support environment for the fielded equipment". The many components of ILS are encompassed in a structured and integrated way through DEF STAN 00-60. The standard includes profiles of existing, internationally recognized standards, which are brought together for consistent use. The baseline standards and specifications are:

- MIL-STD-1388-1A and MIL-STD-1388-2B
- AECMA Specification 1000D (S1000D) - International Specification for Technical Publications Utilising a Common Source Database
- AECMA Specification 2000M - International Specification for Materiel Management Integrated Data Processing for Military Equipment.
- AECMA is currently merging with EDIG, the European Defence Industries Group, and EUROSPACE, the association of the European space industry, into the AeroSpace and Defence industries association of Europe (ASD).

DEF STAN 00-60 is presented in parts. Part 1 describes the overall context of ILS and integrates the remaining parts. Subsequent parts describe the individual processes and their data and information management in detail covering Logistic Support Analysis, Logistic Support Analysis Record, Integrated Supply Support Procedure and Electronic Documentation creation and delivery. On a more specific level, DEF STAN 00-60-Part 22 describes the procedures for the initial stages of codification of equipment provisioned in accordance with AECMA Specification 2000M (S2000M) procedures, showing the link between DEF STAN 00-60 and the NCS.

Summary

This chapter analyzes the adoption of each of these standards within the MoD and will focus on both primary and secondary adoption issues surrounding their adoption. This is keeping with Dedrick and West's (2003) belief that "a richer framework for understanding these decisions (for standards adoption) can be developed through a qualitative study of a specific standards adoption case" (p.237).

ANALYSIS OF THE ADOPTER-CENTRIC MODEL: PRIMARY ADOPTION

Primary adoption within an organization deals with the adoption decision. The adoption decision is impacted or influenced by a number of factors identified within the adopter-centric model developed in Chapter Three and replicated in Figure 1. This

Figure 1. Adopter-centric standards adoption and diffusion model

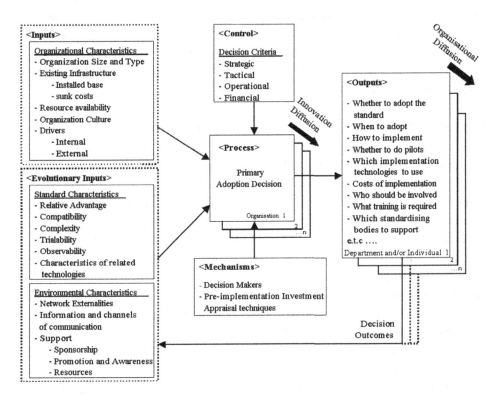

section analyzes, tests and verifies the identified factors against data surrounding the three standards.

Organizational Characteristics

The organizational characteristics that impact the primary adoption of a standard within the MoD, relates to five key issues, namely:

- Organization size and type
- Drivers (motivation)
- Organization culture
- Existing infrastructure
- Resource availability

Chapter Five gave a brief overview of two of the named factors, namely, organization size and type and organization culture. However, Chapter Five was taking an innovation-centric view and offered only a generic analysis of these factors. The remainder of this section is devoted to giving a more detailed analysis of the factors discussed in Chapter Five and the remaining organizational characteristics that impact the adoption of a standard within the specific context of the UK MoD.

Organization Size and Type

This factor relates to how the size and type of organization may impact the adoption decisions of an organization. Chen (2003) ascertains that large government agencies are traditionally known to be strong supporters of standardization efforts. This was found to be true in the case of the MoD. As was previously mentioned, the MoD SSE (Support Solutions Envelope) emphasises that standardization is key to ensuring the interoperability, quality, safety, reliability, maintainability, effectiveness and efficiency of the equipment used by the Armed Forces (UK MoD SSE, 2005a). This strong support for standards is driven by the fact that it is a large organization that is at the top of a supply chain made up of hundreds of contractors and industry partners, and effective exchange and sharing of information and the management of equipment is greatly enhanced by the use of standards. An interviewee who has worked for over 30 years in the MoD stated, *"I have a business to run. It is called the Royal Navy. The best way for me to run my business is by applying standards. That is my corporate rule"*.

In addition, following a number of government programs and initiatives, such as the Strategic Defence Review and the "Modernising Government" initiative, and an internal MoD drive towards implementing Shared Data Environments, plus the impact of the Internet and the explosion of e-business, Enterprise Integration has been seen as a key enabler to facilitate the seamless exchange and integration of information across design, production and engineering support systems in the MoD (UK MoD SSE, 2005b). For this reason, the MoD Support Solutions Envelope states that, "Current policy is that international and application neutral standards are to be used wherever possible, particularly ISO standards such as ISO 10303" (UK MoD SSE, 2005b). Therefore, for projects requiring electronic exchange of product data, STEP is the specified preferred standard within the MoD.

These MoD policies plus statements made by interviewees emphasise and confirm the importance of standards for the effective running of the MoD. This indicates that MoD support of standardization efforts has a positive impact on the potential adoption of any standard within the MoD and is not unique to the adoption of data-exchange standards. Therefore, the theme that emerged from this was:

Theme 1: Due to the MoD's size and position in the defence supply chain, the use of standards is a vital for effective running of its business. Consequently, the MoD has developed policies on standardization that have a positive impact on the decision to adopt standards within the organization.

What is interesting to note about the issues surrounding the size and type of organization was that as one travels down the defence community supply chain, the response of prime contractors to the decision to use a standard is not always positive. This was particularly true in the case of the adoption decision process between an Integrated Project Team (IPT) and a prime defence contractor involved in the RAMP project. The contractor was reluctant to take on the use of an open neutral standard like AP224 because the company believed that this would empower the MoD to take business to any contractor who was willing to comply with the standard, which could result in a loss of their business with the MoD. An interviewee who has worked for over 30 years in the MoD noted, "*Industrial companies are reluctant to apply the standard because they believe it is restraining them or reducing their profit. I remember an encounter with a senior manager with a major ship builder in the UK saying 'why would I apply RAMP because it is just taking money out of my pocket'*". The interviewee went on to explain, that "*if you tell [contractors] that [using standards] does not lose money it gives you a better opportunity in a bigger market place, they do not buy that and it comes back to hard work to convince them.*"

This resistance by industry has an interesting caveat within the MoD because, even though STEP is the MoD's preferred choice of standard for data exchange, as one long-serving MoD project manager went on to explain, "*the MoD have large industry contractors that tend to be very traditionally based and we are not in a good position to say, 'If you do not apply this standard then we will take our business away'. We cannot take it to someone else. These large contractors are very powerful. In the United States they have a larger industrial base so they are able to actually apply these technologies and these standards more easily and we tend to be restrained*". So in the case of the RAMP project, it was important that a balance was reached for benefit to be seen by both the MoD and prime contactor, and this was accomplished through a contractual arrangement explained in later sections. This confirms Meister's finding that adoption of these data-exchange standards needs to be thought of in terms of supply chains rather those individual organizations. Indeed some of SC4 members interviewed by Meister (2004) suggested that customers, like the MoD, should promote STEP by writing it into contracts.

Drivers (Motivation)

Themistocleous (2002), when looking at the adoption of enterprise integration technologies within two large organizations, found that the internal and external

Table 1. Drivers behind the adoption of the case study standards

Standard	Driver	Nature of driver
AP224	Better control of stockholding of spares in order to reduce the size of inventory	Internal Economic
Def Stan 00-60	Reduce the cost of in-service support of defence equipment through an Integrated Logistic Support (ILS) package	Internal Economic
NCS	Managing stock, inventory and duplication of stock and facilitate interoperability between nations	Internal and external Economic and operational

drivers and pressures were key factors in the adoption of technology within an organization. The drivers involved in the adoption of a standard may be internally based on organizational need or pressure from, for example, senior management. The drivers may also be external because of pressure from trading partners in the form of mandatory or legal requirements. The nature of drivers can also be strategic, tactical, operational or economical. Table 1 summarises the main drivers behind the adoption of the three standards.

There were clear drivers for the adoption decision for all three standards. The natures of these drivers were mainly internal from within the MoD and economic in relation to cost savings. In the case of the RAMP project, the key facilitator was the fact that there was a clear motivation and need for the use of the RAMP process. The UK Navy had a desire to better control its stockholding of spares in order to reduce the size of its inventory, which was very large, and predominately made up mechanical parts. Therefore, as the RAMP project leader went on to explain, the main motivation behind the project was that, *"There is a lot of cost [associated with storing parts] and whilst big warehouses full of spare parts can be absorbed in some form of government bureaucracy, if you are in industry with shareholders expecting a dividend you cannot afford to have this asset that is appreciating at 6% per year. And our shareholders are taxpayers!"*

So cost saving and efficiencies were driving the desire for a solution. However, in the case of the NCS, there was an additional external and operational driver to support interoperability both within the MoD and with other nations. One MoD senior manager explained the operational drivers in this way, *"If you look at the codification process, for instance when you have a guy whose out on the front line in the pouring rain in just over freezing, he has not got any time to do a [part] comparison ... By coding one number he is going to get an interoperable part put in his hand, and if that saves him time it is going to deliver operation capability to him and its going to get him into the warm and dry as soon as possible and get his aircraft back in the air, and that is what its about. We are investing time so the guy on the frontline can make quick decisions*".

What was shown from analysis of the RAMP project was that having these clear drivers behind the adoption of the standard had a positive impact on the adoption decision. This was evident in the two other cases but not as significant. In the case of DEF STAN 00-60, it is a defence standard initiated by the MoD and consequently by its very nature it will be adopted by the MoD. It is also mandated, so the drivers are not directly related to the adoption decision although the drivers triggered the development of the standard. Therefore, for DEF STAN 00-60 the primary adoption decision was not in question, the key issues arise in secondary adoption across the MoD. This is discussed in later sections.

In the case of the NCS, the drivers did impact the decision but again to a lesser extent than in the RAMP project because there were also external pressures due to the UK being a member of NATO, and the standard being mandated throughout NATO. Hence, the decision to adopt the NCS was straightforward, unlike in the case of the RAMP project. Thus the resulting theme is:

Theme 2: Having clear economic and operational drivers behind the use of the standard has a positive impact on the adoption decision process. This is particularly true where there are internal and external drivers behind the adoption of the standard.

This result confirms findings of authors such as Themistocleous (2002) and emphasises the validity of this factor.

Organization Culture

This organizational characteristic relates to the cultural beliefs that an organization has relating to change (Mustonen-Ollila & Lyytinen, 2003). Overall, there was a resistance to change. Indeed, resistance to change was the most commonly cited primary adoption barrier. The source of this resistance to change varied among the different MoD representatives. The main sources of resistance included:

- **Reluctance to change current ways of working:** Some representatives resisted adoption purely because they had traditional ways of approaching work and were not willing to change. They had what one interviewee termed as '*not-invented-here syndrome*', which was exactly the response given by potential STEP users in the process industry (Dreverman, 2005). Some stakeholders were resistant to the idea of new technologies being rapidly introduced within the MoD, as one MoD senior manager noted, "*I have old* *directors who tell me Rome was not built in a day, but what they fail to realise is that parts of it were, and what we are doing is parts of it."* The MoD official went on to state that, *"information is now almost fully digital, and hopefully, with young engineers and business students coming out from university, they will be more familiar with this technology, but at this point we have got this old school who do not understand all this"*.

- **Switching costs:** Other end-users were resistant to the possible switching costs involved in having to change their current approaches to work, which would affect budgets and incomes. As one of the RAMP project interviewees noted, *"the contractor is a very large organization and most people would prefer to carry on the way they have done things and use drawings and be able to carry on unchanged. They have had a massive investment in new equipment new machines and new software to support this"*.

- **Fear of loss of power and control:** For IPT representatives, the introduction of this project represented a loss of control and power, as one MoD employee explained, *"The amount of money [MoD managers] receive to buy things per year is power. So therefore, they do not want to see their budget decreased. The civil servant is not naturally a person looking for efficiency... So some people do not want to get into that type of game because of it taking some of their power away"*. In addition, some IPT decision makers saw the impact that the introduction of a system like RAMP might have on their relationships with contractors. One MoD senior manager noted *"[managers] have a large team of people, to some of whom RAMP would represent significant change to their control of how things are ordered and how things are supplied, so it is upsetting their relationship with their suppliers and it is causing them some difficulties and, at the end of the day, it must cause fears of driving unemployment"*.

An MoD end-user pointed out that the traditional military way to overcome resistance to change was a *"you just do it"* attitude. However, the interviewee went on to point out that, even in a military environment, employees will not work with the system whole heartedly and that will frustrate what needs to be done on a project and lead to project overruns. Therefore the resultant theme is:

Theme 3: The adoption decision was negatively impacted by a resistance to change demonstrated by key decision makers. The main causes of resistance were traditional ways of working, switching costs and loss of power and control.

This theme is consistent with the commonly cited resistance-to-change factors identified by Kotter *et al.* (1998) in the Harvard business review. All the factors point to personal characteristics, which show that some potential adopters are more inno-vative than others (Fichman, 1992). This was particularly the case in the resistance by some of the older MoD employees who, because of their age, were resistant to the speed at which new technologies were being introduced. Age was also identi-fied as a key moderator of end-user willingness to accept new technologies in a comprehensive study by Venkatesh *et al.* (2003) into user acceptance of IT.

A second issue relating to organization culture was user attitudes towards stan-dards. In other words, the opinions and beliefs of users towards standards. Some of the common attitudes and perceptions were that the use of standards would restrict the way they worked and bring no real benefits. As one interviewee explained, *"Standards, I believe, are necessary. What we have to be able to do is not frighten people by their implementation and also stress to people that they are not there as a restraint, they are there as a business enabler"*. Meister (2004) had a similar comment from an SC4 member he interviewed; he found that in some countries the term standard meant constriction and a change in current ways of working to match someone else.

Other end-users interviewed perceived the standards as being complex and would therefore cost a lot to implement. In addition, some of the end-users indicated that they had a negative view of ISO standards in general, mainly because of their ex-periences with the ISO standards development community, which they perceived to be a group of academics who were not connected to reality, which was discussed in Chapter 5. In the case of the RAMP project, some interviewees expressed the view that standards like STEP are simply ideas that software vendors and consultants were trying to get them to use and, therefore, there was a reluctance to adopt and implement the standard. Hence, the resultant theme is:

Theme 4: Some decision makers have negative attitudes and perceptions towards standards in general and ISO standards in particular and this has a negative impact on the adoption decision process.

Coombs *et al.* (2001) recognize in their study of the adoption of community information systems that it desirable to attain positive user attitudes towards a system. In their view this may have a beneficial impact upon user behaviour, ultimately influencing user acceptance of a system. Other authors (Zmud, 1983; Davis, 1993; Al-Gahtani & King, 1999) have given insight into the impact of user attitudes on system acceptance and adoption. However, these studies focused on attitudes towards information systems and change, and not on specific standards, and what emerged from the literature was a lack of studies that dealt specifically with decision makers' attitudes and perceptions towards standards from an adopter-centric point of view. These results have, therefore, given insights into some of the issues surrounding attitudes towards standards and offered an opportunity for an interesting further study to test if these perceptions were valid over a wider population of end-users. The findings from the study into attitudes towards standards are presented in Chapter 9.

Existing Infrastructure

This factor is linked with organization culture, and was particularly demonstrated in the RAMP project. What emerged was that investments that had been made in new equipment and machines would be lost with the introduction of the standard. This was particularly the case for the prime contractor involved in the adoption decision. Therefore, the theme that emerged was:

Theme 5: Some stakeholders have investments in technology and software that would be lost with the introduction of the standard, resulting in additional switching costs. This had a negative impact on the adoption decision process.

This is in keeping with findings by authors such as Hovav *et al.* (2003) who explain that, "even if an innovation is considered to be superior on the basis of objective criteria, a potential adopter may still not adopt the innovation. The presence of a large installed base of existing innovation leading to the presence of sunk costs through irreversible investments can introduce a drag on the adoption of a new innovation" (p.470).

The reluctance of some stakeholders is tied to the switching costs that emerge from the need to change systems and ways of working. Kahl (2004) classified switching costs into four categories:

- Technical integration costs: These costs relate to the costs associated with integrating a new system with other infrastructure software such as databases, application servers, operating systems, transaction management, as well as different kinds of hardware and communication protocols.
- Organizational integration costs: These costs deal with the costs associated with change, in particular changes to business processes.
- Training and learning costs: In the introduction of a new system there will be costs associated with training staff to learn and new system.
- Contractual costs: Contractual arrangements can create a form of switching costs. For example contract termination penalties or a maintenance contract, which costs 15-20% of the total license over a three-year period.

The costs in the cases studied here were mainly technical integration and organizational integration costs, mainly due to the fact the these ISO data-exchange standards underpin software that enables the exchange and sharing of information both within and across organizations. In addition, there are learning costs associated with retraining the end-users. These technical- and human-cost issues are generally consistent with the impact of organizational learning upon adoption (West, 1999).

Resource Availability

Resource availability within the MoD is greatly affected by restructuring and review initiatives. This was particularly the case in the RAMP project. After the 1998 pilot there was a major reorganization of the MoD, in addition to that, the associated changes that resulted from the Smart Procurement Initiative started in 1997 (LSC Group, 2002). These activities may explain some of the reasons for the delays that occurred between the first successful pilot in 1998 and the subsequent pilot project in 2001.

In addition to the reviews and restructuring initiatives that take place in the MoD, the other challenge to resource availability is the constant changing of position within the organization. An interviewee who has worked for over 30 years in the MoD explained this situation as follows: *"The MOD is not an easy customer to have. Everybody changes position every two years and there is very little continuity between one set of people to a next, so it is a constant battle to educate people and they are largely fruitless battles to educate people and move forward ...It is probably only with the involvement of a prime contractor as a reasonably significant supplier that we managed to engage one of the IPTs in taking this approach to supply [RAMP] seriously"*.

This reorganization and general moving of people has an impact on the financial and human resources available, as was the case in the RAMP project. To further compound resource availability challenges, the influence and consequences of urgent operational requirements may require people to be reassigned to different projects without notice or warning, again making continuity very difficult. However, this was not a key issue at the primary decision level adoption of the NCS and DEF STAN 00-60. The resultant theme is therefore:

Theme 6: Restructuring initiatives and frequent redistribution of employees within the MoD results in a lack of continuity of financial and human resources, which has a negative impact on the adoption decision process.

One of the key counter factors of this resource availability challenge in the RAMP project was the availability of key champions. Some were internal to the MoD. Some were key external consultants who kept the project moving forward and who were vital in championing the benefits of the standard and were responsible for getting the standard to the current point of implementation in the form of a pilot project. One of the interviewees noted that it was difficult to initially find any internal business champions. However, one interviewee stated, *"once some key managers saw the business benefit and were able to see the changes required in light of these benefits, support for the adoption of the standard grew"*.

Theme 7: Champions and change agents are vital in keeping the adoption decision process moving forward and have a positive impact on the final decision.

Meister (2004) found that having a strong visionary leader or champion was a common element of every successful STEP adoption story. This confirms work by Rogers (2003) and Prescot and Cogner (1995) who did a longitudinal study into the factors that impact adoption of innovations, and they explain that champion support for an innovation means that someone within the organization becomes a special advocate for the innovation, taking actions to increase the probability of successful adoption and implementation and this was demonstrated in the study. This is further affirmed by Fichman (1992) who explains that, "the actions of certain kinds of individuals (opinion leaders and change agents) can accelerate adoption" (p.2).

Standards Characteristics

The standard characteristics factor draws on Rogers' five traditional characteristics, namely: complexity, relative advantage, compatibility, observability and trialability, and the characteristics of the related implementation technologies. At the primary adoption level, the characteristics of DEF STAN 00-60 and the NCS did not have an impact on the adoption decision; again issues surrounding the characteristics of these standards emerged mainly during the secondary adoption stage or implementation process.

However, in the case of the RAMP project, certain characteristics of the standard did impact the adoption decision process. The first was related to the complexity of the standard, and was as a result of decision makers finding it difficult to understand the standard and how it works. Two of the consultant implementers noted, *"When you talk about STEP they think there is some "black magic" there and say 'absolutely no way are we going to understand that' "*. The second characteristic was in relation to relative advantage, and RAMP was seen as the only standard decision makers believed would bring them the benefit they required. One interviewee who has worked for over 30 years in the MoD explained this point by stating that, *"STEP seemed the logical way to go and the STEP-based approach [RAMP] was the best way. It gave us that degree of neutrality that we did not have to rely on single source supplier and [it] gave us a capability of holding a file neutrally that we could exchange. We did not feel a need to try any other standards".*

The next characteristic was in relation to the compatibility of the standard. This was particularly the case with regards to the use of XML to implement the STEP application protocol. This is due to the fact that the UK government and many trading standards bodies have adopted XML as the format for exchanging information. Therefore, the use of XML for data exchange into and out of MOD systems is being encouraged wherever appropriate. Hence, the use of XML to implement the system encouraged the uptake of RAMP because there was compliance with MoD policy, which states that XML must be used to exchange information between systems within the MOD and between MOD systems and external partners (UK MoD CDMA, 2004). The resulting theme is therefore:

Theme 8: Characteristics relating to the complexity, relative advantage and compatibility of the standard have a positive impact on the adoption decision process.

These characteristics have emerged as key issues in the adoption studies of numerous authors (Hovav *et al.,* 2004; Mustonen-Ollila & Lyytinen, 2003; Dedrick & West, 2003), and confirm Rogers (2003) view that standards will be adopted more readily than other standards if they are perceived by organizations as having greater relative advantage, compatibility, trialability, observability and less complexity. In addition, the characteristics of the related technologies should be favourable to support the adoption of the standard.

Environmental Factors

The environmental characteristics describe the set of factors that favour an organization's adoption of a standard by assessing the environmental conduciveness. This includes issues surrounding three factors:

- Network effect
- Support
- Information and communication channels

Network Effects

The key factor within the environmental characteristics is the impact of network effects on the adoption decision. There was a positive network effect on the adoption of RAMP in the UK Navy, based on the fact that this project was first established in the US Navy. As one implementer said, *"It was quite a sensible choice to a use an existing standard that did have some support and use."* The resultant theme is therefore:

Theme 9: Current adoption and use of the standard within the US defence community has a positive impact on the adoption decision within the UK.

These findings point to results found in research on network externalities. In network externalities, each buyer of a technology receives greater benefits as the user network increases in size. Examples of this include the telephone service and fax machines (Warner 2003). These benefits include an increase in support and resources surrounding an innovation. Though this RAMP example is slightly narrow, there was an acknowledgement that by using an international standard there would be an increased benefit as more people work to the standard, and one MoD decision maker noted, *"In the case of an international standard, there is a hope that as more organizations outside the MoD and contractor sector work to the standard, there will be benefit in working with the standard"*. This confirms another hypothesized factor in the economics of standards regarding the role of positive network effects that accrue to all adopters of a popular standard (Von Weizsäcker, 1984). Therefore, the MoD is positioning itself for greater network benefits as the adoption of AP224 increases.

Support

The numerous pilots, demonstrations and seminars had a positive impact on the primary adoption decision of the RAMP project and were beneficial in promoting the standard, gaining interest and proving that the standard and supporting technologies worked. These pilots were also able to show the benefits that could be achieved from using the standard. Nonetheless, there was a delay between the 1998 pilot and the subsequent pilot in 2001. One interviewee suggested that one the reasons for this delay after the successful pilot in 1998 was due to the apathy some MoD employees display towards pilots, and explained that, *"It did not get taken up because it was just another MoD pilot project"*. However, despite this view, the overwhelming view was that pilots and demonstrations are key in supporting the adoption decision process. Hence, the resulting theme is:

Theme 10: The use of pilots and demonstration for promotion and awareness of the standard has a positive impact on the adoption decision process.

This is in keeping Mathieson and Ryan's (1997) findings that users have an important role in evaluating the fit between their tasks and software packages. Mathieson's experiments compared two different types of experience with an information system: direct (such as hands-on testing) and indirect (such as watching a demonstration). Mathieson and Ryan (1997) explained that direct experience resulted in more extreme beliefs and suggested that inexpensive demonstrations should be used initially, since they can help users discriminate between packages, but hands-on testing, though more expensive, is best used when demonstrations do not yield a clear preference. The use of these pilots and demonstrations confirms the importance of the observability and trialability innovation characteristics identified by Rogers (2003).

Another form of support that was made evident was the importance of consultants. A consultant is a person who provides expert advice professionally (AskOxford. com, 2005). In the case of the RAMP project, these consultants helped in facilitating some of the pilots and demonstrations, developed software to implement RAMP and provided key champions who facilitated the adoption process. Therefore the resulting theme is:

Theme 11: The involvement of consultants, who provide expert advice and services, has a positive impact on the adoption decision process.

Authors such as Themistocleous (2002), found that support factors like vendor support and consultant support were key in the adoption of EAI and ERP systems within an organization. In addition, Attewell (1992) ascertains that the availability of external skills (such as through integrators or consultants) is essential for adoption by some organizations, and this has proved true in the case of the adoption of standards within the MoD. This was mainly due to the skills that were made available and needed on the project.

Mechanisms and Control: Decision Makers, Techniques and Criteria

According to Rogers (2003), the innovation decision process is a mental process through which an individual (or other decision-making unit) passes first from knowledge of an innovation to forming an attitude toward the innovation through persuasion, to a decision to adopt or reject the innovation, to the implementation of the new innovation. The process of 'forming an attitude towards innovation through persuasion' is where the decision mechanisms come into play. A common mechanism in the decision making process is the use of some form of pre-implementation investment appraisal techniques such as business cases or doing some form of Return of

Investment analysis. The pre-investment technique used in the RAMP project was the development of a business case to support the adoption decision.

A number of the interviewees noted that developing a business case for the implementation of RAMP was initially difficult to do. They recognised that it was important to have a business case, but that there was a difficulty in establishing what the current costs were, and where improvements would be realised against the current baseline costs. As one MoD technical officer put it, *"Part of what we had to do was predict the usage and savings, and that is a horrendously difficult [task] because the Ministry's figures for stock levels and stock values and item values fluctuate all over the place, and so it is very difficult to target [usage and savings]"*.

What this does is make it difficult to clearly justify where the benefit is without having suspicions being raised, and according to one a MoD project manager, many of the business cases are seen as *"'wet finger in the air' jobs"*, which is a term often used to refer to a 'best guess' based on plausible assumptions (Blakeley *et al.*, 1994). This confirms findings by Parker and Benson (1989) which revealed that most chief executive officers are not comfortable with the current tools and techniques used to justify their investments in IT, because they lack preciseness of definition in the financial methods used.

Other interviewees noted that there were political issues surrounding the development of business cases. As one interviewee explained, *"If cost-benefit analysis could be done very easily, I would say that it has got to be a good thing, but I think that it would be so politically charged it would be like the spin government put out on how much improvement they are going to get from a particular policy... I think so many people have got a vested interest in seeing these standards implemented. I do not think you will ever get a clear picture"*. The theme that therefore emerged was:

Theme 12: Determining the business case for the project was a difficult exercise and will initially have a negative impact on the adoption decision process.

This finding was not unique to the two case study standards. Meister (2004) found that most common problem mentioned by SC4 members he interviewed was the difficulty in establishing a business case for the use STEP. These difficulties were mainly attributed to the fact that while the costs of STEP implementations are tangible, the benefits were less so. As a consequence many of the managers interviewed by Meister found that when a business case was made, it focused primarily on capabilities and opportunities, not on numbers that meet organizational hurdle rates for investments. Subsequently STEP-related funding seemed to come out of what was perceived as research budgets, rather than production budgets. This has been confirmed by a number of authors (Irani, 2002; Irani *et al.*, 1999) who postulate that the justification of IT is a complex issue due to many intangibles and non-financial benefits that are inherent in the implementation of IT. There is no commonly agreed method or way to develop a business case for evaluating the return on investment from IT standards, and as detailed in Chapter 10, further research can be carried out to address this issue.

Small and Chen (1995) have identified various underlying concerns in industry with regard to the justification of new technology that can be applied to the adoption of data-exchange standards. These concerns centre around: (i) many of the achievable benefits are considered to be qualitative rather than quantitative, and hence difficult to quantify; (ii) a lack of readily accessible and acceptable techniques for appraising all project costs and benefits; (iii) the ability to assess the true performance of a system is diminished if all benefits are not quantified during the justification process; and (iv) an insufficient level of internal skills (managerial and technical) to appraise proposed systems. Due to the above concerns, many corporate managers have been forced to adopt one of the following strategies:

Not to undertake IT projects that could be beneficial to the long-term future of the organization

- Invest in projects as an 'act of faith'
- Use creative accounting as a means of passing the budgetary process (Irani *et al., 2002*).

In the end, the solution that countered this difficulty was a "gain-share" arrangement that was initially developed as a business case and then become the contractual arrangement around which the adoption decision was made. This gain-share contractual arrangement was one of the significant factors that encouraged the uptake of the RAMP project by the prime contractor. One implementer explained that the essence of the arrangement was that, "*If [the] MOD says we need 100 spares, the team within this organization looks at the electronic STEP-based stock holding and would say you do not need 100, you need 10 and they would have saved the MoD 90 spares. So half of the cost that they saved goes back to the contractor*".

Another interviewee who was instrumental in developing the contractual arrangement went on to explain that, "*I do not think the project would have been accepted without this business case...the MoD not only saw this as a way to get over their problems they saw it as a way that was reasonable for the contractor to take forward the business proposition*". The decision criteria used in the decision process was based on the economic and strategic benefits that were captured in the contractual arrangement, and represented business benefit and value to both the MoD and the industry prime contractor. In light of this, the resultant theme is:

Table 2. Primary adoption factors

Standard specific factors	Generic organizational factors
Standardization policy (organization size and type)	Attitudes towards change
Attitudes towards standards	Resource availability
Standard characteristics	Existing Infrastructure
Drivers	Support
Network effects	

Theme 13: Having a contractual arrangement that captures the benefits of the adoption of the standard and offers a reward to all relevant stakeholders has a very positive impact on the adoption decision.

This is a key factor and points to the issue of all stakeholders being able to see the business value of a new investment.

Primary Adoption Decision Process: Key Factors and Summary

The study of the primary adoption decision process has led to the emergence of key themes and factors, most of which confirm existing literature. However, these factors have been grounded in a new context, the UK defence community. The results from the case studies have also shown that the factors that impact the primary adoption decision of standards within the MoD are made up of both factors relating specifically to the MoD as an organization and factors directly linked to the standard as shown in Table 2.

In conclusion, this section has tested and verified the factors shown in the original adopter-centric model and offered insights into the details surrounding different factors within the MoD context. However, the adoption and diffusion process does not stop at the primary adoption decision. At some point, as was shown in the case of the RAMP project, a final adoption decision was made between an IPT and the prime contractor and this enabled the first working pilot of the RAMP project to begin. Once the decision has been made, secondary adoption and implementation takes place. Some of the issues surrounding secondary adoption are mentioned in the "output" section of the original model, but were not analyzed in detail. Therefore, the next section aims to give a more detailed analysis of secondary adoption issues that emerged from the case studies.

SECONDARY ADOPTION AND ORGANIZATIONAL DIFFUSION CHALLENGES

Secondary adoption relates to the implementation process and the use of a standard within an organization. Although this was not the focus of the research, a significant number of insights were given into the challenges facing the implementation and uptake of the three case study standards within the MoD. These challenges were viewed as offering valuable insights into the factors that impact the adoption of standards, some of which related specifically to the standard and standards community.

Secondary Adoption Issues Surrounding the RAMP Project

All interviewees involved in the adoption and implementation of the RAMP project were asked to give their view on the current rate of uptake of the standard. The head of the RAMP project within the MoD when asked the question stated, "*I do not believe the uptake in the Royal Navy has been as great as it could be. You're dealing with an organization that tends to be very traditionally based, especially the supply chain, and the take-up of a new technology is not the quickest and they have a need to drive down cost by doing a just-in-time type of supply. We are starting to do some business but it is not been taken up as quick as we had hoped*". Another interviewee described the rate of uptake as, "*fair to middling*". All RAMP project interviewees in the end expressed some disappointment at the currant rate of uptake or diffusion of the standard within the organization. The main reasons for this include:

- Attitude towards change
- Lack of knowledge and understanding
- Working with the STEP conceptual model
- Revisions of the standard
- Fee for purchasing the published standards
- Remoteness of the standards community

1. Attitude Towards Change

Resistance to change emerged in secondary adoption. In primary adoption it related to the managers and decision makers. In this case, it now relates to the individual end-users of the RAMP-based software. The two main reasons for resistance at an individual level were, firstly, end-users not wanting to change from using proprietary systems they were familiar with. Secondly, some end-users were resistant to outsiders and consultants coming in. This was noted by one of the consultant implementers who explained that, "*There is massive resistance to anything [consultants] do, and it is connected to politics… people we should speak to run past our area so they do not talk to us".*

2. Lack of Knowledge and Understanding

What the implementers found is that some of the end-users lacked an understanding of both the standard, and the benefits that would result from the use of the standard. The reasons for this are the perceived complexity of the standard and poor internal promotion of the standard. Consequently, this lack of understanding and ignorance of the standard and the benefits meant, as one interviewee noted, *" [the project] had lower priority with people being assigned to work on it, so we are currently in a delay at the moment".* Another interviewee went on to explain that there is a challenge in countering this understanding problem in relation to how you sell the standard and the benefits to people at the grass-roots level. The interviewee explained that, *"It is a mistake to call it a standard. Do not use the word 'standards' use 'work processes'. The worst thing is to talk about is a standard. Cut the standards element out of the standard, hone in on the bit relevant to the person".* This advice not to use the word "standards" during promotion is based on the idea that some end-users had negative perceptions towards standards. This was demonstrated at the primary adoption level as well.

3. Working with the STEP Conceptual Model

The implementers interviewed felt that the standard was complex which hindered their implementation efforts. Many of them attributed this complexity to the structure of the STEP standard. One interviewee summarised this view by explaining that, *"the concept of the AIM and ARM is preposterous. It is a real impediment to working with the standard".* The AIM (Application Interpreted Model) and ARM (Application Reference Model) are parts of the STEP data model structure, a more detailed description of the STEP architecture can be found at the ISO/TC184/SC4 website (SC4Online, 2009).

4. Revisions of the Standard

In addition to the issues surrounding the STEP data model structure, two implementers found that some revisions of the standard had a negative impact on the implementation process. The implementers found that some of these newer versions at times lacked backward compatibility with earlier versions of the standard. This caused a certain amount of rework to be done, causing delays in the development of software required to use the standard within the RAMP project, as was discussed in Chapter 5.

5. Fee for Purchasing Published Standards

The cost of the standard was an issue that was raised in relation to the fee that had to be paid to access the standard. Although some interviewees believed that the fees relating to the standard were minimal relative to the project costs, other implementers disagreed with this view. They argued that having to justify the cost of purchasing a copy of the standard was not always easy on a day-to-day basis when dealing with managers who could not necessarily see the need for the extra cost. However, eventually the company purchased a membership subscription, which enabled the standard to be easily accessed, and solved the problem.

6. Remoteness of the Standards Community

Two implementers who were interviewed expressed that they felt the standards community was very remote, resulting in a sense of isolation and a lack of a support network. One of the implementers stated, *"The only real mechanism for engaging with the ISO community is to attend their thrice-yearly meetings"*, and went on to explain that, *"When we went to a STEP meeting in Bordeaux and set up a stand showing that we were using the standard, we thought we would have lots of people flocking round, we could not get a person to stop and look at it, they were too busy going to the next meeting"*. The implementers went on to state that, *"There is no community out there that people can turn to and have user group meetings and swap ideas around and get suggestions, it can be pretty lonely."* In their view, *"Developers do not do anything for the standard except propagate it and do not support it"*. Another implementer who had more input and engagement with developers agreed that, *"One barrier is the remoteness of the standards community, the complete lack of anybody to support the implementation process which clearly you would get if you pay for a proprietary system. So it is the underlying marketing and support that you would expect to receive for starting on any of these processes which is transparently absent when you adopt a standard"*.

These factors are the key issues impacting the secondary adoption and rate of uptake of the RAMP project within the MoD. A summary of the key points is shown in Table 3 and linked to the diffusion of innovation (DOI) theories surrounding the standards secondary adoption. In spite of these challenges, work continues on the RAMP project. The first phase is now complete and tangible benefits have been realised. One report states that to date £60,000 of stock reduction has been realised (Dobson, 2005). With these kinds of results, one of the key stakeholders expressed

Table 3. The RAMP project secondary adoption challenges

Issue	Related DOI Theoretical Foundation	Explanation
Attitudes toward change	Cultural values	- Familiarity with proprietary systems - Reluctance to work with consultants
Lack of knowledge and understanding	Complexity	- Perceptions about the complexity of the standard - Poor internal promotion
STEP conceptual model	Complexity	Complexity of the AIM and ARM structure of STEP data structure made implementation difficult
Revisions of the standard	Compatibility	Not all revisions of the standard were compatible
Fee for purchasing the standard	Cost	The fees required to access the standard hampered some implementers
Remoteness of the standards community	Support infrastructure	Lack of support from STEP community to deal with implementation challenges

a belief that if this pilot project is completed and successful, then other IPTs within the MoD could become interested, which would cause the standard to diffuse through the organization. This is in agreement with a secondary adoption strategy described by Gallivan (2001) as the advocacy strategy, where an organization targets specific pilot projects within the firm and the outcomes are observed and used to determine continued adoption of the innovation.

Secondary Adoption Issues Surrounding DEF STAN 00-60

All interviewees involved in DEF STAN 00-60 described the rate of uptake of the standard as good and widespread amongst MoD programmes, mainly because the standard is mandated. However one of the interviewees went on to point out there is a tendency for the standard to not be productively or effectively implemented. One MoD official ascertained that, *"None of the contractors have taken DEF STAN 00-60 the way DEF STAN 00-60 is intended to be used, and that is one of the biggest failings we have had on the whole process"*. Another interviewee, who previously worked within contractor companies, explained this problem by describing how the use of DEF STAN 00-60 is often seen as a *"tick box exercise"* by some contractors, and this was elaborated further by one interviewee's comment that, *"From my experience, I have found that industry has quite a lot of problems with the way DEF STAN 00-60 is mandated, but industry knows they have to give all the right messages to the customer"*. Some of the issues industry has with the standard are:

1. Complexity

A number of interviewees commented on the complexity of the standard. One even stated that, " *[DEF STAN 00-60] is the most complex standard the MoD has. It has lots of bits [part]...The database is extremely complex and has lots of business rules around its construction*". Another interviewee explained that, "*Yes, [DEF STAN 00-60] was needed. It is just the deployment and complexity of [DEF STAN 00-60] that should have been addressed. [DEF STAN 00-60] is just far too complex*".

2. Cost of Implementation

The issue of cost of implementation was often raised as an issue in the uptake of the standard. A former employee of a major prime contractor that used DEF STAN 00-60 on a major defence equipment project found that approximately 8.5% of project costs were associated with implementing DEF STAN 00-60. According to the interviewee the main source of this cost was tied to the complexity of the standard, which lead to unexpected learning costs from what he described as the "*huge learning curve associated with deployment*". Another key issue relating to cost was the training. One interviewee describing his experience stated, "*Once we actually understood what it was about, to actually get these people up to speed [trained] to input into a database was massively expensive*".

3. Understanding the Value

Another challenge is that industry deal with is the MoD actually understating the value that DEF STAN 00-60 would bring. As one interviewee put it, "*Industry does not see the benefit of DEF STAN 00-60 because they find it too prescriptive*". The interviewee went on to explain that, "*I think the way [DEF STAN 00-60] is written, makes it almost impossible to convince people that this it is worth implementing, and I do not think any organization will pick [DEF STAN 00-60] up and implement it, and maybe this is the proof of the pudding. If it was not mandated would [industry] still say this is what we need to do?*". What the MoD employee believed was that unless industry can see the true value of the standard, in his words, "*you are going to get short changed when you try and convince people*".

4. Tailoring of the Standard

This was another key issue that was raised. As one consultant put it, "*I think the only resistance was in that it was not tailored sufficiently. If you take the Astute program, the requirements for DEF STAN 00-60 have not been tailored at all, and it is going to cost Industry a fortune, and it will lead to cost overruns and programme overruns"*.

Despite these challenges, uptake is good but there are still issues relating to the efficient implementation and the benefits of the standard. This is best exemplified in a note made by one senior consultant that, *"I am not aware of a formal business case validating the business benefit achieved through DEF STAN 00-60 ever having been generated, and that is really a serious issue. We made an offer going back three to four years to do that, but as far as the MoD are concerned they have made the investment in developing the standard. Validating that decision or potentially undermining that decision – there is no real merit in it for them"*. However, all agree that the basic concepts that DEF STAN 00-60 represents and what it provides in terms of Integrated Logistic Support is important. New developments are underway to replace DEF STAN 00-60 and this is discussed in Chapter 9.

Secondary Adoption Issues Surrounding the NATO Codification System

Similar to DEF STAN 00-60, the rate of uptake of the NCS was generally described as good. All those interviewed agreed that because it is mandated within the MoD the uptake is good but not as good as they would like. There were six reasons suggested for this and these are:

- Marketing of the standard
- Individual attitudes towards standards
- Resistance by some IPT's
- Dummy stock numbers
- Integration of the data handling systems
- Resistance from industry

1. Marketing of the Standard

A senior member of the Codification team explained that, *"Marketing ourselves is a challenge. Explaining what we offer and the benefits that accrue from it, from my point of view we can do better [at marketing]. We still get phone calls from some IPTs that still do not know anything about Codification and how to get in contact with us, and that surprises me"*.

2. Individual Attitude Towards Standards

Another challenge relates to people's perceptions and views of the standard. The common perceptions were:

- It is expensive to implement.
- The use of a standard would add time to the overall project.

Most of the codifiers agreed that some end-users had these views because of misinformation and argued that none of these perceptions are valid when you have the appropriate technical data, because with the right data codifying does not take that long.

3. Resistance by Some IPTs

One of the senior managers at the UKNCB explained that a recently commissioned study showed that most IPTs use Codification. However, there was still some resistance from IPTs, and the main reasons for this were:

- Reluctance to bear the cost of codifying legacy equipment that was previously not codified.
- Misunderstanding about how long it should take, how much it costs and who pays for it.
- Lack of understanding of what the benefits are. As one interviewee explained, "*It comes back to if there was one sheet of paper that said this is what Codification delivers with good benefit to you, here is why you should use it, they would be tearing our arm off, but its difficult to define those kind of details in hard cash terms. Therefore, it makes it much more difficult to sell to people.*" There was a desire by some IPTs for an item number to be unique to the IPT for their specific material so they can manage it in its entirety. This is not what the Codification system is designed for. This point was further explained by another interviewee who noted that, "*you do get this business where projects want to own their own destiny. If my weapon system is not going to work because that guy over there has not bought enough spares, I will get the blame so I need to manage the spare myself and that mentality starts to deliver high stock piles again*". Consequently, some IPTs prefer not to use the system.

4. Dummy Stock Numbers

There are problems that have emerged due to imperfect implementations, especially when some employees within an IPT might allocate a dummy stock number. This is where an individual will create a stock number that is similar to a NATO Stock Number (NSN) and just allocates a reference to it. This creates all sorts of problems because it gets confused with genuine NSNs, and results in double stocking if the item already exists in the stores. In addition, either party could end up ordering the wrong item if the same number already exists for another item of supply.

5. Integration of the Data Handling Systems

Each of the three services areas has a main data handling system that feeds back to the master catalogue system known as the Item of Supply Information System (ISIS), which stores all the NSNs used in the UK armed services However, as one interviewee explained, "*W have got three systems, the RAF, the Army and the Navy system, and they are all separate... However, different projects commit to buy things that remain in their bespoke system and they do not come back to update ISIS. So the services can create their own records and NSN, but we are now building processes where they cannot do that*".

6. Resistance from Industry Partners

There is also occasional resistance from MoD industry partners. Although on the whole, as one MoD interviewee put it, "*For industry, as long as [DEF STAN 00-60] is contracted they are happy to do as they are told. If you sign a contract with the MoD, it is a cash cow. If we ask for the data, they will give us it*". Nevertheless, there were two areas of slight resistance from industry. Firstly, there is reluctance by some contractors to have their competitors know how much they are charging the MoD for equipment. The second issue relates to the desire by some industry partners to be able to sell the same spare to the MoD under two different descriptions. One interviewee estimated that having a single stockpile could hurt some suppliers' sales by up to 30%.

These challenges have impacted the secondary adoption and rate of uptake of the NCS. Nonetheless, the general uptake of the NCS within the UK MoD is good, and the UK National Codification Bureau has commissioned the next phase of a codification engine, which can generate codified output direct from a STEP file. This initiative is called Smart Codification and is covered in more detail in Chapter Nine. On a more general level regarding the adoption of NCS one of the interviewees pointed out that, "*One of the challenges in recent years with Codification is raising the capability of the newly emerging nations from Eastern Europe who have all been embraced... those nations have all wanted to embrace the Codification system because of the benefits it will deliver in managing their inventory. But that then provided what is a substantial training burden on the rest of the NATO nations to bring them up to speed".*

Secondary Adoption Key Factors

The details of the three case studies give insight into some of the issue surrounding secondary adoption of standards within the MoD. The main factors are discussed in this section using the key secondary adoption factors identified by Gallivan (2001) as a classification of the issues that have emerged. The three main issues that impact secondary adoption, according to Gallivan (2001), are:

- Managerial intervention
- Facilitating conditions
- Subjective norms

The issues that have emerged in this research relate to managerial intervention and facilitating conditions. Subjective norms describe individuals' beliefs about the expectations others have regarding their own secondary adoption behaviour, and were therefore beyond the scope of this research. The remainder of this section discusses the two other factors.

Managerial Intervention

Managerial intervention describes the actions taken and resources made available by managers to expedite secondary adoption, including mandating usage (Gallivan, 2001). Out of the three standards considered, both DEF STAN 00-60 and the NCS are mandated. On the other hand, AP224 according to MoD policy is the 'preferred choice' of the MoD. Interestingly, however, the fact that the standard was the 'preferred choice' is slightly different to what the literature suggests in terms of standards being either mandatory or voluntary (Weston & Whiddett, 1999). The term 'preferred choice' does not fit in either description, industry is not mandated to use the standard, but there is a policy regarding STEP. Nonetheless, if an IPT organization can justify with a business case why using the standard is more costly than not using it, then they are not bound to use the standard. This results in confusion about use of the standard, which takes away from the incentive and benefits of everyone using the same standard.

Similar issues were raised with the uptake of DEF STAN 00-60 and the NCS. Interviewees expressed concern that even though the standards are mandated, there is still a way to opt out of the use of the standards if a strong enough case is given by a project. What this has shown is that the perception in most literature that standards are either mandated or voluntary, is not a complete picture. There are situations, as shown in the MoD case study, where there is a grey area that can cause conflict and counter the benefits of standardization. Consequently, there are efforts underway to make STEP mandatory across the MoD. However, in relation to managerial intervention, the main theme is:

Theme 14: The term 'preferred choice' leaves room for piecemeal secondary adoption, which has a negative impact on the effective secondary adoption of standards.

Facilitating Factors

According to Gallivan (2001), facilitating conditions are made up of a number of sub-factors, which are:

- Individual attributes
- Innovation attributes
- Organization / Department attributes

Issues surrounding each of these sub-factors emerged during analysis of the research data, and in addition to these three sub-factors and additional factor was added, namely:

- Standards community attributes

This additional factor emerged during data analysis.

1. Individual Attributes

The individual attributes relate mainly to an individual's attitude towards change and towards the standards, and how these impact their willingness to adopt the standards. These issues emerged both at the primary adoption decision level and at the secondary adoption level, and confirm findings by Venkatesh *et al.* (2003) who, in their in-depth analysis of the eight main models of user acceptance of IT, discovered four core determinants of intention and usage, which are: performance expectancy; effort expectancy; social influence and facilitating conditions that relate to the degree to which an individual believes that an organizations technical infrastructure exists to support use of the system. These four factors are moderated by the age, gender, experience and the 'voluntariness of use' of the individual (Venkatesh *et al.* 2003). The resulting theme is therefore:

Theme 15: Attitudes of an individual in relation to change and towards the standards and the willingness of an individual to use the system have an impact on the effectiveness of secondary adoption.

Some of the attitudes that the interviewees believed were prevalent among different stakeholders were:

- Standards are complex
- Standards restrict the way work is done

A number of interviews went on to state that the wording used to describe standards, including the word 'standard' itself or ISO were some of the causes of the negative attitudes towards the standards. One final point was made with regards to the fact that these attitudes vary among different managerial role. These assertions are tested in Chapter 9.

2. Innovation Attributes

The main innovation attributes relate directly to Rogers' (2003) DOI theory of innovation characteristics. The main characteristic that emerged was complexity, which was evident in both DEF STAN 00-60 and the RAMP project. The complexity of the standards had a negative knock-on effect on the cost of implementation and on understanding and learning costs. Some of the issues of complexity were as a result of end-user perceptions, the size and rules surrounding the standard, as was the case with DEF STAN 00-60, and the conceptual idea of the model in the case of AP224. The problems surrounding working with the conceptual structure of STEP confirm findings by Edgyedi and Dahanayake (2003) that the conceptual idea behind a standard can impact the implementation of a standard. The RAMP project also highlighted another of Rogers' characteristics; in this case it was compatibility between subsequent revisions of the standard. These compatibility concerns point to issues within the standards development community that relate to managing revisions of a standard, and is discussed in Chapter 5. The key theme is therefore:

Theme 16: The complexity and compatibility of a standard has an impact on the effective secondary adoption of the standard.

A final challenge with regard to innovation attributes relates to the fees required to access the ISO data-exchange standards. There is an ongoing debate with regards to the fees associated with the purchase of completed standards. The implementers interviewed believed that having freely available standards would make life easier for them and result in increased interest and use of the standard in general. In the end a licence was purchased which dealt with the issue surrounding the fee in this specific case, therefore the theme is:

Theme 17: Ensuring that an organization's standards licence is made available to all stakeholders involved in the implementation of a standard, makes secondary adoption more effective.

A number of commentators agreed that providing standards documents at no charge expands the dissemination of the document (Krechmer, 1998; Swann, 2000). Oksala et al. (1996) take this view one step further and declare that, "standards whose dissemination are controlled for the purposes or garnering additional revenue sow the seeds of their own demise" (p.10). However, Krechmer (1998) contests this extreme view and explains that there are only a few market segments where free completed standards will create a significant change in the number of standards stakeholders. In addition, Krechmer explains that accredited standards bodies like the ISO often use document charges to avoid increasing members' dues. Therefore, this raises the issue of innovative pricing schemes for standards (Swann, 2000). One proposal put forward by Krechmer (1998) is to provide committee work-in-progress documents at no charge to increase the number of stakeholders, and for standards bodies like ISO to continue to sell completed standards to minimize any impact on their existing economic model.

3. Organizational Attributes

This related to organizational attributes of both the IPTs and industry and what was seen was that at different points they impacted secondary adoption. Most of the issues were covered in the primary adoption under the organizational characteristics section. However, a key feature that emerged from the NCS case was the unwillingness for some IPTs to engage in the use of the standard due their narrowed view on their own projects' costs and benefits instead of looking at the benefits the use of the NCS would bring to the whole organization. Therefore the theme that emerged was:

Theme 18: When departments in an organization did not perceive the implementation of a standard as a means of offering them direct benefits, there was a reluctance to adopt the standard.

This confirms findings by Weitzel (2003) who explained that independent business units perceive no incentive to invest in compatibility when the benefits from standardization are accredited to the 'entire' firm or any other entity different from the investing unit. This shows the importance of support and internal promotion and marketing within the organization.

4. Standards Community Attributes

This is a factor that has been added specifically as a result of the RAMP project case. In the case study, some implementers expressed concern at a lack of a support infrastructure surrounding the implementation of AP224. The issues surrounding the support infrastructure had to do with communication and implementer relationships with the development community. There appears to be a disconnect between the two communities in this case and a need for better communication channels, which are a key element for successful diffusion of an innovation (Rogers, 2003; Hovav *et al.,* 2003). Available communication channels can also facilitate accessibility to information by organizations regarding a new standard (Nilakanta & Scamell, 1990). Therefore, the final theme is:

Theme 19: The communication between the standards community and implementers is vital to ensure successful implementation of a standard in order to facilitate secondary adoption.

This theme mirrors the findings presented in the innovation-centric Theme 14 in Chapter Five, which states that, '*Poor communication channels among developers, existing adopters and potential adopters have negatively impacted the adoption of the standards'.* These two themes indicate the importance of effective and clear communication between the stakeholders involved in the development, use and implementation of these standards. Steps need to be taken to deal with these communication issues and some recommendations relating to this are presented in Chapter 10.

Summary

This section has looked at the secondary adoption factors that impact the adoption and diffusion of a standard within an organization. The section began by assessing the key factors associated with each of the three case study standards. These individual factors were categorised into two main secondary adoption factors, originally identified by Gallivan (2001), managerial intervention and facilitating conditions.

Figure 2. Revised adopter-centric adoption model

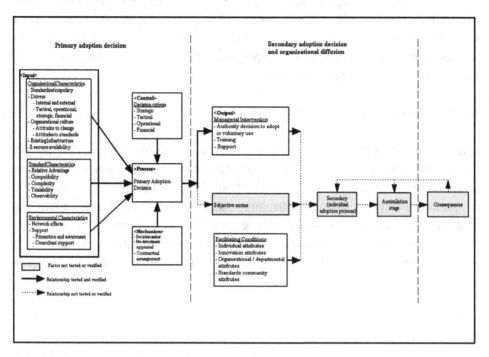

Further work can be done into the additional Gallivan (2001) factors that impact secondary adoption shown in Figure 2.

CONCLUSION

This chapter has shown the factors and barriers critical to the adoption of standards within the MoD. One of the standards chosen for investigation was a data-exchange standard to stay in keeping with the overall aim of the research. However, in order to limit bias, an additional focus was given to the adoption of the NCS and DEF STAN 00-60, a regional and a national defence standard, respectively. The original focus was to look at primary adoption; nonetheless some significant insights also emerged from looking at secondary adoption. The original model has been revised to include the details of the factors that emerged from the case studies and is shown in Figure 2.

What has emerged is that most of the findings have confirmed existing literature. Therefore, one of the main contributions of this work is that the issues surrounding standards adoption within an organization have been grounded in a different context, namely the UK MoD. Nonetheless, there have been some factors where

Table 4. Adopter-centric themes

Primary Adoption Themes
Theme 1: Due to the MoD's size and position in the defence supply chain, the use of standards is a vital for effective running of its business. Consequently, the MoD has developed policies on standardization that have a positive impact on the decision to adopt standards within the organization.
Theme 2: Having clear economic and operational drivers behind the use of the standard has a positive impact on the adoption decision process. This is particularly true where there are internal and external drivers behind the adoption of the standard.
Theme 3: The adoption decision was negatively impacted by a resistance to change demonstrated by key decision makers. The main causes of resistance were traditional ways of working, switching costs and loss of power and control.
Theme 4: Some decision makers have negative attitudes and perceptions towards standards in general and ISO standards in particular and this has a negative impact on the adoption decision process.
Theme 5: Some stakeholders have investments in technology and software that would be lost with the introduction of the standard, resulting in additional switching costs. This had a negative impact on the adoption decision process.
Theme 6: Restructuring initiatives and frequent redistribution of employees within the MoD results in a lack of continuity of financial and human resources, which has a negative impact on the adoption decision process.
Theme 7: Champions and change agents are vital in keeping the adoption decision process moving forward and have a positive impact on the final decision.
Theme 8: Characteristics relating to the complexity, relative advantage and compatibility of the standard have a positive impact on the adoption decision process.
Theme 9: Current adoption and use of the standard within the US defence community has a positive impact on the adoption decision within the UK.
Theme 10: The use of pilots and demonstration for promotion and awareness of the standard has a positive impact on the adoption decision process.
Theme 11: The involvement of consultants, who provide expert advice and services, has a positive impact on the adoption decision process.
Theme 12: Determining the business case for the project was a difficult exercise and will initially have a negative impact on the adoption decision process.
Theme 13: Having a contractual arrangement that captures the benefits of the adoption of the standard and offers a reward to all relevant stakeholders has a very positive impact on the adoption decision.

new insights have been given. For example, in terms of user attitudes towards standardization, the findings provide an opportunity to verify if the attitudes are valid in a wider population. In summary, the main novel contributions of this section of the research are:

- Grounding of the issues surrounding primary standards adoption in a new context, the UK MoD. This is important to the MoD, because the recently published Defence Industrial Initiative states that, *"To remain at the leading edge of military capability will, therefore, increasingly require effective exploitation of commercially-driven ICT... This requires the use of novel approaches, for example: activity at the Government level to make the market attractive; commitment to COTS [Commercial off-the-shelf], common standards and open architectures wherever possible."* (UK MoD, 2005b).

Table 5. Adopter-centric themes

Secondary Adoption Themes
Theme 14: The term 'preferred choice' leaves room for piecemeal secondary adoption, which has a negative impact on the effective secondary adoption of standards.
Theme 15: Attitudes of an individual in relation to change and towards the standards and the willingness of an individual to use the system have an impact on the effectiveness of secondary adoption.
Theme 16: The complexity and compatibility of a standard has an impact on the effective secondary adoption of the standard.
Theme 17: Ensuring that an organization's standards licence is made available to all stakeholders involved in the implementation of a standard, makes secondary adoption more effective.
Theme 18: When departments in an organization did not perceive the implementation of a standard as a means of offering them direct benefits, there was a reluctance to adopt the standard.
Theme 19: The communication between the standards community and implementers is vital to ensure successful implementation of a standard in order to facilitate secondary adoption.

- Grounding of some of the issues surrounding secondary standards adoption within an organization in a new context, the UK MoD. Not all secondary adoption issues have been covered due to limited time and resource and the original scope being limited to primary adoption. Nonetheless, the importance of the standards community during secondary adoption emerged; there are clear opportunities for further research.
- Development of a standards adoption model that considers both primary and secondary adoption factors.
- The development of a list of themes that can be used by managers and practitioners as a frame of reference to support the data-exchange standards adoption and diffusion process within the MoD. These themes are summarised in Table 4 and Table 5.

These contributions attest to the importance and necessity of this research to the standards development community, the MoD and the standard adoption research community. The next chapter chronicles the development of the innovation and adopter centric 'Adoption Checklists'. The checklists are based on the finalised innovation-centric and adopter-centric models developed in Chapter Five and Six respectively.

REFERENCES

Al-Gahtani, S., & King, M. (1999). Attitudes, Satisfaction and Usage: Factors Contributing to Each in the Acceptance of Information Technology. *Behaviour & Information Technology, 18*(4), 277–297. doi:10.1080/014492999119020

Askoxford.Com. (2005). *Compact Oxford English Dictionary*. Retrieved December 6, 2005, from Http://Www.Askoxford.Com/?View=Uk

Attewell, P. (1992). Technology Diffusion and Organizational Learning: The Case of Business Computing. *Organization Science, 3*(1), 1–19. doi:10.1287/orsc.3.1.1

Blakeley, J., Fishman, D., Lomet, D., & Stonebraker, M. (1994). The Impact of Database Research on Industrial Products. *SIGMOD Record, 23*(3), 35–40. doi:10.1145/187436.187455

Chen, M. (2003). Factors Affecting the Adoption and Diffusion of XML and Web Services Standards for E-Business Systems. *International Journal of Human-Computer Studies, 58*(3), 259–279. doi:10.1016/S1071-5819(02)00140-4

Coombs, C., Doherty, N., & Loan-Clarke, J. (2001). The Importance of User Ownership and Positive User Attitudes in the Successful Adoption of Community Information Systems. *Journal of End User Computing, 13*(4), 5.

Davis, F. (1993). User Acceptance Of Information Technology: System Characteristics, User Perceptions And Behavioral Impacts. *International Journal of Man-Machine Studies, 38*(3), 475–487. doi:10.1006/imms.1993.1022

Dedrick, J., & West, J. (2003). Why Firms Adopt Open Source Platforms: A Grounded theory of Innovation and Standards Adoption. In J. King, & K. Lyytinen (Ed.)*: Proceedings of MISQ Special Issue Workshop on Standard Making: A Critical Frontier for Information Systems* (pp. 236-257). Seattle: MISQ Quaterly.

Dobson, B. (2005). Greater Efficiency, Reduced Cost. *Defence Management Journal, 28*, 25–26.

Dreverman, M. (2005). *Adoption of Product Model Data Standards In the Process Industry.* Eindhoven, The Netherlands: Eindhoven University of Technology.

Egyedi, T., & Dahanayake, A. (2003). Difficulties Implementing Standards. In T. Egyedi, K. Jakobs, & K. Krechmer (Ed.), *Proceedings From the 3rd Conference On Standardization and Innovation In Information Technology* (pp. 75-84). Delft, The Netherlands: Tud-Tbm.

Eisenhardt, K. (1989a). Building Theories from Case Study Research. *Academy of Management Review, 14*(4), 532–550. doi:10.2307/258557

Eisenhardt, K. (1989b). Making Fast Strategic Decisions In High-Velocity Environments. *Academy of Management Journal, 32*(3), 543–576. doi:10.2307/256434

Fichman, R. (1992). Information Technology Diffusion: A Review of Empirical Research. In J. Degross, J. Becker, & J. Elam (Ed.), *Proceedings of the Thirteenth International Conference on Information Systems* (pp. 195-206). London: University of Minnesota.

Gallivan, M. (2001). Organizational Adoption and Assimilation of Complex Technological Innovations: Development and Application of A New Framework. *Sigmis Database, 32*(3), 51–85. doi:10.1145/506724.506729

Gladwin, C. (1989). *Ethnographic Decision Tree Modeling (Qualitative Research Methods Series)* (Vol. 19). Newbury Park, CA: Sage Publications.

Group, L. S. C. (2002). *RAMP White Paper - Driving Down the Cost of Spares Provisioning Issue 2.* Bath, UK: Warship Support Agency.

Hovav, A., Patnayakuni, R., & Schuff, D. (2004). A Model of Internet Standards Adoption: the Case of Ipv6. *Information Systems Journal, 14*(3), 265–294. doi:10.1111/j.1365-2575.2004.00170.x

Irani, Z., Grieve, R., & Race, P. (1999). A Case Study Approach to Carrying Out Information Systems Research: A Critique. *International Journal of Computer Applications in Technology, 12*(2), 190–198. doi:10.1504/IJCAT.1999.000203

Irani, Z., Sharif, A., Love, P., & Kahraman, C. (2002). Applying Concepts of Fuzzy Cognitive Mapping to Model: The IT/IS Investment Evaluation Process. *International Journal of Production Economics, 75*(1-2), 199–211. doi:10.1016/S0925-5273(01)00192-X

Kahl, S. (2004). *A Proposal for an Econometric Analysis of Switching Costs in the Software Industry.* MIT Opencourseware: Sloan School of Management, 15.575 Research Seminar in IT and Organizations: Economic Perspectives. Sloan School of Management.

Kotter, J., Collins, J., Pascale, R., Duck, J., Porras, J., & Athos, A. (1998). *Harvard Business Review on Change.* Boston: Harvard Business School Publishing.

Krechmer, K. (1998). The Principles of Open Standards. *Standards Engineering, 50*(6), 1–6.

Mathieson, K., & Ryan, T. (1997). *Users' Evaluations of Packages: Demonstrations Versus Hands-On Use.* Retrieved March 25, 2005, from Electronic Journal of Information Systems Evaluation Web site: http://www.ejise.com/volume-1/volume-issue1/issue1-art2.htm

Meister, D. 2. (2004). *STEP Through 20 Years: Lessons and Theoretical Implications - Working Paper Edn.* Faculty of Information Systems, Richard Ivey School of Business. London, Canada: University of Western Ontario.

Miles, M., & Huberman, A. (1994). *Qualitative Data Analysis.* Newbury Park, CA: Sage Publications.

Mustonen-Ollila, E., & Lyytinen, K. (2003). Why Organizations Adopt Information System Process Innovations: A Longitudinal Study Using Diffusion of Innovation Theory. *Information Systems Journal, 13*(3), 275–297. doi:10.1046/j.1365-2575.2003.00141.x

Nilakanta, S., & Scamell, R. (1990). The Effect of Information Sources and Communication Channels on the Diffusion of Innovation in a Data Base Development Environment. *Management Science, 36*(1), 24–40. doi:10.1287/mnsc.36.1.24

Oksala, S., Rutkowski, A., & Spring, M., & O'donnell, J. (1996). The Structure of IT Standardization. *StandardView, 4*(1), 9–22. doi:10.1145/230871.230873

Pare, G. (2002). Enhancing the Rigor ofQualitative Research: Application of a Case Methodology to Build Theories of IT Implementation. *Qualitative Report, 7*(4).

Parker, M., & Benson, R. (1989). Enterprise Wide Information Economics: Latest Concepts. *Journal of Information Systems Management, 6*(4), 7–13. doi:10.1080/07399018908960166

Prescott, M., & Conger, S. (1995). Information Technology Innovations: A Classification By It Locus of Impact and Research Approach. *ACM SIGMIS Database, 26*(2-3), 20–41. doi:10.1145/217278.217284

Rogers, E. (2003). *Diffusion of Innovations.* New York: Simon & Schuster International.

SC4Online. (2009). *STEP Overview.* Retrieved January 18, 2009, from ISO TC184-SC4.org: http://www.tc184-sc4.org/sc4_open/sc4%20legacy%20products%20(2001-08)/step_(10303)/

Small, M., & Chen, I. (•••). (1995/7). Investment Justification of Advanced Manufacturing Technology: An Empirical Analysis. *Journal of Engineering and Technology Management, 12*(1-2), 27–55. doi:10.1016/0923-4748(95)00003-5

Stirling, A. (2001). Standardization: A Vital Enabler for Acquisition Excellence. *Standards in Defence News* (180), 4-7.

Swann, G. (2000). *The Economics of Standardization*. Retrieved January 21, 2004, from Report for Department of Trade and Industry, Standards and Technical Regulations Directorate: http://www.dti.gov.uk/strd/fundingo.htm#swannrep

Themistocleous, M. (2002). *Enterprise Application Integration*. Brunel, UK: Brunel University.

UK MoD. (2002a). *General MoD Article*. Retrieved June 25, 2005, from UK Defence Standardization website http://www.dstan.mod.uk/mod%20stan%202002.pdf

UK MoD. (2002b). *General MoD Article*. Retrieved June 25, 2005, from UK Defence Standardization website http://www.dstan.mod.uk/mod%20stan%202002.pdf

UK MoD. (2005a). *Def Stan 00-60*. Retrieved June 24, 2005, from Acquisition Management System Web site: http://www.ams.mod.uk/ams/content/docs/ils/ils_web/dstan.htm

UK MoD. (2005b). *Defence Industrial Strategy*. Defence White Paper. Cm 6697. London: The Stationery office.

UK MoD. (2005c). *Recent Trends In Service and Civilian Personnel Numbers, At 1 April Each Year*. Retrieved November 11, 2005, from Defence Analytical Services and Advice Web site: http://www.dasa.mod.uk/natstats/ukds/2005/c2/table21.html

UK MoD. (2006a). *Defence for Researchers - Information for Conducting Research Into the MoD*. Retrieved November 17, 2006, from UK MoD Web site: http://www.mod.uk/defenceinternet/defencefor/researchers/

UK MoD AMS. (2003). *AMS Additional Information - Addressing Standardization*. Retrieved July 18, 2005, from Acquisition Management System Web site: http://www.ams.mod.uk/ams/content/docs/addrstan.doc

UK MoD CDMA. (2004). *Ministry of Defence Policy On the Use of XML*. Retrieved June 4, 2005, from Central Data Management Authority Web site: http://www.cdma.mod.uk/suppinfo/xmlpolicy-v1_0.doc

UK MoD SSE. (2005a). *Support Solutions Envelope - Engineering & Asset Management*. Retrieved March 16, 2005, from Acquisition Management System Web site http://www.ams.mod.uk/ams/content/docs/sse/v3_3_archive/eam.htm

UK MoD SSE. (2005b). *Support Solutions Envelope – Data Standards*. Retrieved March 11, 2005, from Acquisition Management System Web site: http://www.ams.mod.uk/ams/content/docs/sse/v3_3_archive/ikm%20&%20c4i/gp_3_ed1.htm

UK NCB. (2002). Retrieved November 4, 2002, from The United Kingdom National Codification Bureau Website: http://www.ncb.mod.uk/index.html

Venkatesh, V., Morris, M., Davis, G., & Davis, F. (2003). User Acceptance of Information Technology: Toward A Unified View. *MIS Quarterly, 27*(3), 425–478.

Von Weizsacker, C. (1984). The Costs of Substitution. *Econometrica, 52*(5), 1085–1116. doi:10.2307/1910989

Warner, A. (2003). Block Alliances In formal Standard Setting Environments. *International Journal of IT Standards and Standardization Research, 1*(1), 1–18.

Weitzel, T. (2003). A Network ROI. In J. King, & K. Lyytinen (Ed.), *Proceedings of MISQ Special Issue Workshop on Standard Making: A Critical Frontier for Information Systems* (pp. 62-79). Seattle: MIS Quaterly.

West, J. (1999). Organizational Decisions for I.T. Standards Adoption: Antecedents and Consequences. *Proceedings of the 1st IEEE Conference on Standardisation and Innovation in Information Technology* (pp. 13-18). Washington, DC: IEEE.

Weston, L., & Whiddett, R. (1999). Factors Affecting the Adoption of IS Standards. In B. Hope, & P. Yoong (Ed.), *Australasian Conference on Information Systems* (pp. 1158-1169). Wellington, New Zealand: Victoria University of Wellington.

Yin, R. (1994). *Case Study Research: Design and Methods.* Newbury Park, CA: Sage Publications.

Zmud, R. (1983). The Effectiveness of External Information Channels In Facilitating Innovation Within Software Development Groups. *MIS Quarterly, 7*(2), 43–58. doi:10.2307/248912

Section 3
Adoption and Diffusion Checklists

In this section the revised innovation-centric and adopter-centric models developed in Section 2 are used to create adoption checklists. These checklists are then used to assess both the innovation-centric and adopter-centric adoptability of a specific data-exchange standard known as Product Life Cycle Support (PLCS). All case study information presented in this section is based on data collected and analysed between October 2002 and July 2006.

Chapter 7

Emergent Innovation–Centric and Adopter–Centric Checklists

INTRODUCTION

Data-exchange standards adoption research is important to both the SC4 community and the IT standards research community. Chapter Five and Six presented case studies of four standards to assess the factors and barriers critical to the adoption of standards. Two models were developed and these models sought to shed light on the relationships between factors and barriers critical to the adoption of data-exchange standards. However, as part of this research it was deemed important to develop two novel standards 'Adoption Checklists' from both an innovation- and adopter-centric point of view. The purpose of these checklists is to act as a frame of reference to support the decision-making process in the development and adoption of new and emerging data-exchange standards. The checklists are a series of ques-

DOI: 10.4018/978-1-60566-832-1.ch007

Figure 1. High level view of innovation-centric factors

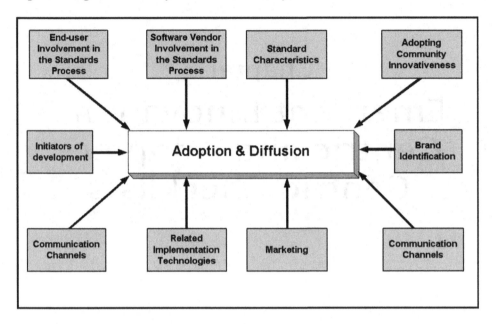

tions that can be used to assess the adoptability of a data-exchange standard. The checklists have been developed so that positive answers to the series of questions indicate that a standard is more likely to be adopted. In addition, these checklists act as a foundation for the action research into the adoption of PLCS, which is detailed in Chapters Eight and Nine. This chapter begins by chronicling the development of the innovation-centric 'Adoption Checklist'. Following on from that is the development of the adopter-centric 'Adoption Checklist.' The final section summaries and concludes this chapter.

INNOVATION-CENTRIC 'ADOPTION CHECKLIST'

In the innovation-centric approach, the unit of analysis was the data-exchange standard. Figure 1 is a top-level diagram of the main factors that directly impact the adoption of the two data-exchange standards studied in Chapter Five.

Figure 6 in Chapter 5 outlined four main categories that contain the factors that impact the adoption and diffusion of data-exchange standards. These four categories are: Conception, Standards Process, Standard Specifications, and Adoption conduciveness. The eleven factors displayed in Figure 1 fall into these four categories as follows:

- **Conception:** Initiators of development.
- **Standards process:** End-user involvement and software vendor involvement.
- **Standards specifications:** Standards DOI characteristics, completeness of the entire standard, brand identification and IPR.
- **Adoption conduciveness:** Adopting community innovativeness, communication channels, marketing, and related implementation technologies.

The categories represent the sections that will be used to develop the questions that will be part of the innovation-centric 'Adoption Checklist'. Apart from the conception category, the questions in the checklist are based only on the factors that directly impact the adoption of a standard, shown in Figure 1.

Conception

The three factors under the conception category are drivers behind development, initiators of development and the conceptual idea and scope of the standard. The drivers behind the development of a standard did not directly impact the adoption of the standard, but as was pointed out in Chapter Five, these drivers are the trigger behind the standardization process and what emerged is that it is important that there are economic drivers behind the development of a standard. Therefore, the first question is:

1.   Are there economic drivers behind the development of the standard?

The initiator of development of a standard directly impacted the adoption of a standard on two levels. Firstly, the likelihood of adoption is greatly increased in end-users and software vendors are involved in the initiation of the standard. The results in Chapter Five also indicate that the initiators of the development of a standard can have an indirect impact on the adoption of a standard, when the head of a supply chain initiates development of a standard. This is due to the fact that end-users further down the supply chain and software vendors make an effort to join the standards development process in order to keep in step with the activities of these large organizations at the head of the supply chain. Therefore the next three questions are:

2.   Were end-users among the initiators of the development of the standard?
3.   Were software vendors among the initiators of the development of the standard?

4.   Were any organizations at the head of a supply chain among the initiators of the standard?

The final factor under the conception category looked at the impact the conceptual idea and scope of a standard has on the adoption of a standard. What emerged was that although this factor does not directly impact adoption, standards that cover a wide domain area tend to be more complex. This complexity has a negative impact on the adoption of a standard. Therefore the final question in the 'conception' category is:

5.   Is the scope of the standard targeted at one industry sector?

Standards Process

The first factor that directly impacts the adoption of a standard in the standards process category is end-user involvement in the development process. The innovation-centric model indicated that having end-users involved in the development process meant the end-users believed they were getting a standard that met their requirements, which had a direct positive impact on the end-users subsequently adopting the standard. The resulting question is therefore:

6.   Were end-users involved in the development of the standard?

The second factor relating to the standards process was software vendor involvement in the development process. Software vendors were described as critical for adoption to take place because of the contributions they make during the development stages, and in the development of tools that end-users can use. The resulting questions are therefore:

7.   Were software vendors involved in the development of the standard?
8.   Have software applications, which are based on the standard and support end-user business processes, been developed?

From the finalised model presented in Figure 6 of Chapter 5 the two main factors that impacted end-user and software vendor involvement in the development process were the initiators of development and the development timescales. Questions relating to initiators of development are covered in later sections. Therefore the final question in the standards process category looks at the indirect impact of development timescales on the adoption of a standard:

Table 1. Factors that impacted the DOI theory characteristics

Characteristic	Influencing factors
Complexity	Conceptual idea and scope, balance and diversity of development team
Relative advantage	Development timescale
Compatibility	Revisions
Trialability	Pilots, demonstrations, workshops
Observability	Verified benefits

9. Was the standard developed in the originally projected timescales? If not, how long was the overrun?

Standard Specifications

The first set of factors that relates to standard specifications is Rogers' (2003) DOI theory characteristics. Table 1 below presents the five characteristics and the main factors that impact these characteristics.

Taking these influencing factors in consideration, the resulting six questions are:

10. Was there a balance between academic- and business-orientated individuals in the development team? If not, is the business side sufficiently represented?
11. Is there a positive perception relating to whether the standard is complex or not?
12. Is the standard unique in the capability it offers?
13. Are the current editions of the published standard compatible with previous editions?
14. Have there been any pilots, demonstrations or workshops during the development of the standard?
15. Have the benefits of the standard been verified in a cost-benefit analysis, Return on Investment analysis or success stories? If so, are they publicly available?

The final three factors surrounding the standard specifications category that directly impact the adoption of a standard are completeness of the entire standard, brand identification and IPR. These factors are not directly influenced by any other factors. Nonetheless, they are the basis of the following four questions:

16. Have all remaining parts of the standard that directly impact the implementation of the standard been finalised or developed? If not, what remains to be specified?
17. Was the standard developed by a recognised traditional standards development organization? If so, please specify.
18. Was the standard developed by a consortium? If so, please specify.
19. Are all parts of the standard available in the public domain?

Adoption Conduciveness

Adoption conduciveness covers a number of different factors. The first factor is the innovativeness of the adopting community. The results from the two case studies showed that this factor is generally impacted by the size, type and culture of an organization. An objective measurement of the culture factor is difficult to assess from an innovation-centric perspective, and is best assessed when analyzing a specific organization. Therefore, culture factor is addressed in the adopter-centric checklist. Nonetheless, the size and type factors are relevant to this section, and are expressed in the following three questions:

20. Are large multinational organizations part of the targeted adopting community?
21. Are SMEs (organizations between 50 to 250 employees) part of the targeted adopting community?
22. Are organizations from within any of the following industries part of the targeted adopting community: defence, oil and gas, energy, automotive?

The next relevant factor concerns communication channels, which were described as important and key to adoption. A communication channel is defined as a means by which a message gets from one individual to another (Rogers 2003). In the case of standards development, the stakeholders include end-users, developers, software vendors and implementers. So this factor assessed whether there are communication channels between the various stakeholder groups. Closely related to the communication channels is another factor, marketing. This factor looks at how the standard is marketed and promoted amongst the different stakeholder groups. Based on these two factors, three further questions emerged:

23. Does the standard have an implementer's forum that allows implementers to discuss their challenges and successes?
24. Is there a marketing strategy for the standard? If so, who manages it?

Table 2. Innovation-centric 'Adoption Checklist' – Conception and Standards Process

Questions	Y/N
Conception	
1	Are there economic drivers behind the development of the standard?	
2	Were end-users among the initiators of the development of the standard?	
3	Were software vendors among the initiators of the development of the standard?	
4	Were any heads of an industry supply chain among the initiators of the standard?	
5	Is the scope of the standard targeted at one industry sector?	
Standards Process	
6	Were end-users involved in the development of the standard?	
7	Were software vendors involved in the development of the standard?	
8	Have software applications, which are based on the standard and support end-user business processes, been developed?	
9	Was the standard developed in the originally projected timescales? If not, how long was the overrun? ……	

25. Does the standard have a website or other form of central outlet that enables potential adopters (end-users) or software vendors to find information about the standard and current developments?

The final main factor in adoption conduciveness is the related implementation technologies, which the interviewees in the original case study described as very important. Their main argument was that a key issue surrounding the adoption of these standards is their link to mainstream technologies. Therefore a final question is:

26. Is the standard implemented using current mainstream technologies, such as XML, UML, or OWL?

Finalised Innovation-Centric 'Adoption Checklist'

The questions developed around the main factors were collected and tabled using the four categories identified in the innovation-centric model. The finalised checklist is presented in Tables 2, 3 and 4. The table indicates the questions in relation to the four main categories identified in the model. The number of positive answers determines the adoptability of a standard. The more 'Yes' responses the greater the likelihood of adoption.

Table 3. Innovation-centric 'Adoption Checklist' – Standard Specifications

Questions		Y/N
Standard Specifications		
10	Was there a balance between academic- and business-orientated individuals in the development team? If not, is the business side sufficiently represented? Y/N	
11	Is there a perception that the standard is not complex?	
12	Is the standard unique in the capability it offers?	
13	Are the current editions of the published standard compatible with previous editions?	
14	Have there been any pilots, demonstrations or workshops during the development of the standard?	
15	Have the benefits of the standard been verified in a cost-benefit analysis, return-on-investment analysis or success stories? If so, are they publicly available? Y/N	
16	Have all remaining parts of the standard that directly impact the implementation of the standard been finalised or developed? If not, what remains to be finalised?	
17	Was the standard developed by a recognised traditional standards development organization? If so, please specify.	
18	Was the standard developed by a consortium? If so, please specify.	
19	Are all parts of the standard available in the public domain?	

In the tables, the darkened table cells indicate questions that linked to key factors that impact the adoption of data-exchange standards. The determination of these key factors was based on the responses of the initial interviewees with regards to what they believed were the very important factors that impact the adoption of a

Table 4. Innovation-centric 'Adoption Checklist' – Adoption Conduciveness

Questions		Y/N
Adoption Conduciveness		
20	Are large multinational organizations part of the targeted adopting community?	
21	Are SMEs (organizations between 50 to 250 employees) part of the targeted adopting community?	
22	Are organizations from within any of the following industries part of the targeted adopting community: defence, oil and gas, energy, automotive?	
23	Does the standard have an implementer's forum that allows implementers to discuss their challenges and successes?	
24	Is there a marketing strategy for the standard? If so, who manages it?	
25	Does the standard have a website or other form of central outlet that enables potential adopters (end-users) or software vendors to find information about the standard and current developments?	
26	Is the standard implemented using current mainstream technologies, such as XML, UML, or OWL?	

Table 5. Key adopter-centric factors

Adoption stage	Key factors
Primary adoption	Organizational characteristics, standard characteristics, environmental characteristics, decision criteria and decision mechanisms
Secondary adoption	Managerial intervention, facilitating conditions

data-exchange standard. A 'No' response in any of the darkened table cells means that adoption is still likely, but there will be significant challenges that need to be addressed for successful adoption of a standard to take place. A 'No' in any of the non-darkened table cells indicates that adoption is likely with some points of concern.

This innovation-centric 'Adoption Checklist' is a tool that can be used by standards developers to assess the adoptability of new and emerging standards or data-exchange standards currently in use, and steps can be taken to facilitate adoptability where concerns may be raised. End-user organizations can also use these checklists to assess whether or not to invest time and effort into adopting a new or emerging standard. Likewise, software vendors can also use the checklist to assess whether or not to invest time and effort to develop tools for new or emerging standards.

ADOPTER-CENTRIC 'ADOPTION CHECKLIST'

The development of the adopter-centric 'Adoption Checklist' follows a similar approach to the innovation-centric checklist. The checklist is based around the adopter-centric model developed in Chapter Six, which established the factors and barriers critical to the adoption and diffusion of standards within the UK MoD. The key factors were broken down into primary and secondary adoption issues. The "Adoption Checklist" has been developed as a tool to support decision makers involved in the adoption and diffusion of data-exchange standards within the UK MoD, or similar organizations.

The main factors for both the primary and secondary adoption are summarised in Table 5. The section starts by developing questions around the primary adoption factors. Following on from that, the key questions that emerged within secondary adoption are presented.

Primary Adoption Questions

This section looks at the development of questions from the primary adoption perspective and breaks the section down into the four main categories:

Organizational Characteristics

The first factor in primary adoption is 'organizational characteristics', and this covers issues concerning organizations' policies towards standards, the drivers behind standards, organization culture and resource availability. Based on the themes surrounding these issues, the main questions that emerge include:

1. Does the organization have a policy that relates to the standard?
2. Is there a need for the standard within the organization?
3. Are there any external pressures to use the standard?
4. Was the organization involved in the development of the standard?
5. Is the organization currently free from any re-organization or restructuring initiative?
6. Does the organization adapt well to change?
7. Is the use of standards prevalent within the organization?
8. Is there a key strategic champion for the use of the standard within the organization?

Standards Characteristics

The three main standard characteristic issues that emerged within this factor were the five DOI characteristics described by Rogers (2003), namely: complexity, compatibility, relative advantage, trialability and observability. Based on these characteristics the main questions are:

9. Is there a perception that the standard is not complex?
10. Is the standard compatible with existing infrastructure and technologies used in the organization?
11. Is the standard unique in the capability it offers the organization?
12. Have any pilots and demonstrations been carried out to show the use of the standard? If so, have they been of benefit?
13. Have the benefits of the standard been verified internally within the organization?
14. Have the benefits of the standard been verified externally by any other user of the standard? If so, have they been made available?

Environmental Characteristics

This factor relates to the wider stakeholder community and users of the standards and looks at issues concerning network effects and support. Therefore, the main questions are:

15. Is the standard being used in any other organization?
16. Are there tools available to implement the standard?
17. Are there consultants available to support adoption and implementation of the standard?
18. Does the standard have a website or other form of central outlet that enables potential adopters to find information about the standard and current developments?

Decision Criteria and Mechanisms

The key issues linked to these factors, which emerged amongst the themes of Chapter Six, were in relation to the pre-investment appraisal techniques and the influence of the key decision makers. So the final questions in relation to primary adoption are:

19. Is there a compelling business case for the adoption of the standard that allows all stakeholders to identify the benefits?
20. Have key decision makers bought into the idea of using the standard?

Secondary Adoption Questions

Secondary adoption was not the original focus of this research but some key issues emerged within the research, which would be likely to affect secondary adoption. These were managerial intervention and facilitating conditions such as individual attributes, innovation attributes, departmental attributes and standard community attributes. These main factors resulted in the following questions:

1. Is there a policy relating to the standard that impacts the adoption of the standard within the department? If so, is there a choice of whether to use the standard?
2. Is funding being made available to facilitate adoption of the standard throughout the organization?
3. Is training being made available to facilitate adoption of the standard throughout the organization?
4. Is there a team of people devoted to promoting the standard throughout the organization?
5. Have any pilots and demonetisation been carried out to show the use of the standard? If so, have they been of benefit?

Table 6. Adopter-centric 'Primary Adoption Checklist'

Primary adoption questions	Y/N
Organizational characteristics	
1 Does the organization have a policy that relates to the standard?	
2 Is there a need for the standard within the organization?	
3 Are there any external pressures to use the standard?	
3 Was the organization involved in the development of the standard?	
5 Is the organization currently free from any re-organization or restructuring initiative?	
6 Does the organization adapt well to change?	
7 Is the use of standards prevalent within the organization?	
8 Is there a key strategic champion for the use of the standard within the organization?	

6. Does the implementation of the standard offer direct benefit to the department?

7. Is the standard compatible with existing infrastructure and technology within the department?

8. Does the department have any external business partners? If so, are these business partners positive towards the use of the standard?

9. Does the organization or department have a standards licence, which will allow implementers to access the standard?

10. Does the department adapt well to change?

11. Is the use of the standard compatible with individual end-users current ways of working?

12. Does the end-user understand the benefits of the standard?

13. Is there a positive perception in relation to whether the standard is complex or not?

14. Have all remaining parts of the standard that directly impact the implementation of the standard been finalised or developed? If not, what remains to be finalised?

15. Do implementers of the standard have a forum to discuss their challenges and successes with other implementers?

These questions attempt to tackle some of the secondary adoption issues that have emerged.

Table 7. Adopter-centric 'Primary Adoption Checklist'

Primary adoption questions	Y/N
Standard characteristics	
9 Is there a perception that the standard is not complex?	
10 *Is the standard compatible with existing infrastructure and technologies used in the organization?*	
11 Is the standard unique in the capability it offers the organization?	
12 Have any pilots and demonstrations been carried out to show the use of the standard? If so, have they been of benefit? Y / N	
13 Have the benefits of the standard been verified internally within the organization?	
14 Have the benefits of the standard been verified externally by any other user of the standard? If so, have they been made available? Y / N	
Environmental characteristics and decision mechanism	
15 Is the standard being used in any other organization?	
16 Are there tools available to implement the standard?	
17 Are there consultants available to support adoption and implementation of the standard?	
18 Does the standard have a website or other form of central outlet that enables potential adopters to find information about the standard and current developments?	
19 Is there a compelling business case for the adoption of the standard that allows all stakeholders to identify the benefits?	
20 Have key decision makers 'bought into' the idea of using the standard?	

Finalised Adopter-Centric 'Adoption Checklists'

The questions developed around the main factors were collected and tabled using the main categories identified in the original model. The finalised checklists are presented in Tables 6 and 7, 8 and 9.

The tables give a complete picture for the adoption from a primary and secondary perspective and can be used together. Like the innovation-centric checklist, the greater the number of 'Yes' responses the greater the likelihood of adoption. However, unlike the innovation-centric checklist there is no indication of the main factors because interviewees were not asked to rate the main factors. Therefore each section has to be analyzed separately to establish the adoptability of a data-exchange standard.

This adopter-centric 'Adoption Checklist' is a tool that can be used by end-user organizations in two ways. Firstly, using the primary adoption checklist as a frame of reference, an organization can answer the following questions:

Table 8. Adopter-centric 'Secondary Adoption Checklist'

Secondary Adoption		Y/N
Managerial Intervention		
1	Is there a policy relating to the standard that impacts the adoption of the standard within the department? If so, is there a choice of whether to use the standard?	
2	Is funding being made available to facilitate adoption of the standard throughout the organization?	
3	Is training being made available to facilitate adoption of the standard throughout the organization?	
4	Is there a team of people devoted to promoting the standard throughout the organization?	
5	Have any pilots and demonetisation been carried out to show the use of the standard? If so, have they been of benefit?	
Department attributes		
6	Does the implementation of the standard offer direct benefit to the department?	
7	Is the standard compatible with existing infrastructure and technology within the department?	
8	Does the department have any external business partners? If so, are these business partners positive towards the use of the standard?	
9	Does the organization or department have a standards licence, which will allow implementers to access the standard?	
10	Does the department adapt well to change?	

Table 9. Adopter-centric 'Secondary Adoption Checklist'

Secondary Adoption		Y/N
Individual attributes		
11	Is the use of the standard compatible with individual end-users current ways of working?	
12	Does the end-user understand the benefits of the standard?	·
Standard attributes		
13	Is there a positive perception in relation to whether the standard is complex or not?	
14	Have all remaining parts of the standard that directly impact the implementation of the standard been finalised or developed? If not, what remains to be finalised?	
Standards community attributes		
15	Do implementers of the standard have a forum to discuss their challenges and successes with other implementers?	

- Is this the best standard to use to meet our business requirements?
- Do we have the resources to adopt the standard?
- Is this the best time to adopt the standard?

Secondly, using the secondary adoption checklist, an organization can assess what steps can be taken to takes steps to facilitate successful of the standard throughout the organization.

CONCLUSION

This brief chapter has focused on the development of two 'Adoption Checklists' based on the models developed in Chapters Five and Six. The purpose of these checklists is to act as a frame of reference to support the decision-making process in the development and adoption of data-exchange standards. Their applicability has not been tested, so the aim of the following chapters is to apply the checklists to the adoption of PLCS from both an innovation-centric and adopter-centric vantage point. It is hoped that by doing this the adoptability of PLCS can be determined and the checklists can be evaluated to investigate if there are any emergent adoption factors within the PLCS community that have not been identified in the original case studies.

REFERENCES

Rogers, E. (2003). *Diffusion of Innovations.* New York: Simon & Schuster International.

Chapter 8

Innovation–Centric Checklist Application:
Product Life Cycle Support Adoption and Diffusion

INTRODUCTION

PLCS (Product Life Cycle Support) was one of the motivations behind this research and triggered the research question into the factors and barriers critical to the adoption of data-exchange standards. A review of the literature showed that there was a gap within the SC4 community with regards to the factors critical to the adoption of the standards and there was a need for more empirical studies in IT standards adoption research. In light of this, a novel combined innovation- and adopter-centric approach was taken to establish the factors and barriers critical to the adoption of data-exchange standards. A retrospective case study of two SC4 standards was carried out to test and verify the factors identified in the original model, developed in Chapter Three. The finalised model, shown in Figure 6 of Chapter 5, identified the

DOI: 10.4018/978-1-60566-832-1.ch008

key factors and showed the interrelationships amongst the key factors. Therefore the aim of this chapter is twofold:

- To verify and test the factors identified in the innovation-centric model and note any emergent factors or issues based on the current factors surrounding the adoption of PLCS.
- To predict the adoptability of PLCS in light of the issues and factors that emerged using the 'Adoption Checklist'.

By carrying out this analysis, steps can be identified that will help to facilitate the adoption of PLCS. On a more general level, this chapter will predominately demonstrate the applicability of the 'Adoption Checklist' as a tool for stakeholders and decision makers involved in the adoption and diffusion of data-exchange standards such as PLCS.

PLCS Overview

Application protocols are the implementable data specifications of STEP. Therefore, 'STEP implementation' refers to the practical incorporation or implementation of an Application protocol within a company for the purpose of data exchange. Studies have been undertaken into the implementation of various other STEP Application protocols within industry (Pratt & Anderson, 2001; Peng & Trappey, 1998). However, this chapter is focused on the development, implementation and more importantly, adoption of Application protocol 239, known as the standard for Product Life Cycle Support (PLCS).

The purpose of the PLCS is to "establish structured data exchange and sharing capabilities for use by industry to support complex engineered assets throughout their total life cycle" (OASIS PLCS TC, 2005). PLCS was developed to meet the needs of governments, original product and/or equipment manufacturers, operators and third party service providers. Subsequently, the following industry groups can benefit from the adoption of PLCS (PLCS Inc., 2002):

- Transportation – commercial and military aircraft and associated aero engines
- Transportation – commercial and military truck fleets
- Transportation – commercial and military ships
- Transportation – locomotives and trackside equipment
- Heavy industrial machinery
- Power generation
- Oil and gas process plant.

Therefore, the common attributes of the products for which PLCS is most appropriate are:

- Complex high value products
- Many unique parts and product configurations
- Long service life
- Demanding in-service support requirements
- In-service support costs that encompass a significant portion of the total cost of ownership.

Further details with regards to the history, development and makeup of PLCS emerge in the remainder of the chapter.

Chapter Overview and Data Analysis Process

For this phase of the research, the research approach adopted is action research. Action research is often uniquely identified by its dual goal of both improving the organization participating in the research project, usually referred to as client organization, and at the same time generating knowledge (Kock *et al.*, 1997). The questions identified in the 'Adoption Checklist' were answered using data retrieved from using documentation, archival records, and interviews. The interviews were carried out with six PLCS stakeholders. One stakeholder was the chair of SC4 committee; two interviewees were STEP AP developers who were also consultants for a software company heavily involved in the STEP standard. The final three interviewees were members of the UK MoD product data standards team, who have been involved with the development of PLCS. In addition to these data retrieval methods, the author was actively involved in investigating methods to implement PLCS using XML within LSC Group. The results of these investigations were not only used to answer one of the key questions, but were also the foundation upon which a pilot implementation was based.

The chapter starts by answering questions from the checklist using the four main categories that impact the adoption of a standard from an innovation-centric viewpoint. For each category, details of the development and issues surrounding PLCS are provided. Following on from this is an analysis of the various XML implementation strategies for PLCS. The concluding section summarises the results from the checklist and offers some predictions relating to the adoption of PLCS and discussions on the way forward for PLCS.

Table 1. PLCS responses to 'Conception' questions

Conception		
1	Are there economic drivers behind the development of the standard?	Y
2	Were end-users among the initiators of the development of the standard?	Y
3	Were software vendors among the initiators of the development of the standard?	Y
4	Were any heads of an industry supply chain involved among the initiators of the standard?	Y
5	Is the scope of the standard targeted at one industry sector?	N

CONCEPTION

The conception category deals with three main issues, the drivers behind development, the initiators of the development and the conceptual idea and scope. The key questions and responses for this category are detailed in Table 1. The remainder of this section discusses the issues surrounding these findings.

Drivers and Initiators Behind Development

This looks at the drivers and initiators behind development of PLCS, and addresses questions one to four in Table 1. The main driver behind the development of PLCS was the need for a mechanism by which to ensure support information is aligned with the evolving product definitions over the entire life cycle of a product. There is a clear economic benefit in protecting the information surrounding complex assets. This information is of vital importance to a business or, as King (2002b) notes it is the 'strategic through life asset' of the enterprise. This is largely due to the importance of information as a tool to be able to undertake new tasks in the decision-making process.

The development of PLCS was initiated through a consortium known as PLCS Inc. in September 1999. PLCS Inc. was supported by both industry and national governments with the aim of accelerating development of new standards for product support information. The initiative brought together the Ministries of Defence of the United Kingdom, Finland, Sweden, and Norway, the United States Department of Defence and multinational manufacturers including Boeing, Lockheed Martin, BAE Systems, Rolls-Royce, and Saab Aerospace. A third group of companies involved in the PLCS initiative comprised of suppliers of engineering software applications, namely, LSC Group, PTC, Aerosystems International, and Pennant. PLCS Inc. was run as a not-for-profit vehicle, and was established to allow the partners to co-operate in the development and delivery of PLCS as an international standard (Sloss *et al.*, 2002). Therefore, as can be clearly seen, end-users and software vendors were involved in the initiation of the standard. In addition, the presence of the MoDs of various European countries and the DoD from the US, plus the large multinational original equipment manufactures, indicates that heads of supply chains were involved in the initiation of the standard. These results indicate positive adoptability of PLCS.

Conceptual Idea and Scope

This section addresses question five, which looks at the scope of a standard. The ultimate aim of PLCS is to service four key areas for owners of complex engineering assets. The areas include:

- Configuration Management (CM): Manage product and support information throughout the product life cycle.
- Support Engineering (SE): Develop the support solution and provide and sustain the support infrastructure.
- Resource Management (RM): Manage the supply chain, including the purchase, management, storage, moving, issue and disposal of physical resources.
- Maintenance and Feedback (M&F): Maintain, test, diagnose, calibrate, repair and modify the product. Record and feedback information relating to all these activities. (King, 2002a)

One interviewee described the scope as a *"very, very big scope"*. Like the two case study standards, the conceptual idea and scope of PLCS is wide, and not limited to a specific domain. Indeed, PLCS has a wider scope than the previous case studies because it covers a wide range of industries, unlike ISO 15926-2, which is focused on oil and gas industries.

The challenges of the wide conceptual idea and scope of PLCS is that, like other data-exchange standards, it results in a complex standard, and all interviewees agreed that the standard was complex. In addition, this wide scope means that PLCS has a large and generic information model that is larger in scope than most business processes require or most IT applications can manage (Eurostep, 2005). However, this problem is addressed by the development of DEXs (Data EXchange sets). Details of DEXs are discussed in section later sections. The results show that the large scope does pose some challenges for the adoptability of PLCS, but steps have been taken to mitigate some of the challenges.

Table 2. PLCS responses to 'Standards process' questions

	Standards Process	
6	Were end-users involved in the development of the standard?	Y
7	Were software vendors involved in the development of the standard?	Y
8	Have software applications, which are based on the standard and support end-user business processes, been developed?	Y
9	Was the standard developed in the projected timescales? **If not, how long was the overrun?**<u>3 years</u>	N

STANDARDS PROCESS

This section assesses the standards process factors that impact the adoption of PLCS. A summary of the key responses as they relate to the standards process questions is shown in Table 2. The key issues relating to each of the questions are answered in remainder of this section.

Development Process Timescales

This section focuses on the development of the standard and discusses in more detail the responses to question nine from Table 8.2. The development of PLCS began within PLCS Inc. in November 1999. The standard was first registered as a new project within the SC4 sub-committee on the 23rd of February 2002 and published as an ISO standard on 3rd of October 2005 (ISO, 2006c). The chairman of the SC4 subcommittee explained that the targeted development period was 3 years. However, the data indicates an overrun of 3 years meaning a 6-year development time to get to ISO publication. The interviewees gave a number of reasons for these delays including:

1. Pioneering Module Structure

One of the interviewees pointed out that PLCS lost a year through pioneering the modular structure. The modular structure in STEP application protocols, counters the traditional structure that created monolithic complex standards that covered a wide area. Details of the STEP modular structure can be found in Kemmerer's (1999) book on STEP.

2. ISO Publication Process

There was a challenge with the ISO publication process because of the revolution-ary approach that PLCS took to publish the standard in HTML using a module repository. These challenges with the ISO process were the main cause of delay. The SC4 chairman explained, *"PLCS really has broken down all the barriers. ISO do not have a publication stream for doing mass HTML standards. It was only last year that we got them to do the first HTML standard and that was just one of them. Then we submitted for publication, just before Christmas [2004], 145 standards in a package and nobody has ever done that before in ISO. We got the congratulations from the Secretary General downwards... So one of the key features of this is that we are making new rules as we go long"*.

3. Difficulty in Getting Organizations to Agree their Requirements

One interviewee put the time delays down to difficulty in getting different organi-zations to agree what their requirements were. One PLCS interviewee explained that this tied in with some of the research aspects of standards development where organizations spend a long time trying to understand their business in a consistent manner, and find difficulty in encoding what is assumed common practice within the organization.

4. ISO Hurdles

There are ISO hurdles relating mainly to the consensus process. However, one developer pointed out that though these hurdles take time, they do increase the quality of the standard.

Two of the reasons for delays are similar to the reasons that emerged within the case studies detailed in Chapter 5. However, there were two additional reasons that emerged, the first being the modular approach that was introduced into STEP application protocols. The second was the revolutionary approach of HTML pub-lication in ISO. Nonetheless, the negative impact of these delays remain the same, and one of the developers went on to point out that these delays are costly and may cause some companies to lose interest. However, ISO is taking steps to combat the long development times and, as one developer explained, *"f you to take up the new work item, you have to tell ISO in advance whether you are going to deliver in two years, three years or four years. If you want to go beyond four years, the technical management board must give you a waiver. You have to tell them when you are going to do your committee draft ballot, when you are going to do your draft international standard ballot... You have to give them a date for those and if you do not achieve those, the project gets cancelled within six months unless you do something about it".*

End-User and Software Vendor Involvement

End-user and software vendor involvement in the development process is an important factor, and this sections looks at these factors in relation to PLCS, and addressees question six, seven and eight from Table 2. There was a good level of representation of vendors and end-users in the development of PLCS, which is vital and important for its adoption. Nonetheless, one of the senior developers pointed out that, *"The real conflict we have is vendors trying to protect their share of the market against industry who want to have a solution".* One of the developers pointed out that one of their biggest challenges right now was how to get vendors back and interested in the standard. As the SC4 chair explained, *"One of the things we are looking at doing is structuring the SC4 meetings to have an implementers day on the Thursday, which will be focusing on specific implementation problems ...We are going to find something of value for the vendors to come together and do. That is something we are exploring over the next couple of meetings".* Nonetheless, some vendors have come on board, for example, a software consultant company called Eurostep has developed a tool for PLCS, and this is important. As one interviewee noted, *"Unless you have got [a tool] to sell [the standard] through it is not going to work".*

STANDARD SPECIFICATIONS

The questions in this category deal with issues concerning the balance and diversity of the development team, the DOI theory characteristics of the standards, completeness of the standard and IPR and brand identification. Table 3 presents the answers to the questions in this category, based on PLCS development. The remainder of this section discusses the issues surrounding these findings.

Balance and Diversity of the Development Team

The discussion in this section details the response to question 10 in Table 3. One of the developers explained that there was a very good dedicated team involved in the development of PLCS, despite a few organizations coming in and out of the process. Having a dedicated team was one the key issues described as lacking in the development of ISO 15926-2 and hampering the development process. However, as one of the interviewees pointed out, having a dedicated team for developing standards like PLCS which cuts across a number of industries, as opposed to ISO 15926-2

Table 3. PLCS responses to 'Standard specifications' questions

Standard Specifications		
10	Was there a balance between academic- and business-orientated individuals in the development team? **If not, which was predominant?**Business-orientated	N
11	Is there a positive perception relating to whether the standard is complex or not?	N
12	Is the standard unique in the capability it offers?	Y
13	Are the current editions of the published standard compatible with previous editions?	N/A
14	Have there been any pilots, demonstrations or workshops during the development of the standard?	Y
15	Have the benefits of the standard been verified in a cost-benefit analysis, return-on-investment analysis or success stories? **If so, are they publicly available?**No	Y
16	Have all remaining parts of the standard that directly impact the implementation of the standard been finalised or developed? **If not, what remains to be finalised?**DEXs and Reference Data	N
17	Was the standard developed by a recognised traditional standards development organization? **If so, please specify.**ISO	Y
18	Was the standard developed by a consortium? **If so, please specify.**PLCS Inc. originally and currently through OASIS	Y
19	Are all parts of the standard available in the public domain?	Y

which is targeted at the oil and gas industry, can pose a few challenges. As one interviewee explained, *"The main culprits stayed the same pretty much throughout the whole process, which is good from one aspect in terms of continuity, but again you are trying to build a much bigger consensus, so you do not want to end up with a niche standard because you have got a dedicated team – that is why we have these conferences, which give the opportunity for people to throw bricks at us."*

Another issue emerged in relation to the balance between academics and business orientation in the development team. Unlike what emerged in the original case studies where there was more of an academic emphasis, in the case of the development of PLCS, the SC4 Chairman pointed out that there were no academics. This could be due, in part, to having a combination of consortium development and ISO process development so more industries and end-users were involved, and as a consequence there was more of a business focus during development. Nonetheless, one of the interviewees did point out that this tension between academics and the business minded was to be expected. The interviewee stated that, *"Yes, I think there were some cases [of tension] there, but one has to ask, is there any more or any less than what you would expect in a commercial organization"*. The developer went on to point out that in some situations the comments made by the purists were ignored.

DOI Standard Characteristics

This section, covers questions eleven to fifteen, which deal directly with the five DOI characteristics. The details of the responses include:

1. Complexity

In relation to complexity all the interviewees agreed that the standard was complex. However, as one interviewee noted, *"complex solution, complex problem"*. The interviewee went on to explain that after twenty-six years of data-exchange experience, the issue of complexity always comes down to trying to get a common understanding and building an interface that supports a wide range of information. This relates to the conceptual idea and scope of these standards. However, one of the software developers questioned whether this complexity was stopping people using the standards. This confirms the view of the previous case study interviewees, who noted that the complexity of the standards should be absorbed by the software vendors who develop tools that make the standards transparent to the end-users. Having usable software tools is the key issue.

2. Compatibility

Compatibility in relation to PLCS is not an issue yet, because there have not been revisions of the standard. However, steps are being taken to overcome the potential challenges of having new editions of a standard. PLCS has a modular structure and these modules are produced as technical publications that have to be reviewed within three years, and at the end of the first three years these modules can be renewed as technical specifications. However, after six years these technical specifications have to either be withdrawn or made into an international standard. One interviewee agreed that if you implement a different version, there is no guarantee of compatibility, but steps are being taken to mitigate this challenge by having a clear publication profile of which editions of which modules are being brought together. There is a hope to secure funding to do that in an automated, rather than manual, way.

3. Relative Advantage

According to the SC4 chairman there is no standard that competes with PLCS at a global level. This is positive in relation to adoption because the standard appears to have no real competitors, although some of the ISO 15926-2 developers would argue that ISO 15926-2 competes with PLCS. However, ISO 15926-2 is not yet implemented for in-service support.

4. Trialability

A number of pilots and demonstrations have been carried out over the years, which the interviewees described as beneficial to the standards process and showing the usability and benefits of the standard. However, one of the interviewees noted that it was now time to move from pilots and demonstrations to real exchanges, similar to that which was proven on the Norwegian Navy frigate project, which met and resolved several challenges of a PLCS implementation (Hansen, 2004).

5. Observability

As with the case studies described in Chapter Five, the interviewees agreed that having observable, verified benefits would be an advantage for the standard. However, a problem that emerged in the original case studies was that there was a reluctance by some organizations to show the benefits or savings that had emerged as a result of use of the standards. Indeed, one software vendor interviewee explained the story of a US defence contractor who supposedly saved so much from the use of a STEP application protocol that they were afraid, if they published how much money they had saved, the air force would want their money back. Another software vendor who had been directly involved in determining the benefits for an organization using PLCS explained in the interview that even though benefits has been realised, they were not allowed to divulge that information. This has a negative impact on the overall adoption of the standard, as was posted on the Cover Pages website (2003), "The Return on Investment (ROI) from PLCS is still to be proven" (p.15). However, these results show benefits have been proven, but not disseminated.

Completeness of the Standard

This section looks in more depth at the response to question sixteen in Table 3. The completeness of the standard was a factor that emerged as key in ISO 15926-2 because the reference data libraries were not complete and there was concern by some developers that this would hinder uptake. In the case of PLCS, some reference data is available, and the role of reference data in ISO 15926 is more critical than PLCS, so reference data is not a main issue. According to the MoD Coherence Project final report (McCann, 2006), "*The necessary reference data required to give PLCS business context has not yet been fully defined.*" Therefore, though this may not be a main issue, it is a point of concern and an issue that must be resolved.

The challenge in relation to completeness for PLCS is the development of the DEXs (Data EXchange sets). According to the OASIS (Organization for the Advancement of Structured Information Standards) technical committee responsible for PLCS, a DEX is defined as follows: "A Data EXchange set [DEX] is a subset of the overall PLCS information model, comprising one or more capabilities, which in turn are based on the common data modules. DEXs support a specific business process or purpose and can be related to existing information. The developers of ISO 10303 AP 239 used their knowledge and Product Support domain expertise to identify and define the capabilities enabled by each DEX. The use of DEXs will facilitate modular implementation of AP 239. Those applying PLCS and/or vendors providing software applications may claim conformance against a single DEX or a combination of DEXs" (OASIS PLCS, TC, 2005).

In 2004 the PLCS Inc. project defined a range of 30 potential DEXs, however, to date only eight are currently under development (McCann, 2006). The DEXs are initially being standardised by publishing the subset of PLCS and associated usage guidance material as OASIS standards. Once they have been used extensively, they will be included as conformance classes of PLCS. DEX development has not been finalised, though different DEXs are at different stages of development. Nonetheless, one of the key developers described the incompletion of the DEXs as a major barrier to adoption of PLCS at the current time. One of the developers explained that a particular challenge at the moment was that the DEXs were quite large and the DEX development team are looking at creating smaller DEXs that meet the requirements of, for example, workflow within the US DoD.

Other challenges have emerged from working within OASIS. One of the SC4 members points out that, *"Certainly over the last 3 years I have spent more time arguing and fighting OASIS procedures than I have ISO... The only advantage is that [in] most consortia you can get direct membership, but in many cases that will exclude SMEs because they can attend national standards bodies meetings, and any company can be a member and form part of the UK view. How would they get into OASIS? Oh, it is cheaper, but how many trips do SMEs want to pay for their one IT man?".*

Another challenge developers are facing with developing standards within OASIS is similar to the challenges faced by traditional standard development organizations like ISO. Participation is voluntary, consequently funding is required to get specific tasks done. The funding arrangement in PLCS Inc. was that each organization paid $50,000 a year for four years and one of the developers pointed out that over that four-year period, $2 million was spent on the development programs for PLCS. However, as one developer said, *"In OASIS, you do not have any of that dedicated resource, you have just got projects collaborating, so we cannot say, someone go away and write a document, you have got to find a project that has got somebody available to write that document, or somebody that has the lead, and when they get desperate enough, the job gets done. So that is why we are trying, at the moment, to fund the core team of modellers to finish the core activities on DEXs, which is basically an overhead for everybody, that everybody benefits from, so the teams can go away and finalise the DEX contents. Frankly, I think we have lost a lot of momentum by not having dedicated resource".* The other side of this funding challenge is that the people who really need the standard, like the MoD and the Norwegian MoD, are covering the majority of the cost for things to get done. The MoD employee involved with PLCS indicated that this is a problem. In addition, one of the interviewees noted, "What we do not want to do is make [these PLCS DEXs] into a UK MoD standard, so we want someone else to pay for it".

Brand Identification and Intellectual Property Rights

The first part of this section deals with the issues concerning brand identification and explains the responses to questions seventeen and eighteen in Table 3. In relation to brand identification, one of the interviewees found that the fact they were dealing with ISO standards was positive. The interviewee went on to explain that there was a perception that although ISO standards may take a while to get developed, once developed they are set and secure. The interviewee went on to point out that there was further evidence of the benefit of ISO brand in his experience where he has seen work done in consortiums like CEFACT and OASIS, and explained that, *"once it is complete they will push it [CEFACT and OASIS work] through ISO and get an ISO stamp of approval. It does still have some meaning".* However, two of the interviewees did concede that that some people have a negative perception of not just ISO, but standards in general. Indeed, one of the American interviewees stated that, during his thirteen-year experience at one of largest software companies in America, they never used ISO. He argued that there may also be an American and European cultural effect on people's perceptions of standards, and noted that he believed that the W3C has more weight than ISO when it comes to IT standards. One of the other interviewees also pointed out that brand identification with ISO was based on the type of company, and that large organizations with a global presence tended to be more favourable than SMEs to ISO. These findings relate to issues discussed in Chapter 5.

Answering the questions relating to brand identification, questions seventeen and eighteen, also opened up discussion with regards to development of PLCS using both a consortium and the ISO process. An SC4 member noted that, *"It is very easy to do a first draft [of the standard] and we have demonstrated, I think quite successfully in PLCS, that by combining the best of the consortium process and the international standards process, we can make much more rapid progress. PLCS launched in November 1999. By the end of 2003, we had a draft standard".* This confirms the assertions made by some of ISO 15926-2 developers that the best form of standards development combines the benefits of consortia and traditional standards bodies such as ISO.

The final part of this section seeks to address question nineteen, which deals with IPR. The interviewees agreed that IPR was a valid issue in relation to the adoption of standards such as PLCS. However, in relation to PLCS, IPR was not an issue because an agreement was made within six months of the PLCS Inc. consortium forming. Everybody signed up to this agreement, which stipulated that everything was to be made publicly available.

Fee for the Standard

This final section looks at the issues surrounding the fees paid for standards. The debate relating to the fees for the standards was not seen as a key issue in the case study standards, in Chapter Five and Six but was an issue that emerged in the discussions surrounding PLCS. The interviewees argued that this is a key issue not just for PLCS but all ISO standards that are disseminated with a fee. One interviewee expressed, "*unlike W3C or OMG where you can find the standards free on the Web, you have to pay for [ISO standards]...you cannot go off and find a reference [for these standards] on the Web and that is just unacceptable in today's world – totally unacceptable*".

The problem is best explained by one of the developers who notes that, "*The big problem is [that] the ISO business model is currently based on selling paper or CDs. What is [the] alternative business model?...Our parent group, TC 184 has authorized us as SC4 to go and break our heads on the gate at ISO and try and solve this issue. We have their full support for getting free of charge standards. But at the moment, [the] people who are blocking it are not ISO in Geneva– their money comes from national [standards] bodies. The people who are blocking it are BSI, ANFOR, ANSI, and DIN who are all struggling to generate revenue, so that they can pay for ISO fees among other things...These organizations [BSI, ANFOR, ANSI, and DIN] could try and sell services to gain revenue, for example by selling consultancy on how to use the standards, but that will not work because then BSI will be in competition with its members that already provide these services. So it is a big challenge.*" This is an ongoing problem often debated in the literature and discussed in Chapters Five and Six.

ADOPTION CONDUCIVENESS

Adoption conduciveness covers the adopting community innovativeness, communication channels, marketing, and related implementation technologies. The first

Table 4. PLCS responses to 'Adoption conduciveness' questions

Adoption Conduciveness		
20	Are large multinational organizations part of the targeted adopting community?	Y
21	Are SMEs (organizations between 50 to 250 employees) part of the targeted adopting community?	Y
22	Are organizations from within any of the following industries part of the targeted adopting community: defence, oil and gas, energy, automotive?	Y
23	Does the standard have an implementers' forum that allows implementers to discuss their challenges and successes?	N
24	Is there a marketing strategy for the standard? **If so, who manages it?**SC4	Y/N
25	Does the standard have a website or other form of central outlet that enables potential adopters (end-users) or software vendors to find information about the standard and current developments?	Y
26	Is the standard implemented using current mainstream technologies, such as XML, UML or OWL?	Y

three issues are discussed in this section. The final factor is discussed separately. The results of the questions for this section are shown in Table 4. The remainder of this section discusses the issues surrounding these findings.

Adopting Community Innovativeness

This section addresses question twenty, twenty-one and twenty-two, in Table 4. The main issue raised in relation to the adopting community innovativeness was organization culture. One interviewee who works for a major defence contractor and is a developer of PLCS stressed the point about organization culture, and noted that there is a tendency for organizations to not recognise the value of information. The interviewee went on to suggest that organizations need to find ways to address this tendency because when organizations do not understand the value of information there is a greater chance of perceiving that the standard will not meet their needs and this can be a barrier to adoption. One of the results of this information mismanagement is that, as was noted by one software vendor, "*there is a challenge of mapping traditional custom and practice to what is actually included in the standard*". In the end it was agreed that innovativeness is dependent on an organization's culture, and not just in relation to its attitude towards change or standards but information as well, which has added a new dimension to the culture issue, and presents an opportunity for further research detailed in Chapter 10.

Communication Channels and Marketing

This section addresses question twenty-three, twenty-four and twenty-five, in Table 4. The communication channels were seen as important and currently there are no communication channels for implementers of PLCS although steps are being made to start an implementers' forum. Closely related to communications channels is the marketing of PLCS. In the case studies this was described as an important issue. Table 4 shows a Yes/No answer to question twenty-four was given because a Committee for Education and Outreach has been established in SC4 to look specifically at marketing. However, an SC4 member pointed out that a key challenge was trying to establish a team fully committed to building this committee. The committee is currently on its third chairman and lacking in funding. Marketing is a key factor and not having a stabilised committee for education and outreach is not positive for the adoption of PLCS.

RELATED IMPLEMENTATION TECHNOLOGIES

The main purpose of this section was to aid the researcher in having an in-depth understanding of the STEP standard and XML. It was vital for the researcher to have this understanding in order for action research, detailed in Chapter 4, to be effectively carried out. In addition to that, one of the important factors that emerged in the innovation-centric analysis was that the use of technologies like XML for implementation will positively impact adoption of data-exchange standards like STEP. Therefore, the second purpose of this section is to present work that was done to investigate different implementation techniques for PLCS and XML. Thus, answering question twenty-six in Table 4 by showing that PLCS could be implemented using XML

There is a debate within the STEP community about moving to more mainstream technologies like UML, XML and OWL. One of the software vendors interviewed noted that using tools around technologies like EXPRESS involves a large learning curve and cost, and this can become a barrier to other vendors or end-users getting involved with STEP standards. However one of the developers countered this view and pointed out that, *"The value in EXPRESS is that it moves through the generations of information technology. The disadvantage is that it doesn't tie into the major tool sets, the pre-tools and so on that are around, so we need to build a bridge to UML [and] XML just as we built a bridge to databases after we did the original flat file"*. One of the vendors found that about a third of the STEP community he dealt with wanted to stay with their traditional ways of working, which was slightly hindering progress towards more mainstream technologies. However,

ISO 10303 Part 28 of STEP is focused on creating an EXPRESS-XML mapping and another standard, ISO 10303 Part 25, is being developed for transforming EX-PRESS schemas into UML models (Lubell *et al. 2004*). There is agreement that these technologies are vital and that the STEP community cannot afford to ignore the work in these communities.

PLCS and XML Implementation

In September 2001, two teams of PLCS Inc. members independently developed PLCS technology demonstrations based on a part of the single integrated information model (Sloss *et al*. 2002). The demonstrations concentrated on the core of the model dealing with product structures, configuration management and exchange of information in the form of a STEP Part 21 file. The two technology demonstrations were sponsored by:

- UK MoD, Rolls-Royce and the LSC Group
- US DoD, Boeing, Aerosystems International and PTC

Following the success of the demonstrations, in November 2002 further investigations were carried out by the author while based at the LSC Group office in Tamworth, UK working with part of the LSC Group STEP/PLCS team. The investigations looked into the different technologies that could be used to fully implement PLCS.

Investigated Implementation Architectures

Three implementation options were investigated based on the exchange of data originating in a relational database. All three investigated architectures were built on the following initial steps:

- First the schemas, entities and attributes within the PLCS application modules that corresponded to the tables and columns of the relational database had to be identified. For example, the Asset table in the relational database would be equivalent to the Product entity in the PLCS schema.
- Next all the relevant PLCS entities and attributes were validated and compiled to create one schema that contained all the entities and attributes that represent the relational database.

Once these steps were established the three different methods of implementation could be investigated.

Figure 1. PLCS implementation options

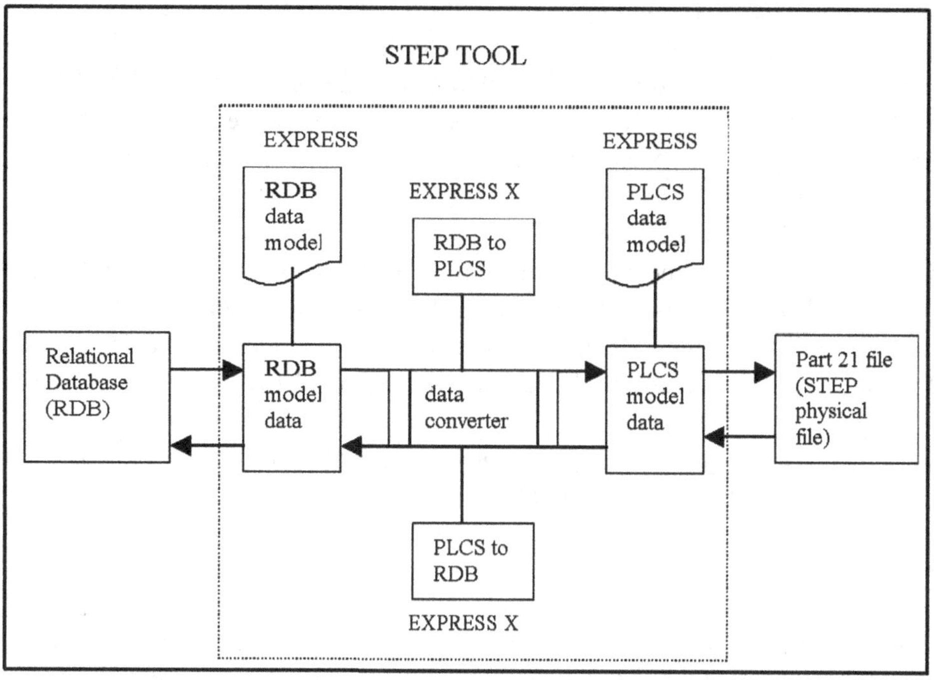

Method One

This section introduces the architecture used for Method 1 and analyzes the potential costs associated with this method.

Method 1 was investigated based on Figure 1, which has been adapted from the PLCS demonstrator to only detail the data exchange process within the STEP tool. The following steps were carried out prior to the use of the STEP tool:

- The relational database was converted into a series of object types using SQL statements. The object type names corresponded to table names and the object type attributes corresponded to table columns.
- Each object type was then directly converted into EXPRESS entities, with object type names and attributes represented as EXPRESS entities and attributes respectively.
- All the entities created from the object types were then combined into one EXPRESS schema.

This resulted in the creation of two EXPRESS data models, one that represented the relational database and the other the PLCS data model, which is based on all the entities and attributes that correspond to the relational database. Both data models were then loaded into the STEP tool. The next step involved creating the EXPRESS-X procedure that details the mappings between the relational database data model and the PLCS data model.

How Method 1 Works

Data is imported into the STEP tool from the relational database to populate the relational data model. Once the relational database data model is populated it is mapped to PLCS using EXPRESS-X. The resultant PLCS model data is exported from the STEP tool as a Part 21 file. Likewise a Part 21 file can be loaded into a STEP tool and converted into relational database data. Method 1 provided a basis for initial research into practical implementation; the following two methods build on Method 1 by introducing the use of XML.

Method Two

There have been arguments on the use of XML within STEP community. However, Fry (2001) explains how "STEP and XML are complementary technologies and are both necessary with appropriate recognition of the respective strengths and purposes of the two standards" (p.4).

Method 2 built on Method 1 by creating object views on top of the object types, using SQL statements. These object views were then run through the Oracle's PL/SQL XML Developers Kit in conjunction with SQL statements, producing an XML file and an XML Schema (XSD). Once the XML file and Schema were produced, two approaches were identified:

- Using the eXtensible Stylesheet Language with Transformations (XSLT) to convert the XML file directly into a Part 21 file - This removed the need for the use of EXPRESS-X or a STEP tool. However, the Part 21 file can still be loaded into a STEP tool. This approach offered an alternative but was still seen as a "point-to-point solution", and a method of generically using XSLT to produce a Part 21 file is still being investigated.
- The second approach was to load the XML file and Schema into a STEP tool that has XML to EXPRESS conversion capabilities; this approach is still under consideration.

Method Three

The final method built on ideas generated from the first approach of Method two and incorporates the use of web services. This was carried out using a Remote Procedure Call protocol known as the Simple Object Access Protocol (SOAP). This architecture is built around a web-based user interface with SOAP used to extract product data from a relational database, and data exchange carried out using XML files. The XML files are validated by an XML Schema (XSD), which is based on the relevant PLCS entities and attributes. In addition, this architecture enables conversion of the XML file into a Part 21 file using XSLT, thereby allowing the file to be validated and exchanged using a STEP tool. Further research needs to being carried out to ensure that the XML files and the XML Schema are Part 28 compliant. The two initial methods provided the basis for understanding ways of practically implementing PLCS and were the means by which the final implementation architecture, Method 3, was established.

SUMMARY AND CONCLUSION

The results presented in this chapter have looked at the innovations-centric issues that impact the adoption of PLCS. The findings of each of the sections have been collated and are summarised in Table 5 and 6. It is evident from the table that there are more 'Yes's than 'No's, which shows positive signs for the adoptability of PLCS. However, some of the key factors have been answered negatively indicating that there could be some concerns. The first concern is the timescale, which could have impacted the involvement of some end-users and software vendors. Nonetheless, now that the standard is published, this factor is no longer considered a major issue. The next main factor with a 'No' response is completeness of a standard, and this has more immediate causes for concern. With no DEXs completed and available, uptake of the standard will be delayed until the DEXs are available, what this means is that in the short term there is a potential for missed opportunities. Indeed this sentiment is reiterated in a statement made in the MoD Coherence Project final report, which states, "The future validity of PLCS as a global information standard as opposed to the basis for bespoke interfaces will depend on the degree to which this work can be effectively managed to deliver business driven DEXs in a timely manner". Nonetheless, the report goes on to state that US DoD has expressed a desire to be involved in DEX development, which if successful could result in an injection of funding to take the DEX work forward.

In addition to the DEX development concern, there is still not a clear marketing strategy, which, until rectified, will also negatively impact adoption. Nonetheless,

Table 5. Application of innovation-centric 'Adoption Checklist' to PLCS

Question		Y/N
Conception		
1	Are there economic drivers behind the development of the standard?	Y
2	*Were end-users among the initiators of the development of the standard?*	Y
3	Were software vendors among the initiators of the development of the standard?	Y
4	Were any heads of an industry supply chain involved among the initiators of the standard?	Y
5	Is the scope of the standard targeted at one industry sector?	N
Standards process		
6	Were end-users involved in the development of the standard?	Y
7	Were software vendors involved in the development of the standard?	Y
8	Have software application, which are based on the standard and support end-user business processes, been developed?	Y
9	Was the standard developed in the projected timescales? **If not, how long was the overrun?**3 years	N

Table 6. Application of innovation-centric 'Adoption Checklist' to PLCS

Question		Y/N
Standard specification		
10	Was there a balance between academic- and business-orientated individuals in the development team? **If not, which was predominant?**Business-orientated	N
11	Is there a perception that the standard is not complex?	Y
12	Is the standard unique in the capability it offers?	Y
13	Are the current editions of the published standard compatible with previous editions?	N/A
14	Have there been any pilots, demonstrations or workshops during the development of the standard?	Y
15	Have the benefits of the standard been verified in a cost-benefit analysis, return-on-investment analysis or success stories? **If so, are they publicly available?**No	Y
16	Have all remaining parts of the standard that directly impact the implementation of the standard been finalised or developed? **If not, what remains to be finalised?**DEXs and Reference Data	N
17	Was the standard developed by a recognised traditional standards development organization? **If so, please specify.**ISO	Y
18	Was the standard developed by a consortium? **If so, please specify.**PLCS Inc. originally and currently through OASIS	Y
19	Are all parts of the standard available in the public domain?	Y

Table 7. Application of innovation-centric 'Adoption Checklist' to PLCS

Adoption conduciveness		
20	Are large multinational organizations part of the targeted adopting community?	Y
21	Are SMEs (organizations between 50 to 250 employees) part of the targeted adopting community?	Y
22	Are organizations from within any of the following industries part of the targeted adopting community: defence, oil and gas, energy, automotive?	Y
23	Does the standard have an implementers' forum that allows implementers to discuss their challenges and successes?	N
24	Is there a marketing strategy for the standard? **If so, who manages it?**	N
25	Does the standard have a website or other form of central outlet that enables potential adopters (end-users) or software vendors to find information about the standard and current developments?	Y
26	Is the standard implemented using current mainstream technologies, such as XML, UML or OWL?	Y

adoption of PLCS is still very positive, these issues are more points of concern. The reason why adoption is positive despite the 'No's in some of the key issues is that there is sill a majority of 'Yes' answers to the key issues. The important ones being:

- The involvement of large multinational organizations in the standards process, these organizations have a tradition of working with standards. In addition, some countries, for example Norway, have specific policies regarding the use of PLCS.
- Software vendor involvement and the development of tools that will facilitate the uptake of PLCS.
- The linking of implementations of PLCS with mainstream technologies like XML.

In summary, the adoption of PLCS is still very positive, although there are a few concerns, which, the author believes, will not stop the adoption of PLCS but, PLCS will fail to achieve adoption as fast as could be possible. All interviewees also agreed that there would be eventual widespread adoption of PLCS.

The aim of this chapter was:

- To verify and test the factors identified in the innovation-centric model and note any emergent factors or issue based on the current factors surrounding the adoption of PLCS.

- To predict the adoptability of PLCS in light of the issues and factors that have emerged using the 'Adoption Checklist'.

Both aims were met and the checklist was applied to PLCS, and an outcome predicted. During the application of the checklist one new factor emerged relating to how an organizations attitude towards information can impact the adoption of a standard within an organization. What emerged from the data is that the likelihood of the adoption of a data-exchange standard is positively impacted by the importance an organization places on the efficient management of information. One way to measure this importance is through the existence of a department or individual responsible for the effective management of information within the organization. Therefore, a new question has been added to the adopter-centric checklist, and the question asks: *Does the organization have an individual or department devoted to the management of information throughout the organization?*

This question is by no means exhausts the possible ways of determining whether an organization has a positive attitude towards information, but is one indication. There is an opportunity for further research to be done to establish how to measure an organizations attitude towards information, and what impact that attitude has on the adoption of data-exchange standards.

In addition to this new factor, what emerged from the data were different perspectives on a number of existing factors like the reasons for the time delays in development, two new reasons emerged, the modular approach and the revolutionary HTML publication in ISO. In addition, the stakeholders involved in PLCS gave the fees paid for standards a much higher priority. Therefore, from a research perspective this chapter has offered the opportunity to confirm and ground the original factors and findings in a new context, and offer new insights into existing factors. The next chapter looks at the application of the adopter-centric 'Adoption Checklist' on the adoption of PLCS within the UK MoD.

REFERENCES

Cover Pages. (2003). Retrieved October 31, 2004, from XML.Coverpages.org, http://xml.coverpages.org/PLCSInc-FAQv2-20030804.pdf

Eurostep. (2005). *Product Life Cycle Support*. Retrieved December 3, 2005, from http://Www.plcs-resources.org/

Fry, T. (2001). *STEP & XML*. White Paper, Technologies for Digital Product Integration.

Gilman, C., Aparicio, M., Barry, J., Durniak, T., Lam, H., & Ramnath, R. (1997). Integration of Design and Manufacturing. In *A Virtual Enterprise Using Enterprise Rules, Intelligent Agents, STEP, and Workflow. Proceedings- SPIE the International Society for Optical Engineering*, (Vol. 3203, pp. 160-171).

Hansen, T. (2004). *Synchronise Work On DEXs and Reference Data Between PLCS Pilots and OASIS/PLCS*. Oslo: Det Norske Veritas As.

ISO. (2006c). *ISO Website*. Retrieved February 9, 2006, from http://www.iso.org/Iso/En/Isoonline.frontpage

Kemmerer, S. (1999). *STEP: The Grand Experience*. Gaithersburg, MD: National Institute of Standards and Technology.

King, T. (2002a). *Early Practical Realisation of Product Life Cycle Support*. Retrieved October 3, 2003, from OASIS-OPEN Web site http://www.oasis-open.org/committees/download.php/7626/03_Product_Lifecycle_Support_Pdt-Eu.pdf

King, T. (2002b). Requirements for Access To Technical Data -- An Industrial Perspective. *The 18th International Codata Conference — Frontiers of Scientific and Technical Data - Book of Abstracts* (pp. 40-41). International Council for Science: Committee On Data for Science and Technology.

Kock, N., McQueen, R., & Scott, J. (1997). Can Action Research Be Made More Rigorous In A Positivist Sense? the Contribution of An Iterative Approach. *Journal of Systems and Information Technology*, *1*(1), 1–24.

Lubell, J., Peak, R., Srinivasan, V., & Waterbury, S. (2004). STEP, XML, and UML: Complementary Technologies. *Journal of Computing and Information Science in Engineering*, *4*(4), 379–390. doi:10.1115/1.1818683

McCann, C. (2006). *Joint Engagement Group Coherence Project Final Report*. Document Number: 20060421-U-Final Report Version 2.0. England: UK MoD.

OASIS PLCS TC. (2005). Oasis Product Life Cycle Support (Plcs) Technical Committee. Retrieved November 4, 2005, from OASIS Web site: http://www.oasis-open.org/committees/tc_home.php?wg_abbrev=plcs

Peng, T., & Trappey, A. (1998). A Step Toward Step-Compatible Engineering Data Management: The Data Models of Product Structure and Engineering Changes. *Robotics and Computer-integrated Manufacturing*, *14*(2), 89–109. doi:10.1016/S0736-5845(97)00016-1

Pratt, M., & Anderson, B. (2001). A Shape Modelling Applications Programming Interface for the Step Standard. *CAD Computer Aided Design, 33*(7), 531–543. doi:10.1016/S0010-4485(01)00052-5

Sloss, I., King, T., & Turner, T. (2002). *PLCS Demonstrator Has World Premiere.* Tamworth, UK: LSC Group.

Starly, B., Lau, A., Sun, W., Lau, W., & Bradbury, T. (2005). Direct Slicing of STEP Based NURBS Models for Layered Manufacturing. *CAD Computer Aided Design, 37*(4), 387–397.

Chapter 9
Adopter–Centric Checklist Application:
Product Life Cycle Support Adoption and Diffusion in the UK MoD

INTRODUCTION

Standardization is the key to ensuring the interoperability, quality, safety, reliability, maintainability, effectiveness and efficiency of the equipment used by the Armed Forces (UK MoD SSE, 2005a). To realise these benefits, standards have to be effectively adopted and implemented within the MoD. However, what emerged in Chapter Six was that there are a number of factors and barriers critical to the adoption of standards within the MoD. Some factors like organization culture are applicable to the adoption of any standard or innovation within the MoD. However, other factors like standardization policies, standard characteristics and support from the standards community are unique to a particular standard. Therefore the aim of this chapter is two fold:

DOI: 10.4018/978-1-60566-832-1.ch009

- To verify and test the factors identified in the adopter-centric model and note any emergent factors or issues based on the current factors surrounding the adoption of PLCS within the MoD
- To predict the adoptability of PLCS in light of these issues and factors that have emerged using the 'Adoption Checklists'

By carrying out this analysis, steps can be identified to help facilitate the widespread adoption of PLCS. This analysis will also demonstrate the potential of using the 'Adoption Checklists' as a tool for key stakeholders and decision makers involved in the adoption and diffusion of data-exchange standards within organizations such as the MoD.

As was stated in Chapter 4, the collection of data in this chapter was carried out using a number of methods. The main methods used, and the purposes of the chosen methods are detailed below:

- Interviews: Two group interviews were carried out. One with three members of the product data standards team and the other with an IPT leader and four members of his team. They provided details on some of the primary and secondary adoption issues that emerged. The interviews were carried out from April 2005 to august 2005.
- Observations: The observation method was used during the PLCS workshop to note the main questions and concerns raised during the workshop. These were used during analysis of secondary adoption. The attendees were made aware that the author was taking notes of all questions and concerns raised.
- Questionnaire: This was given out at the end of the workshop to assess participants' attitudes towards PLCS and to establish if the workshop had impacted the attitudes of the participants.
- Documentation: Documentation was used to verify and add information regarding different issues raised during both primary and secondary adoption.

The data collected from the above methods was used to answer the questions in the 'Adoption Checklist'. The completed checklist was used to assess the adoptability of PLCS and provide a basis for recommendations to support the standard's continued adoption. The methodological approach used in this chapter is, like in Chapter 8, action research, as was detailed in Chapter 4.

The chapter begins by going through the primary adoption questions. The next sections present the results of the questionnaire and observations made during the workshop that demonstrated the use of PLCS. The concluding section brings together the completed checklist and data from the workshop to assess the secondary adoptability of PLCS and looks at the uptake of PLCS within the UK MoD.

PRIMARY ADOPTION

Primary adoption represents the adoption decision that needs to take place at a high level in an organization. There are a number of key factors that emerged within the adopter-centric study in Chapter Six, the key factors fall into four main categories: organizational characteristics, standard characteristics, environmental characteristics and decision mechanisms. This section seeks to test and verify if these factors are valid within the adoption process of PLCS.

Organizational Characteristics

Five key factors emerged within the organizational characteristics. These are: standardisation policy, drivers, organization culture, existing infrastructure and resource availability. Each of these factors is addressed below:

1. Standardization Policy

MoD policy is that STEP is the standard of preferred choice for all data exchange. For this reason, it has been announced in the Defence Contracts Bulletin (UK MoD SSE, 2005b) that, ISO 10303 STEP is the uniform standard of preference for the electronic exchange of product model data. This statement was reiterated by the then head of the product data standards team during a PLCS forum, that, *"Importantly, it has been announced in the Defence Contracts Bulletin that as from January 2003, STEP will be the uniform standard of preference for the electronic exchange of product model data." (Margaret Christison, Defence Logistics Organisation)*

One of the product standard team went on to explain that this policy came into place after some STEP Application Protocols (APs) had started to be used within the MoD. Indeed, PLCS was very much part of the motivation for this policy, as the current head of the product data standards team explained, *"[certain MoD officials] recognised that STEP was a standard that had CAD model control, so they thought 'Why don't we have that through life?'...I think the idea was to mandate PLCS and then someone said, 'Not just PLCS, we ought to mandate the rest of STEP'"*. PLCS, therefore, has an advantage over AP224, because this policy was not in place when AP224 was first considered. Having this policy in place means that there has been adoption at the primary level due to the recognition of the importance of STEP standards.

2. Drivers (Need for the Standard)

The drivers for use of PLCS are at two levels. The first is the need within the MoD to integrate information. What emerged from the research data is that, over the years, there has been an emergence of silos of information across the MoD to meet the needs of specific purposes and projects. These silos or stores of information are generally systems that meet a specific, narrow area of business requirements. This has resulted in over two hundred information systems that store and manipulate data across different departments within the MoD. These numerous systems run on bespoke software, which is expensive and difficult to modify, with high support costs. The IPT leader interviewed said that, *"It is an absolute fact of life that [the three services] will always operate together, I cannot envisage an operation where the Navy and Army would do something by themselves, it just does not happen, all warfare and operations are joint from now on"*. Therefore, it is important that the systems within each of the three services interoperate and interact with each other.

In light of this, a number of government programs and initiatives, such as the Strategic Defence Review, the "Modernising Government" initiative, and an internal MoD drive towards shared data environments, plus the impact of the internet and the explosion of e-business, has seen enterprise integration emerge as a key enabler to facilitate the seamless exchange and integration of information across the design, production and engineering support systems in the MoD (UK MoD SSE, 2005b). Hence, there is a clear driver for the use of data-exchange standards like PLCS within the MoD.

The second issue with regards to drivers behind the use of PLCS was that, in addition to the need for standards to support integration in general, there was a specific need for a standard that supports a product through life. What emerged from the data was that Def Stan 00-60 did not offer full life cycle support for a product, and one of the product data standards team pointed out that they realised they needed a through-life information standard. In 1999, an employee of the Defence Procurement Agency presented a paper at a ministerial level about the need for PLCS, and according to the product data standards team, the *'powers that be'* were convinced enough of the importance of PLCS that they agreed that the MoD should become one of the founding sponsors of PLCS Inc. and become involved in the development of the standard. So there were drivers for PLCS at two levels, the need for standards to support data integration and the need for a specific data standard to support a product through life. Therefore, there is a clear need for the standard. This worked positively in favour of adoption of the standard at a primary level.

3. Organization Culture

This factor relates to an organization's general attitude towards change, information and standards. Based on the interviews from the original case studies, many of the interviewees working for the MoD described the MoD as a traditional organization that is not always favourable to change. Sull (2002) describes this as an organization's tendency to persist in established behaviour. Nonetheless, although attitudes towards change is an issue, the head of the IPT who was interviewed, pointed out that this is a challenge most organizations face. Nonetheless, on a primary adoption level, what is evident is that the organization as a whole has a positive attitude towards standards and has a culture that is favourable towards data-exchange standards on a general level. With regards to the organizations attitude towards information the MoD has placed increased importance on the effective management and utilisation of information within the MoD. This is evidenced by the presence of a Director of Logistics Information (DLogInfo). The role of the team devoted to logistics information is described on the MoD DLO website as: "Its role is to identify and remedy gaps in defence logistics information capability. It introduces information discipline and derives maximum benefit from Defence information infrastructure (DII), which brings clarity and simplicity to logistics applications and data storage. [It] reduces the likelihood of failure, delay and waste, by improving programme, project and service management"[1]. Statements such as this highlight the fact that the MoD recognises the importance of information and consequently has a culture that indicates a positive attitude toward information.

The main cultural issues emerged during secondary adoption and are linked towards the culture of a department or an individual. Therefore, a more in-depth analysis of the culture issues that impact adoption is discussed within secondary adoption analysis.

4. Existing Infrastructure

This factor points mainly to switching costs and to the impact the adoption of a standard has on the current ways of working. Due to the policy and the apparent need for a standard like PLCS, the issues surrounding existing infrastructure will be more dependent on the specific IPTs and departments that have to adopt the standard and how this impacts their current ways of working. This is considered in more depth in secondary adoption analysis.

5. Resource Availability

This concerns two issues, the first being organizational restructuring. At the time of the interviews, the Defence Logistics Organisation was going through a reorganization. The head of the product data standards team saw this reorganization as an opportunity to bring the ownership and management of all the STEP APs used in the MoD under the control of the product data standards team and explained, *"If we can get the new reorganization done properly then we ought to own all of those [APs] as well. We might not develop them but we would own them as a focal point".* This implies that reorganization can be used as means to facilitate better management, ownership and control of STEP APs. Despite this opportunity, there was still concern and debate with regards to how the product data standards team would continue to operate after the restructuring.

The second issue in resource availability relates to resources to support the secondary adoption of the standard. This relates more specifically to having a champion or owner of the standard within the MoD to promote secondary adoption. In the case of the forward uptake of PLCS within the MoD, the members of the product data standards team emphasised that the Director of Logistics Information (DLogInfo) was the person who would be key in taking the standard forward. Members of the IPT agreed with this and pointed out that successful secondary uptake is dependent on having a champion with clarity of vision that can see the way forward for the standard across the three services. At the time of data collection, there was still no clear policy from the office of DLogInfo with regards to a strategy for the adoption of PLCS across the MoD. However, in January 2006 a new project, called the MoD Coherence Project, was launched to define the rules, tools and standards that will enable the MoD and Industry to accelerate the transformation of end-to-end logistics information capability. PLCS was one of the standards considered in this project, and details of this new initiative are discussed in later sections. One of the recommendations of this project is that DLogInfo and his team be responsible for the daily management and control of future work suggested by the project.

Standard Characteristics

The standard characteristics refer to Rogers' DOI characteristics, namely: complexity, compatibility, relative advantage, trialability and observability. Each of these factors is discussed below:

1. Complexity

The members of the product data standards team described PLCS as complex, which is in agreement with statements made by interviewees during data collection for the innovation-centric approach. Whether a wider population of stakeholders is in agreement with this view was assessed during the workshop questionnaire and is presented in later sections.

2. Compatibility

Like all STEP APs, PLCS can be implemented using modern technologies like XML; therefore, the standard is in line with best general commercial practices. The importance of XML is verified in the questionnaires. Nonetheless, compatibility will also be vital at a secondary adoption level again depending on the IPT or department that is to use the standard.

3. Relative Advantage

There was unanimous agreement among the interviewees that there was no competing standard available that could meet the needs of the MoD. The MoD became involved in the development of PLCS because they recognised there was a need to be met and PLCS would fulfil that need.

4. Trialability

There have been pilots and demonstrations that have taken place to display the benefits of PLCS, and these activities have acted as a platform to market the standard within the organization. According to the head of the data standards team, the workshop detailed in the next sections is the largest promotion and demonstration of PLCS that has been carried out so far. There was agreement amongst the interviewees that all demonstrations have been beneficial and are important. However, a member of the product data team did express that, *"there should be a fixed set of presentations from the OASIS PLCS technical committee which describes PLCS [in a consistent manner] ... so that whoever [receives the presentations] will be confident about what [the standard] means ".* The concern expressed here points to the need for a coordinated set of presentations to promote the standard. This indicates the need for a more definitive marketing strategy for PLCS from within the OASIS technical committee or ISO/TC184/SC4. However, as was stated in Chapter Five, efforts are being made for a clearer marketing strategy for all SC4 standards.

5. Observability

All the interviewees agreed that doing a pre-implementation business case was difficult due to the common problem of establishing a current baseline to work from. Therefore, it was frequently expressed that the key is to emphasise the enabling power of PLCS. Post-implementation, cost-benefit analysis of STEP APs has been done, to some extent, on the RAMP project involving AP224. However, with regards to PLCS, although some cost-benefit analysis has been carried out in other organizations, as was discussed in Chapter 5, the organizations involved in producing these figures have not made them publicly available. Having these benefits publicly available would be a powerful tool as it could show verified benefits of the standard and would support secondary adoption and promotion of the standard within the MoD.

Environmental Characteristics

The environmental characteristics look at two issues: network effects and support from the community. Network effects look at whether the standard is being used in other organizations. PLCS has been used as a basis for development of several point-to-point interfaces in the UK, Sweden, Norway and elsewhere, and for the LLM POC integrated data repository (McCann, 2006). In addition to that, the United States Unique Identification (UID) Program office is exploring the data exchange possibilities enabled by PLCS. There are tools available to use the standard, and consultants like the LSC Group and Eurostep are working on projects with the MoD regarding PLCS. Indeed, the workshop was a collaborative effort between the MoD and the LSC Group. So, there are network effects in place due to the defence community in countries like Norway and the USA taking on PLCS. This in turn leads to an increase in the proliferation of tools. In addition, there are consultancies such as the LSC Group that can support the secondary adoption of PLCS within the MoD.

Primary Adoption Summary

The issues discussed in this section are used to answer the questions posed in Table 1. From Table 1, it is evident that the primary adoption of PLCS is not in question There are a majority of 'Yes' responses, and there is a clear need for the standard and the MoD has a policy towards the use of STEP. One of the main organizational challenges at the time the interviews were carried out was that the Defence Logistics Organisation was going through a reorganization, which meant that coordination of efforts surrounding the standard was not as clear as it could have been. However,

Table 1. Application of the 'Primary Adoption Checklist' to PLCS

Primary adoption questions	Y/N
Organizational characteristics	
1	Does the organization have a policy that relates to the standard?	Y
2	Is there a need for the standard within the organization?	Y
3	Are there any external pressures to use the standard?	Y
3	Was the organization involved in the development of the standard?	Y
5	Is the organization currently free from any re-organization or restructuring initiative?	N
6	Does the organization adapt well to change?	N
7	Is the use of standards prevalent within the organization?	Y
8	Is there a key strategic champion for the standard?	Y/N
* new	Does the organization have an individual or department devoted to the management of information throughout the organization?	Y

this reorganization is now complete and work continues on the initiatives related to PLCS. Another challenge faced by the organization is dealing with the issue of change management and coordinating the change efforts associated with implementing systems based on standards such as PLCS. Later sections assess the change issues associated with implementing new systems based on data-exchange standards.

The other key challenge is having buy-in for the standard at the top level to promote and support effective secondary adoption of the standard. A yes/no response has been given to the question relating to having a strategic champion because though there has been some commitment form senior management that has resulted in pilots like the LLM Proof of Concept, and suggestions have been made regarding who should be responsible for taking the various initiatives forward, there is still no definitive answer to this question at the present time. Therefore, in summary, the issue is not whether there will be primary adoption of PLCS within the MoD, the main issue relates to getting a strategy in place to effectively manage and promote the secondary adoption and use of the standard within the MoD. If this issue is not resolved, data-exchange standards like PLCS will not get effectively adopted within the MoD.

SECONDARY ADOPTION: INVESTIGATION OF ISSUES SURROUNDING THE DIFFUSION OF PLCS WITHIN THE MoD

Although this was not the original focus of the study, it seems that secondary adoption is the main issue surrounding the adoption of data-exchange standards

Table 2. Application of the 'Primary Adoption Checklist' to PLCS

Standard characteristics		
9	Is there a perception that the standard is not complex?	N
10	Is the standard compatible with existing infrastructure and technologies used in the organization?	Y
11	Is the standard unique in the capability it offers the organization?	Y
12	Have any pilots and demonstrations been carried out to show the use of the standard? **If so, have they been of benefit? Y / N**	Y
13	Have the benefits of the standard been verified internally within the organization?	N
14	Have the benefits of the standard been verified externally by any other user of the standard? **If so, have they been made available? Y / N**	Y
Environmental characteristics and decision mechanism		
15	Is the standard being used in any other organization?	Y
16	Are there tools available to implement the standard?	Y
17	Are there consultants available to support adoption and implementation of the standard?	Y
18	Does the standard have a website or other form of central outlet that enables potential adopters to find information about the standard and current developments?	Y
19	Is there a compelling business case for the adoption of the standard that allows all stakeholders to identify the benefits?	Y
20	Have key decision makers 'bought into' the idea of using the standard?	Y/N

within the MoD. To establish the specific nature of the issues relating to secondary adoption, data was collected from a workshop run by the MoD that demonstrated the use of PLCS for systems integration. The data collected during the workshop included a full list of all the questions and concerns raised by the attendees of the workshop. In addition, a questionnaire was administered at the end of each workshop to establish the attendees' attitude towards PLCS and the impact the workshop had on their attitudes. This section starts by giving an overview of the workshop and then details the main issues and concerns that were raised from the questions and comments made during the workshop. The final section presents the results of the analysis of the questionnaire.

Workshop Overview: Aim of the Lean Logistics Model Proof-of-Concept Workshop

The purpose of 'Lean Logistics' in the context of the Defence Logistics Organisation (DLO) change program implies the complete elimination of waste so that all activities along the defence supply chain add value (LSC Group, 2006). To support this, LSC Group is currently involved in a number of initiatives, one of which was creating a Lean Logistics Model (LLM). The objective of the LLM was to bring together information from supply management systems, and engineering and asset management systems, into one single, coherent and consistent repository that is based on open neutral data standards, the primary standard being PLCS.

The Lean Logistics Model Proof of Concept Conference Room Pilot was run as a series of workshops sponsored by MoD Corporate Technical Services. The aims of the workshops were:

- To demonstrate the role new technologies and international information standards can play in delivering new ways of working.
- To evaluate what has been achieved by the Proof of Concept.
- To identify opportunities for implementation of the Lean Logistics Model. (Edwards, 2005)

The basis for the development of the Lean Logistics Model Proof of Concept (LLM POC) was the Through-Life Information Value Stack shown. The value stack emerged from work carried out by the joint MoD/Industry, Through-Life Management Group (Sloss, 2005). A detailed explanation of the value stack can be found in the LLM POC project development report (Sloss, 2005), but the key elements are:

1. CADMID Collection
2. Repository &Document
3. Business Intelligence and Modelling
4. KPI Identification
5. Coherent and Relevant reports
6. Workflow-Business Process Management
7. Business Enterprise Portal
8. Knowledge Management

The value stack represents the steps that need to be taken to enable information to be fully exploited by moving data collected from disparate systems into an integrated repository, where there is a common understanding of the meaning of data elements. Information management capability and functionality is built on top of the repository, and culminates in a knowledge management capability that is coherent throughout a business community. Figure 1 shows a top-level view of the system designed against the value stack. The four main layers of the system correspond to the value stack as follows:

- Donor systems and transactional systems - CADMID Collection
- Data integration layer – Repository and document

Figure 1. System developed for the LLM POC based on the value stack

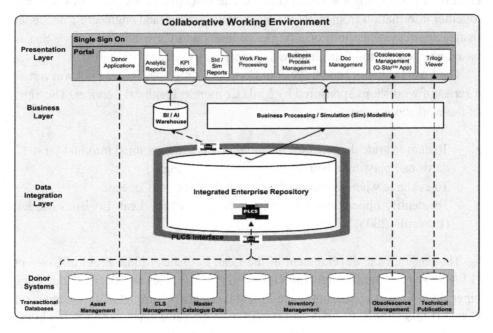

- Business layer – Business Intelligence and modelling, KPI identification
- Presentation layer – Coherent and relevant report, workflow and business enterprise portal.

During the actual workshop, the functionality of the LLM POC system was demonstrated through a series of scenarios. The scenarios were used to demonstrate the business benefit that could be achieved by the exploitation of the repository. The developed scenarios covered: narrative fault reporting, obsolescence management and enterprise performance management. Data to perform the scenarios was obtained from the nine donor systems shown at the base of Figure 1. There were four supply management systems, three engineering and asset management systems, a technical publications system and an obsolescence management system. The LLM POC was demonstrated to 211 people between February and April, 2005. Attendees at the workshop sessions ranged from the Chief of Defence Logistics and Chief of Defence Procurement to IPT desk officers. During the workshops attended by the author, all questions and concerns raised by the attendees were recorded by the author and are presented in the next section.

Observations: Emergent Questions and Concerns

The questions and comments raised during the workshop were noted during each session. At the end of each week a complete list of all questions was documented by the author and distributed to all members of the LSC Group POC team. Some members of the team then formally categorised the observed questions and comments under five headings for a formal MoD report (Edwards, 2005). These five headings are duplicated here to present a summary of the main questions asked. The headings are:

1. PLCS Related Questions

The PLCS-related questions can be broken down into six main areas.

- What it is? – These questions mainly revolved around what PLCS is and the difference between PLCS and STEP.
- How long it took to develop and publish? – There were a number of questions relating to how long and whether the standard has been published.
- The general uptake of PLCS – A number of attendees were curious as to whether PLCS had been adopted elsewhere, particularly in the US Department of Defence.
- The relative advantage of PLCS – Some of the attendees inquired as to whether the LLM POC could have been done without PLCS. The LLM POC team pointed out that though it could be done, there was extra benefit from working with open neutral standards like PLCS.
- Compatibility of PLCS as it evolves and is revised.
- Mapping exercise – Numerous questions were asked about whether all product data could be mapped to PLCS. The LLM POC team explained to the attendees that all the main features of product data for the life cycle of a product are covered by PLCS, and additional sections, particularly relating to geometry and design data, are covered by other APs in the STEP standard. In addition, questions were raised with regards to how long mapping takes (in terms of the nine donor systems used in the conference room pilot, mapping took six months). A final point was made about updating mappings when changes are made to the donor systems.

2. Donor System Questions

There were numerous questions relating to the donor systems. The main question was in relation to how over 200 MoD donor systems would be integrated into the repository. However, what was made clear to the attendees was that the integration of donor systems would be driven by business requirements and only where positive benefit could be identified.

3. Technical (System and Data) Questions

The next set of questions were classed as technical questions, and related to the main system. The questions raised related to the following issues:

- Bandwidth requirements
- Refresh rates and feedback to donor systems
- Off-line access to information
- Software packages used by LLM POC
- Why the POC will succeed where other projects have failed
- How access can be managed, especially on multi-national projects
- The link between this systems and other MoD technology initiatives
- IPR issues surrounding ownership of data
- Data cleansing issues
- Data security

All these issues are common concerns that emerge with the implementation of any integrated database, and are commonly cited in literature surrounding integrated databases (Lin & Brown, 2000; Hernandez & Stolfo, 1998).

4. Business Issues Questions

The business issues questions covered the following:

- Specifics about the scenarios
- Impact of the system on business processes
- SME involvement with the system
- Business benefits of the approach
- How to include the concepts of LLM POC within a contract
- Mandating the system
- Deployment of the system on the battlefield
- The fit of LLM POC with MoD strategy
- Understanding the value stack
- The reactions of top-level management to the presentation. Many of the attendees wanted to know how the top-level management viewed the workshop.

One of the main business questions was whether the MoD was going to mandate PLCS. Some of the attendees advocated that the standard be mandated, in order to make it easier to get their industry partners to use the standard. However, at the time of the workshops, the standard was still described as being the preferred choice in the MoD Support Solutions Envelope. Therefore, another option could be justified because PLCS was still not mandated. Nonetheless, the head of the product data standards team often explained during the workshops that there were steps being taken to review the policy.

5. Future Considerations

The final set of questions related to the way forward from the LLM POC. The key questions asked were with regards to where the project goes from here. The main issues raised were with regards to funding and the steps senior officials will be taking to drive the project forward.

There were many responses given to the different questions, and a full list of responses can be found in the LLM POC Conference Room Pilot user evaluation report (Edwards, 2005). Nonetheless, what emerged during the workshop are some of the key issues surrounding secondary adoption of PLCS within the MoD. The next section looks at the responses given to the questionnaire developed and administered by the author during the workshop.

Questionnaire Results: Attitudes towards PLCS and the Impact of the Workshop on End-user Attitudes

At the end of each workshop session, a questionnaire was given to the attendees. A copy of the questionnaire used can be found in Appendix C. The questionnaire was designed to retrieve information about user attitudes and perceptions of data-exchange standards such as PLCS and the impact the workshop had on their attitude. The propositions this questionnaire sought to verify were: -

Proposition 1: The participants of the workshop have a positive attitude towards data-exchange standards such as PLCS.

Proposition 2: Workshops are helpful in altering attitudes towards standards.

Proposition 3: There is a difference in attitudes towards data-exchange standards between different categorical groups.

Proposition 4: The workshop attendees have identified the benefits of using data-exchange standards like PLCS

Proposition 5: The workshop attendees perceive the standard to be complex.

Proposition 6: The workshop attendees perceive PLCS will limit the way they can do their work.

Proposition 7: It is important to the workshop attendees that data-exchange standards like PLCS are implemented using XML.

Proposition 8: The workshop attendees' attitudes towards the use of a standard are dependent on the wording used to describe the standard.

There were 211 attendees at the workshop over the entire period, and the total number of collected questionnaires for the research was 140. This represented 66.4% of the total attendees; a higher number was not achieved because the author was not able to attend every workshop session. However, in the sessions the author did attend, all but five workshop attendees filled in questionnaires. The analysis presented in this section is based on the number of questionnaires returned and the questions answered. Where respondents missed a question, these results were described as 'missing' within the SPSS tool used to analyze the data. A number of background steps were taken before data analysis was carried out,

1. Negatively worded items were reversed, which meant the responses to questions 6, 8, 9, 11, 13 and 16 were reversed. This was done so that when describing the analysis, higher responses or scores indicated a more positive attitude.
2. All responses from question 5 to 16 were added together to find the total attitude value for each interviewee. Therefore a new variable **TotalAttitude** was created to indicate the total attitude score for each respondent of the questionnaire. With the Likert response scale ranging from 1 to 5, the lowest possible negative attitude would be 12 (1 x 12 questions) and a highest possible positive attitude would be 60 (5 x 12 questions). The following range was created to categorise the results:
    ◦   12 to 21 – very negative
    ◦   22 to 31 – negative
    ◦   32 to 40 – average
    ◦   41 to 50 – positive
    ◦   51 to 60 – very positive

Pallant (2001) suggests that the choice of statistical techniques can be determined depending on whether a researcher is seeking to explore the relationship among variables or to explore the differences between groups. In addition, the choice of statistical technique is also determined by whether a researcher chooses parametric or non-parametric statistical techniques. Parametric techniques are more powerful, but have assumptions that make them more stringent. If the assumptions are not met, one alternative is to use a corresponding, non-parametric technique. An additional categorisation is in relation to the nature of the variables used in the study. In this categorisation Pallant (2001) lists three main categories:

1. Categorical

In this research there are seven categories, namely:

- Whether the individual is a PLCS developer (Yes or No)
- Whether the individual is a PLCS implementer (Yes or No)
- Whether the individual is an implementer or developer of any other data-exchange standard (Yes or No)
- Whether the individual has been to other pilots for data-exchange standards (Yes or No)
- The managerial role of the individual (Senior/board-level management, Other-level management, Non-managerial)
- The technical ability of the individual (Mostly technical, mostly non-technical)
- Whether the pilot had impacted their opinion or not (Yes or No, if Yes are they more favourable or less favourable?)

2. Ordinal

A Likert scale was used to measure attitudes. Therefore, all the responses to the attitudes statements are ordinal variables. This enabled the additional ordinal variable, **TotalAttitude,** to be created to represent the total scores of the attitude questions for each respondent.

3. Continuous

There were no continuous variables.

The choice of statistical techniques is based on these three main categorisations mentioned above. Due to the fact that there is only ordinal and categorical data, only non-parametric tests are appropriate for this research. As Pallant (2001) explains, "Non-parametric techniques are ideal for use when you have data that are measured on nominal (categorical) and ordinal (ranked) scales" (p.210). However, there is much debate within the statistical world with regards to the issue of parametric versus non-parametric analysis of the Likert scale scores. Dawis (1987) and Adams *et al*. (1965) address this debate, and the majority perspective is that parametric tests should only be used where the ordinal scale has more than five categories. Nonetheless, some authors argue that exceptions can be made and parametric tests can be used in cases where the scale is five or less if the population size is very large, at least above 400. In this research, since the ordinal scale had only five categories and the size of the population is limited to 140, non-parametric tests were used, where

Figure 2. Bar chart of attitudes towards PLCS

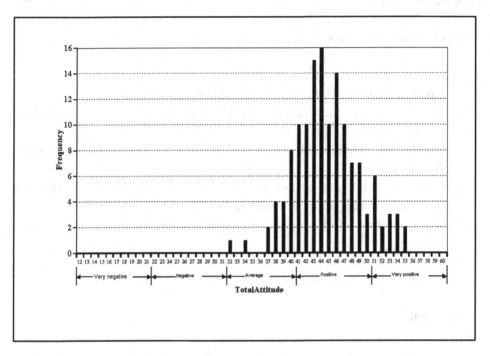

appropriate. Using the chosen statistical tests, the eight propositions were verified, and the results are presented in the remainder of this section.

Proposition 1: The participants of the workshop have a positive attitude towards data-exchange standards such as PLCS.

This proposition was put forward to establish if the attendees of the workshop had a positive attitude towards the standard. As was noted in Chapter 6, positive attitudes have a positive impact on user acceptance of a system. Therefore, to verify this proposition, descriptive techniques were used to determine the median of **TotalAttitude**. TotalAttitude being the summation of the results of question 5 to 16 for each individual, and the median is determined from the bar chart shown in Figure 2.

From the results shown in Figure 2, the median is 44. These results are based on the responses of 138 valid cases, as two cases were missing data. Using the range described in the introduction to this section, a median of 44 indicates a generally positive attitude towards data-exchange standards like PLCS. What needs to be established is if this positive attitude was influenced by the workshop, and if this attitude varies among different groups. These issues are addressed in the next two propositions.

Proposition 2: Workshops are helpful in altering attitudes towards standards.

Ideally this proposition would have been answered by taking the end-users attitudes before and after the workshop. However, it was not possible to administer a questionnaire at the beginning of the workshop, so the attendees were asked to determine if the workshop had impacted their attitude to data-exchange standards, which was question 20 in the questionnaire. Question 20 has a part 'b' that asked the attendees who had been impacted by the workshop, if the workshop had made them more or less favourable toward the standard. Again, to verify this proposition, a descriptive test was performed. The simple descriptive test carried out revealed that 95 of the 140 (67.9%) respondents indicated that the workshop had impacted their attitude. Of the 95 respondents, 94 said the workshop had made them more favourable towards the standard, with the remaining respondent not giving a response to this question. Therefore 98.9% who were impacted were more favourable towards the standard. This result shows that the workshop was helpful in altering attitudes toward the standard. This result was expected, and confirms the findings in Chapters Five and Six, which indicate that pilots and workshops are important in facilitating the adoption and diffusion of a standard. However, 45 respondents indicated that they had not been impacted by the workshop. The next proposition postulates that there are significantly different attitudes among different categorical groups.

Proposition 3: There is a difference in attitudes towards data-exchange standards between different categorical groups.

Six of the category groups were assessed using the Mann-Whitney U test, which is used to compare the medians of two different groups. The median of the TotalAttitude variable of each category group was used, and a significant difference in attitude is shown when Sig. (2-tailed) or p is equal to or less than 0.05. The results of the different groups were:

- **PLCS developers and non-developers** (question 1)

The Mann-Whitney U test used to compare the attitude towards PLCS for PLCS developers and non-developers revealed that ***there was a significant difference*** between the attitudes of PLCS developers (Median = 46.50) and non-developers (Median = 44, p=0.015). The developers were more favourable towards the standard than the non-developers. This result was expected given the developers close involvement with the standard.

- **PLCS Implementers and non-implementers** (question 2)

The Mann-Whitney U test used to compare the attitude towards PLCS for PLCS implementers and non-implementers revealed that *there was a significant difference* for PLCS implementers (Median = 46) and non- implementers (Median = 44, p=0.046). The implementers were more favourable towards the standard than the non-implementers. Again, this was expected given the implementers close involvement with the standard.

- **Whether they are an implementer or developer of any other data-exchange standard or not** (question 3)

The Mann-Whitney U test used to compare the attitude towards PLCS between developers or implementers of other data-exchange standards and non-developers/implementers revealed *there was a significant difference* between developers/implementers (Median = 46) and non-developers/implementers (Median = 44, p=0.012). The developers/implementers were more favourable towards the standard than the non-developers/implementers of other data-exchange standards. This was expected given the developers/implementers exposure to other data-exchange standards.

- **Whether the individual has been to other pilots for data-exchange standards or not** (question 4)

The Mann-Whitney U test used to compare the attitude towards PLCS between individuals who attended other data-exchange standard pilots and those who had not revealed *there was a significant difference* between those who had (Median = 47) and those who had not (Median = 44, p=0.023). Those who attended other pilots had a more favourable attitude that those who had not. This result was expected due to the fact that proposition two had indicated that the workshops had made some of the attendees more favourable to the standard.

- **Technical ability** (question 19)

The Mann-Whitney U test used to compare the attitude towards PLCS for individuals whose job role was mostly technical and those whose job role was mostly non-technical revealed *there was no significant difference* for mostly technical (Median = 45) and mostly non-technical job roles (Median = 44, p=1.000). However, this result may have been influenced by the impact of the workshop on the attendee's attitudes towards the standards.

- **Influenced by the current workshop** (question 20)

The Mann-Whitney U test used to compare the attitude towards PLCS for those who were impacted by the workshop and those who were not, revealed there *was no significant difference* for those who were impacted (Median = 45) and those who were not (Median = 44, p=0.65). This result shows that the remaining 45 attendees who were not impacted by the workshop already had a positive attitude towards the standard. This could be explained by the fact that 22 of them had had exposure to PLCS and other data-exchange standards. The remaining 23 of the 45 had not had any exposure to PLCS or other data-exchange standards but still had a positive attitude. These results show that the workshop had a positive impact on attitudes towards data-exchange standards like PLCS. Some of the interviewees in the product data team believed that this was due to two factors:

- The focus that was given to the enabling capability of PLCS
- The hands-on opportunity that was given to the attendees during the workshop.
  - **Managerial role** (question 18)

The seventh categorical group was tested using the Kruskal-Wallis test. This test is used when a categorical variable has three or more levels. In this case the managerial roles are broken into three levels so this test is appropriate. In the Kruskal-Wallis test scores are converted to ranks and the mean rank for each group is compared. The results suggest that there is *no significant difference* in the attitudes between managerial responsibilities because the Kruskal-Wallis significance level is 0.202 which is greater that 0.05. Again, this result may have been influenced by the impact of the workshop on the attendee's attitudes towards the standards.

The results show that the workshop contributed to most of the attendees having a generally positive attitude to the standard. This attitude varies amongst developers and implementers of PLCS and other data-exchange standards, and non-developers and implementers. In addition, attitudes varied amongst those who had attended other pilots and those who had not. Again this points to the fact that they had had previous exposure to data-exchange standards and would therefore more readily identify the benefits of the standards. This is to be expected since they have close involvement with the standard. The remaining three categories indicated no significant difference in attitude, and this can be explained by the impact of the workshop on their attitudes.

Proposition 4: The workshop attendees have identified the benefits of using data-exchange standards like PLCS

What emerged from question five was that over 99.3% of the attendees see benefit in using data-exchange standards like PLCS for integrating systems. Interestingly only one attendee disagreed, and on further analysis it emerged that the person was a developer, which suggests the developer may actually have developed a dislike for the standard. Question six of the questionnaire explored a different aspect of the same issue addressed in question five. Question six sought to establish if the attendees could see a significant difference between the benefits of standards based and non-standards based system integration. 104 (74.3%) of the respondents believed that there was a significant difference between the benefits of standards based and non-standards based system integration .Only 7.1% disagreed with this view. This points to the fact there is general agreement that there are benefits in using data-exchange standards like PLCS for systems integration.

Proposition 5: The workshop attendees perceive the standard to be complex.

Only 89 of the attendees answered question seventeen in the questionnaire, since it was added halfway through the workshop. It was apparent that a slightly larger proportion, 33.6%, agree with the idea that PLCS is complex rather than disagree, 22.4%. The fact that these potential end-users think the standard is complex may not have a negative influence because, as was mentioned in the interviews in Chapter Five, the standard will be hidden from the end-users, because software vendors will develop tools based on the standard.

Proposition 6: The workshop attendees perceive PLCS will limit the way they can do their work.

What emerged was that 80.7% disagreed that PLCS would restrict the way they do their work, and they saw the standard as an enabler rather than something that will limit the way that they work. Nonetheless a small percentage, 2.8% agreed with this view. Therefore, the observations made by some of the interviewees in Chapter 6 were not completely unfounded. However, overall, this result shows that there is an understanding of the benefits of data-exchange standards like PLCS that are enablers of new ways of working.

Proposition 7: It is important to the workshop attendees that data-exchange standards like PLCS are implemented using XML.

A large proportion of the respondents neither agreed nor disagreed with this view, and this shows a possible lack of understanding of XML technology. Nonetheless, there was a slightly larger proportion, 29 (20.8%), who disagreed with the need for XML than the 13 (9.4%) who agreed with this view. This could possibly be attributed to the understanding the stakeholders have about the enabling benefits of PLCS, and the fact that these benefits are not dependent on the use of XML. However, Chapter 5 highlighted the fact that adoption of a data-exchange standard can be hampered if the standard is not implemented using mainstream technologies like XML.

Proposition 8: The workshop attendees' attitudes towards the use of a standard are dependent on the wording used to describe a standard.

The aim of this proposition was to verify the opinion held by some interviewees that some potential users of data-exchange standards are reluctant to come on board because the wording used to describe standards, including the word 'standard' itself or ISO, were the cause of some of the negative views held. To verify this proposition, results were assessed according to whether the respondents were developers or not. This was done because there was a significant difference between the attitudes of developers and non-developers. Three statements were made and the attendees were asked to agree or disagree with the statements using a five-point Likert scale. The three statements were:

- I think it is important that systems integration is based on commonly agreed data meanings
- I think it is important that systems integration is based on a data-exchange standard
- I think it is important that systems integration is based on an ISO data-exchange standard

Each of these statements represented a different way to describe an ISO data-exchange standard. A summary of the findings is found in Table 3. The medians reveal that developers did seem to have stronger agreement when the words 'standard' and 'ISO standard' were used and this could be due to their exposure to ISO data-exchange standards. However, on hindsight and further reflection of the statements, it became evident that the statements were not worded in the best way to verify the proposition. The different terminologies were deemed very subjective depending on the background of a respondent. For example, one developer indicated that he was contrasting the terms 'common data meaning' and 'data-exchange' standards on a technical level, and not in the way the statements were intended. Therefore, as detailed in Chapter 10, more research is required to establish a methodology to

Table 3. Summary of responses to different standards terminology

Terminology	Non-PLCS developer Median	PLCS developer Median
Common data meanings	4	5
Data-exchange standard	4	4
ISO data-exchange standard	4	5

better verify and examine the issue surrounding the terminology used to describe a 'standard' and how that has an impact on user attitudes towards a standard.

Summary of Findings from Workshop

Through the observations made during the workshop, the concerns of the different end-users were established and they were classed around five main topics, PLCS, donor system issues, technical issues, business issues and the way forward for the standard. In addition, the questionnaire revealed the general attitude of the end-users, the benefits they identified in using data-exchange standards like PLCS, and some of the specific issues they consider with regards to use and perceptions of the standard. All these issues provide a means by which the secondary adoption questions on the checklist can be answered, and the next section looks at this.

SECONDARY ADOPTION: APPLICATION OF THE CHECKLISTS

Secondary adoption looks at the diffusion of a standard within an organization. Using data from the workshop, the interviews carried out and data from a report published by the recently completed MoD Coherence Project, the secondary adoption of data-exchange standards such as PLCS within the MoD is assessed. The Coherence Project was formally launched on the 16th of January 2006 to define jointly with Industry the rules, tools and standards that will enable the MoD and industry to accelerate the transformation of the end-to-end logistic information capability. The aim of the project being to: *"Define a joint target architecture underpinned by common processes, standards, information flows and measures of information performance; together with an agreed compliance regime"* (p.i). A high-level review of the available information standards was carried out to provide an initial assessment of the standards applicable to the generic functions of Engineering and Asset Management and Material Flow. The findings recommended: PLCS as the applicable standard for engineering and asset related information; OAGIS 9.0 as

Table 4. Application of 'Secondary Adoption Checklist' to PLCS

Secondary Adoption		
Managerial Intervention		
1	Is there a policy relating to the standard that impacts the adoption of the standard within the department? **If so, is there a choice of whether to use the standard?**Yes	Y,R
2	Is funding being made available to facilitate adoption of the standard throughout the organization?	R
3	Is training being made available to facilitate adoption of the standard throughout the organization?	NK
4	Is there a team of people devoted to promoting the standard throughout the organization?	R
5	Have any pilots and demonetisation been carried out to show the use of the standard? **If so, have they been of benefit?**Yes	Y
Department attributes		
6	Does the implementation of the standard offer direct benefit to the department?	Y
7	Is the standard compatible with existing infrastructure and technology within the department?	NK
8	Does the department have any external business partners? **If so, are these business partners positive towards the use of the standard?**NK	Y
9	Does the organization or department have a standards licence, which will allow implementers to access the standard?	NK
10	Does the department adapt well to change?	NK

the applicable standard for Material flow transactions and ASD S1000D as the applicable standard for technical documentation.

The secondary adoption questions are answered in Table 4 and 5. Two additional responses have been added to the table. The first is a 'R', which represents situations where a recommendation has been made in the Coherence Project final report regarding a particular question. The second new response is 'NK' which represents a situation where a response to a question is not known because data is not available to give a conclusive response.

From the table it is evident that some of the responses to the questions are not yet known so there is future work to de done to evaluate secondary adoption. However, the issues surrounding each of the answers to these questions are discussed below using the categorisation that emerged in the model shown in Figure 2 in Chapter 6. The main categories are managerial intervention, department attributes, individual attributes and standard and standard community attributes.

Table 5. Application of 'Secondary Adoption Checklist' to PLCS

Individual attributes		
11	Is the use of the standard compatible with individual end-users current ways of working?	NK
12	Does the end-user understand the benefits of the standard?	Y
Standard attributes		
13	Is there a positive perception in relation to whether the standard is complex or not?	N
14	Have all remaining parts of the standard that directly impact the implementation of the standard been finalised or developed? **If not, what remains to be finalised?** DEXs and Reference Data	N
Standards community attributes		
15	Do implementers of the standard have a forum to discuss their challenges and successes with other implementers?	N

Managerial Intervention

Managerial intervention covers three issues: the authoritative decision, funding and support. With regards to the authoritative decision, this topic was constantly raised during the workshop and is an issue that caused much discussion in the interviews. The fact that the standard is the preferred choice means that IPTs cannot force their industry partners to use the standard. However, the head of the product data standards team pointed out that the change by the MoD to move *'from provider to intelligent decider'* means that industry will be more responsible for the data about and related to products and, as a consequence, standards will be vital to industry. Industry will see the benefit of this due to these new arrangements. The IPT leader interviewed said that it would be desirable for the standard to be mandated. However, the issue comes down to who will pay for it, or in other words, who will cover the costs of mandating it. Indeed in the Coherence Project final report (McCann, 2006) the following statement is made, "The potential benefits to be derived from the adoption of open standards for information exchange can only be realised through mandation of the standards" (p.11). The report goes on to specifically recommend that an authoritative policy regarding the mandation of the standards be established through appropriate channels, with emphasis placed on mandating the standards both within the MoD and up to and including the Industry boundary, in order that the benefits of the project can be realised.

Funding was another key issue that came up during the workshop and the main question was whether IPTs would have to pay for the implementation of the standard from their own budgets or would commitment to see widespread adoption come from a central push. This lack of resources and funding was identified in the

Coherence Project as a major barrier to the investing in projects that could save money across Defence Logistics.

The final main point relating to managerial intervention is support through training. Members of the IPT and the IPT leader interviewed all agreed this was vital for the successful uptake of systems based on the standard. Training that is coordinated could also be used to ensure that communication about activities relating to the standard would be systematically disseminated through the organization. In light of this, having a strategy or policy that is managed through a specific department or team will be key to coordinating the communication efforts, so that mixed messages do not stream through the organization. Indeed, one of the product data teams pointed out that all these efforts need to be coordinated by DLogInfo. Therefore, until that coordinated view is finalised, implementation will be a challenge, a clear strategy and program still needs to be finalised. One of the product data standards team explained that, *"One of our tasks is to write a programme of awareness. I do not know how you do that, and whether you go to every single IPT [to do the program of awareness] ...we should have a marketing strategy - but we do not, based on the fact that there are only four of us. There needs [to be] prioritisation of what we are doing and maybe marketing is more important than development [of the standard]"*. This ties in with the issue of marketing the standard within the MoD to promote secondary adoption of the standard. The Coherence Project final report addressed some of these issues and they are briefly discussed in a later section of this chapter. In the report, recommendations have been made regarding marketing and promoting the initiatives based around the standards, using short-term and long-term strategic work plans.

Department and Individual Attributes

This section looks at how department and individual attributes impact the secondary adoption of data-exchange standards within the MoD. The majority of the data that was used for this section was obtained from a group interview carried out with an IPT leader who had attended the workshop and four members of his team. The main departmental and individual attributes that impact secondary adoption, that emerged in Chapter Six also emerged in the data in this section and can be summed up in these four issues:

- Attitudes towards change
- Attitudes towards standards and information
- Whether the standard offers direct benefit to the department or individual
- Industry partners' buy-in

'Attitude towards change' deals mainly with resistance to change. At a department level there may be resistance because of the reluctance of some departments or IPTs to change their current ways of working, but as the head of the product data standards team stated, *"You cannot implement STEP without process change, or any standard without process change"*. This will cause some departments to be resistant where they want to keep their current ways of working. The IPT leader also pointed out that the individualistic nature and attitude of some departments or IPTs can cause them to be reluctant to come on board. He described the scenario that some IPT leaders have where they say, *"This works for me. I do not care about [the rest of the MoD]. Do not bother me. It works, and I do not care about what is happening elsewhere"*. The leader went on to explain that, *"The attitude is further enhanced by the modern way of doing business in individual IPTs that are now starting to set their own rules, and are now starting to have support arrangements which are different and perhaps partnered with industry. This breeds a very stove-piped culture"*. However the IPT leader interviewed went on to point out that, *"I think we are quite privileged because our IPT is not [limited to a particular domain] dealing with our own head down problem; we tend to be able to see the problem across the different areas"*. What this shows is that different IPTs identify varying benefits from using data-exchange standards, and this will be dependent on their service area (land, sea or air) and the function of the IPT.

The change issues are true at an individual level; one of the IPT team members described a scenario where change can be an issue even at the physical moving level. In the department where they were working, a person was "in hysterics" because a change required them to move to another side of the desk. In relation to PLCS, the IPT leader said that people might be resistant to change when they believe the automated processes enabled by standards like PLCS will result in a loss of work for them. All interviewed said they had experienced or witnessed change issues, and they went on to state that it is a key issue for secondary adoption of any innovation within the MoD. Indeed, "initiative overload" was something they agreed was an issue or as one of the team put it, "change on change". The head of the IPT explained that sometimes, at an individual level, it might just be "lethargy" towards a new initiative. Kegan and Lahey (2002) point out that this 'lethargy' is not necessarily a reflection of opposition to change or merely a result of inertia, but an unwitting application of productive energy toward a hidden competing commitment. Kegan and Lahey explain that, "The resulting internal conflict stalls the effort in what looks like resistance but is in fact a kind of personal immunity to change" (p.85). They go on to give an example of a person's reluctance being tied to the fear of not being able to handle tougher assignments, which might follow if the new initiative is successfully taken on. In dealing with change issues, one IPT team member suggested that it was important to demonstrate the standard and its benefits, and explained that, "My experience with a depot was, once we demonstrated *it, within a level of weeks everyone was on board*". Therefore, demonstrations are key, and moving from conference room pilots to live pilots will be important factor in facilitating secondary adoption of data-exchange standards like PLCS.

The next issue was the reluctance of industry to buy into the initiative. However, positive steps have been taken to deal with this. One of the main positive steps was the large number of both Industry and MoD stakeholders who were engaged throughout the Coherence Project process (McCann, 2006). This should assist in securing stakeholder buy-in as deliverables from the Coherence Project and subsequent, follow-on, projects are formally endorsed and mandated.

Standards Attributes

In a similar manner to AP224 and other STEP standards, the PLCS standard will be transparent to the end-user, and when the IPT leader and his team were asked if it was important to them to know the details of the standard, they said 'no'. The leader pointed out that he drives a car without knowing the specific details of how it works. The main issue for him was that his car gets him where he needs to go and he knows the basics in how to keep it running. Relating that to PLCS, the team stated that it was more important to them to have a system that delivered the capability promised by the standard, than to know the details of how the standard works. The specifics of the standard become important when the implementers and consultants start developing systems and databases around the standard. As was the case in the RAMP project, the availability of a support network and implementers forum will be important. This can be a challenge as one of the product data team noted, "*Like other [standards] [PLCS] has limited take-up so you cannot nip round and see another organization using it, because it is a long way away. There is nothing in the UK*". Therefore, the establishment of an implementer's forum is vital for successful secondary adoption of PLCS within the MoD and any other organization looking to adopt the standard.

The next issue concerns whether all the relevant parts of the standard had been completed. As was pointed in Chapter 8 the slow progress of the development of the DEXs will impact the rate at which PLCS is adopted and may result in missed opportunities. Indeed in the Coherence Project final report it was noted that, "*The way development [of the DEXs] is being managed through OASIS is insufficient to deliver fully developed DEXs within the timescales required for Defence Logistics Transformation*". Subsequently, the danger is that other initiatives, which deliver possibly less benefit, may take priority if these delays continue, and the efforts of initiatives like the Coherence Project could be undermined.

SUMMARY

This chapter has looked at the primary and secondary adoption of PLCS within the UK MoD using the adopter-centric standards adoption checklist. This section seeks to provide a summary of the key issues that have emerged and assesses the way forward for data-exchange standards within the MoD.

Summary of Primary and Secondary Adoption of PLCS within the MoD

Based on the adopter-centric 'Adoption Checklist', the primary adoption of PLCS within the MoD is not in question. The MoD has had a clear commitment to PLCS from the initiation of the standard, and they continue to be committed to the standard today. Therefore, the main prediction is that PLCS will be adopted in the MoD. The question is how successful will the adoption be, and whether there will be widespread adoption of the standard within the MoD and across the defence supply chain. Consequently, the important issues are having top management buy-in and having a clear strategy for the way forward that coordinates all the MoD efforts surrounding the adoption of data-exchange standards such as PLCS. This was reiterated by the head of the product data standards team who stated that, "*I think [the adoption of PLCS] has to be a success, and there is no reason why it should not be, so long as we have the appropriate management buy-in. Now, if we make it a success as the defence industry, then maybe that will be the example for others to buy into [PLCS], and we can sell [PLCS] forward from there*". Another product data team member agreed with this and stated that, "*[PLCS] will be successful, but the concern is final buy-in from DLogInfo*". Therefore, successful secondary adoption is very much dependent on having a central push and only time will tell if this will indeed be the case. The other key issue relates to dealing with change management. Dealing with change is important. Indeed one of the identified potential barriers that emerged during a Coherence Project brainstorming exercise, in March of this year, was the need for cultural change. Therefore, the following section assesses the change management issues that need to address.

The Way Forward for Data-Exchange Standards in the MoD: Dealing with Change Management

Dealing with change is vital to any organization, and with the recently completed MoD Coherence Project, it was deemed that an important contribution of this research would be to assess how the results and recommendations of this initiative measure up against the change management steps outlined in the Harvard Business

Review on Change (Kotter *et al.* 1998) and the Harvard Business Review on Culture and Change (Munck *et al.* 2002). The field of change management as a whole is a vast research area in itself, so the assessment presented in this section is by no means exhaustive. However, it offers an initial assessment of the progress being made in the adoption of the rules, tools and standards that will enable the MoD and Industry to accelerate the transformation of end-to-end (foxhole to factory) logistic information capability.

In his analysis of over 100 organizations, Kotter (1998) came up with eight steps to facilitate successful change in an organization, they are:

- Establishing a sense of urgency
- Forming a powerful guiding coalition
- Creating a vision
- Communicating the vision
- Empowering others to act on the vision
- Planning for and creating short-term wins
- Consolidating improvements and producing still more change
- Institutionalising new approaches

The remainder of this section discusses these actions in relation to the results and recommendations that emerged from the Coherence Project.

Action 1: Establishing a Sense of Urgency

This initial step deals with identifying and discussing the crises, potential crises or major opportunities related to a change initiative (Kotter, 1998). The sense of urgency is demonstrated by the three Joint Engagement Group meetings held between September and December 2005, where senior MoD officials and heads of defence industries jointly agreed the need for a short sharp project to define the way ahead for defence logistics information transformation, and this short sharp project was the Coherence Project.

The emphasis of the Coherence Project was on the opportunities to be gained from the adoption of rules, tools and standards that will enable the MoD and Industry to accelerate the transformation of end-to-end logistic information capability. The project developed a jointly agreed Functional Business Process Model with supporting standards mapped to the information exchanges. The final report of the Coherence Project explains that, "This [Functional Business Process Model] provides an unprecedented opportunity to simplify the way information is exchanged" (McCann, 2006, pp. i). The Coherence Project brought together a wide stakeholder community with many differing views and priorities and produced a robust framework which they believe will pave the way for accelerating the development of IS logistics.

Kotter (1998) recommends that information derived from the discussion, such as those held over the course of the Coherence Project, should be communicated widely and broadly. In relation to the Coherence Project there is now a final report available, presentations have been and continue to be carried out, and there are plans to further disseminate information about the project. Therefore, in the case of the UK MoD, the establishment of a sense of urgency was evidenced in previous meetings, which culminated in the Coherence Project that was formally launched in January 2006. This gives evidence that Action 1 has been fulfilled, and the opportunities have been identified and captured in the Coherence Project final report and are being disseminated throughout the organization.

Action 2: Forming a Powerful Guiding Coalition

This next step looks at the importance of having a powerful guiding coalition, and assembling a team with enough power to lead the change effort. Duck (1998) refers to it as a transition management team who will commit all their time and energy to managing change until the process has stabilised. Kotter (1998) points out that whenever some minimum mass is not achieved early in an effort, nothing much worthwhile happens. In addition, the team should have a balance of titles, information and expertise, reputations and relationships, with at least 20 to 50 people.

Now that the Coherence Project has come to an end, a section of the final report is devoted to giving recommendations on how the deliverables of the Coherence Project are to be owned, and how configuration and changes of the underlying model are to be managed and agreed. Therefore, recommendations have been made for a guiding coalition. In summary the Coherence Project recommends that the Chief of Defence Logistics is the process owner and should be responsible for, "strategic direction of logistics at the department level and improvement for operational effectiveness" (McCann, 2006, pp. 16). The report goes on to suggest that ongoing governance of the output of the Coherence Project be managed by two teams, the Through Life Management Group and the Joint Information Group. A Steering Group should also be created to be responsible for overseeing the development and sustainment of the information architecture. In addition, they recommend creating wider user-stakeholder engagement forums, to keep the momentum of the gains made in the Coherence Project, and to facilitate buy-in from the different stakeholder groups. Finally, the report recommends that the daily management and control of the functional business process model be the responsibility of DLogInfo and his team.

This comprehensive list of groups indicates that the recommendations given in the report have fully taken into consideration Action 2. However, care must be taken as so that the activities of these various teams, if they should materialise, do not become isolated from the organization's mainstream activities (Levy, 2002). There needs to be constant communication and feedback that can help the organization. These issues have been taken into consideration in the Coherence Project final report.

Action 3: Creating a Vision

This step relates to creating a vision to help direct the change effort. A vision is something that helps clarify the direction in which an organization needs to move, and gives a clear and compelling statement of where all the initiatives are leading to (Kotter 1998). All the efforts surrounding the adoption of data-exchange standards such as PLCS are linked back into the overarching vision of the DLO, which states: 'The DLO strives to grow confidence in Logistics' (DLO, 2006). Collins and Porras (1998) believe a vision is made up of two parts, the core ideology and envisioned future. The core ideology or mission of the DLO, states that, "DLO exists 'to Deliver Logistics for Operations'". The output of the Coherence Project captures the envisaged future, the report executive summary states that, "The project has developed a jointly agreed Functional Business Process Model with the supporting standards mapped to the information exchanges ...It subsumes many of the process models being utilised across the MoD and it will provide a robust model for future convergence". Therefore, the Coherence Project has provided a framework for the envisioned future and if fully taken on board, Action 3 would be fulfilled.

Action 4: Communicating the Vision

In this action, every vehicle possible is used to communicate the new vision and strategy. If these efforts are not taken on board, the risk of cynicism among employees' increases, while belief in the communication goes down (Kotter, 1998). However, as was pointed out by the head of the MoD product data standards team, any communication efforts need to be managed and coordinated so that mixed messages are not communicated. Again this action has been addressed in the Coherence Project final report and is captured in the recommended Coherence Project Campaign Plan. The plan suggests that all efforts relating to the promoting and taking forward of the project deliverables be developed by two parallel workstreams. The first workstream will list short term tasks required to sustain the model and engage IPTs and Industry. The second workstream will focus on the development of longer-term strategic plans. These efforts have to be jointly taken forward by the MoD and Industry. Again, the Coherence Project has made provision for Action 4.

Action 5: Empowering Others to Act on the Vision

This is where some of the key issues relating to change emerge. This action deals with looking at getting rid of obstacles to change, and changing systems or structures that seriously undermine the vision (Kotter, 1998). Some of these obstacles may be at a department level or individual level, therefore these change challenges need to be dealt with at both levels. Some of the barriers will be departmental and individual attitudes towards change and possibly the standards, as has been detailed in Chapter 6. Some of the potential obstacles are the lack of an authoritative decision with regards to the initiatives surrounding the standards. Mandating the standards would be a way of overcoming this obstacle. This sentiment to mandate the data-exchange standards was echoed by the attendees of the workshops, the MoD officials interviewed as part of the research, and was a recommendation of the Coherence Project. Therefore, steps need to taken deal with this barrier. In addition, the Coherence Project suggests that funding be made available for the IPTs to act on the recommendations. This would empower the IPTs to act on the vision.

Action 6: Planning for and Creating Short-Term Wins

Schaffer and Thomson (1998) stress the importance of translating long-term vision into achievable but ambitious short-term goals. Without these short term wins there is greater potential for many to give up or join the ranks of those who have been resisting change (Kotter, 1998), and this kind of action helps keep the urgency levels up. The Coherence Project proposes that the development of an implementation strategy for an open standards based architecture can be accelerated through the implementation of early-adopter projects (McCann, 2006). The report goes on to practically suggest that, "In parallel to defining longer term strategy, a range of different IPTs will be engaged to test and validate the Project outputs against real scenarios which are bounded by time and cost and more importantly which assist the IPTs with their transformation plans" (p.16). Therefore, live IPT pilots would ensure that this action is fulfilled.

Action 7: Consolidating Improvements and Producing Still More Change

Kotter (1998) explains that the short-term can be used to tackle even bigger problems. This action deals with looking for new opportunities to widen the scope of the vision. These kinds of actions and the way forward could be incorporated into the second workstream, which is focused on long-term strategy.

Action 8: Institutionalising New Approaches

Change sticks when it becomes part of the way things are done (Kotter, 1998). Schaffer and Thomson (1998) propose periodically reviewing a strategy, learning from both successes and failures, institutionalising the changes that work and getting rid of the rest. Again this action is tied into the long-term strategy of the second workstream. The Coherence Project report explicitly recognises that a lack of alignment of this project with the 'master strategy' would cause a barrier to the successful uptake of the deliverables of the project.

What this assessment has shown is that the Coherence Project has effectively and efficiently taken into consideration the key steps to facilitate effective change management. The critical action that needs to take place is an endorsement of the recommendations and strategies put forward by the Coherence Project and immediate action to create some short term wins in order to facilitate the adoption of these rules, tools and standards that will enable the MoD and Industry to accelerate the transformation of the end-to-end logistic information capability.

CONCLUSION

This chapter has sought to highlight the factors and barriers critical to the adoption of PLCS within the MoD. The aim of this chapter was:

- To verify and test the factors identified in the adopter-centric model and note any emergent factors or issues based on the current factors surrounding the adoption of PLCS within the MoD.
- To predict the adoptability of PLCS in light of these issues and factors that have emerged using the 'Adoption Checklists'.

Both aims were met and the checklist was applied to the adoption of PLCS within the MoD, and an outcome predicted. During the application of the checklist no new factors emerged. Nonetheless, from a research perspective this chapter has offered the opportunity to confirm and ground the original factors and findings in a new context, and offer new insights into existing factors that impact the adoption of data-exchange standards within an organization.

REFERENCES

Adams, E., Robert, F., & Richard, R. (1965). A Theory of Appropriate Statistics. *Psychometrika, 30*(2), 99–127. doi:10.1007/BF02289443

Collins, J., & Porras, J. (1998). Building Your Company's Vision. In H. B. Review, *Harvard Business Review on Change* (pp. 21-51). Boston: Harvard Business School Press.

Dawis, R. (1987). Scale Construction. *Journal of Counseling Psychology, 34*(4), 481–489. doi:10.1037/0022-0167.34.4.481

DLO. (2006). *The 2006 PLan*. Retrieved June 11, 2006, from MoD webiste: http://www.mod.uk/NR/rdonlyres/3DF7FB22-6725-4CE3-9C65-3FDBB946A859/0/TheDLOPlan2006.pdf

Duck, J. (1998). Managing Change: The Art of Balancing. In H. B. Review, *Harvard Business Review On Change* (pp. 55-82). Boston: Harvard Business School Publishing.

Edwards, K. (2005). *Lean Logistics Model Proof of Concept Conference Room Pilot - User Evaluation Report*. Report No: D/Zu/02/28/4 - Llmpoc-0000005761 Rev 2. Lichfield, CT: LSC Group.

Group, L. S. C. (2006). *Lean Logistics*. Retrieved May 23, 2006, from LSC Group Web site: http://www.lsc.co.uk/markets/defence/collaborative_working/lean_logistics_cw.html

Hernandez, M., & Stolfo, S. (1998). Real-World Data Is Dirty: Data Cleansing and the Merge/Purge Problem. *Data Mining and Knowledge Discovery, 2*(1), 9–37. doi:10.1023/A:1009761603038

Kegan, R., & Lahey, L. (2002). The Real Reason People Won't Change. In *Harvard Business Review On Culture and Change* (pp. 37-58). Boston: Harvard Business School Press.

Kotter, J. (1998). Leading Change: Why Transformation Efforts Fail. In *Harvard Business Review on Change* (pp. 1-20). Boston: Harvard Business School Publishing.

Kotter, J., Collins, J., Pascale, R., Duck, J., Porras, J., & Athos, A. (1998). *Harvard Business Review on Change*. Boston: Harvard Business School Publishing.

Levy, P. (2002). The Nut Island Effect: When Good Teams Go Wrong. In *Harvard Business Review On Culture and Change* (pp. 1-20). Boston: Harvard Business Publishing.

Lin, A., & Brown, R. (2000). The Application of Security Policy To Role-Based Access Control and the Common Data Security Architecture. *Computer Communications, 23*(17), 1584–1593. doi:10.1016/S0140-3664(00)00244-9

McCann, C. (2006). *Joint Engagement Group Coherence Project Final Report.* Document Number: 20060421-U-Final Report Version 2.0. England: UK MoD.

Munck, B., Kegan, R., Lahe, L., Meyerson, D., Sull, D., Hudson, K., et al. (2002). *Harvard Business Review On Culture and Change.* Boston: Harvard Business School Press.

Pallant, J. (2001). *SPSS Survival Manual: A Step-By-Step Guide to Data Analysis Using SPSS for Windows.* Buckingham, UK: Open University Press.

Schaffer, R., & Thomson, H. (1998). Successful Change Programs Begin with Results. In *Harvard Business Review on Change* (pp. 189-213). Boston: Harvard Business School Publishing.

Sloss, I. (2005). *Lean Logistics Model Proof of Concept Conference Room Pilot - Project Development Report.* Report Number: D/Zu/02/28/4. Lichfield, CT: LSC Group.

UK MoD SSE. (2005a). *Support Solutions Envelope - Engineering & Asset Management.* Retrieved March 16, 2005, from Acquisition Management System Web site: http://www.ams.mod.uk/ams/content/docs/sse/v3_3_archive/eam.htm

UK MoD SSE. (2005b). *Support Solutions Envelope – Data Standards.* Retrieved March 11, 2005, from Acquisition Management System Web site: http://www.ams.mod.uk/ams/content/docs/sse/v3_3_archive/ikm%20&%20c4i/gp_3_ed1.htm

ENDNOTE

[1] As of 1 April 2007 the DLO was merged with the Defence Procurement Agency to form a new organisation called Defence Equipment & Support.

Chapter 10
Summary and Recommendations

RESEARCH OVERVIEW

The benefits of standardization are realised through the effective adoption, implementation and use of standards. Nonetheless, there are a cross-section of factors that impact the adoption and diffusion of standards. Indeed, within the IT standards research community, there is a research area devoted to looking at IT standards adoption. However, there are currently a limited number of peer-reviewed, empirical studies that look at the adoption of IT standards. One particular set of IT standards where this is true is ISO data-exchange standards, particularly those produced by the ISO subcommittee ISO/TC184/SC4, and to date there are only two known studies that have looked at the adoption of the 614 standards published by the SC4 subcommittee. The limited research within both the ISO/TC184/SC4 and IT standards

DOI: 10.4018/978-1-60566-832-1.ch010

research communities led to the emergence of the two main research questions that were the basis for the research aims.

- What are the factors and barriers critical to the adoption and diffusion of data-exchange standards across their target population?
- What can be done to facilitate and accelerate the adoption of data exchange standards across their target population?

In order to answer these questions and fulfil the aims of the research, the objectives of the research were:

1. Develop a preliminary conceptual model that identifies the factors and barriers critical to the adoption of data-exchange standards, through the study of published literature.
2. Revise and refine the preliminary conceptual models by analyzing the information obtained from interviews and other data sources related to the adoption and diffusion of two ISO/TC184/SC4 standards and two military standards, and.
3. Further refine and test the preliminary conceptual model against the current adoption and implementation of PLCS using a 'Standards Adoption Checklist' developed from the conceptual model.
4. Present recommendations to facilitate the adoption of data-exchange standards in general and PLCS specifically, from the experience gained in the above objectives.

These objectives were achieved and presented in the various chapters within this book. The following sections give a summary on how each objective was fulfilled.

RESEARCH FINDINGS, NOVELTY AND LIMITATIONS

This section gives an overview of the results of the first three objectives. The findings, deliverables and novelty related to each of these objectives are also presented. The final part of this section details the limitations of this research.

Development of Conceptual Models

The first objective was to develop a preliminary conceptual model through a study of the published literature surrounding IT standards adoption. What emerged, as

Table 1. Summary of findings and novelty based on Objective 1

Objective 1				
Approach	**Findings**	**Deliverables**	**Novelty**	**Chapter**
Conducting a comprehensive literature review to develop a conceptual model	Two main approaches, innovation-centric and adopter-centric based mainly on DOI theory and Economics of standards	Preliminary innovation-centric and adopter-centric conceptual models	Developing both innovation and adopter centric models to carryout a combined analysis using both approaches in one study	Chapter Three

detailed in Chapter Three, is that there are two main approaches used in IT standards adoption research, these are the innovation-centric and adopter-centric approaches. Therefore, a decision was made to take a novel stance and incorporate both approaches into one study in order to limit the bias of doing a single approach and to get a more balanced picture of the factors and barriers critical to the adoption of data-exchange standards. Consequently, the scope of Objective 1 was extended to incorporate the development of both an innovation-centric and adopter-centric adoption conceptual model. These findings and the novelty of this approach are summarised in Table 1.

Revision and Refinement of Conceptual Models

The second objective was to revise and refine the models through the analysis of interviews, documentation and archival records. The innovation-centric model was tested and revised against the adoption process surrounding two ISO/TC184/SC4 standards namely, ISO 15926-2 and ISO 10303-224. What emerged from the analysis was that there was a complex array and interaction of factors relating to the adoption of data-exchange standards, from conception through the standards process and subsequent adoption of a standard. In the innovation-centric analysis, what emerged was that there were eleven factors that directly impact the adoption and diffusion of data-exchange standards. These factors were summarised around four main categories:

- **Conception:** Initiators of development
- **Standards process:** End-user involvement and software vendor involvement
- **Standards specifications:** Standards Diffusion of Innovation (DOI) characteristics, completeness of the entire standard, brand identification and IPR.

Table 2. Key adopter-centric factors

Adoption stage	Key factors
Primary adoption	Organisational characteristics, standard DOI characteristics, environmental characteristics, decision criteria and decision mechanisms
Secondary adoption	Managerial intervention, facilitating conditions

- **Adoption conduciveness:** Adopting community innovativeness, communication channels, marketing, and related implementation technologies.

The adopter-centric model was tested against the adoption of three different standards within the MoD. The three standards were ISO 10303-224, the NATO Codification System (NCS) and Def Stan 00-60. There were key factors that emerged within the primary and secondary adoption of the standards, and these factors are summarised in Table 2. All these factors were confirmed in the literature and were analysed for both models, with deeper insight provided for some of the factors.

In both the innovation- and adopter-centric analysis, a list of themes and a revised conceptual model were developed. What emerged from the analysis was that most of the factors confirmed the existing literature. However, novelty can be claimed on two levels:

- Grounding of the factors within the ISO/TC184/SC4 standards community
- Grounding of the factors within the UK MoD

In addition, new perspectives were offered on existing factors. In the case of the innovation centric-approach, new perspectives were offered on the following:

- The impact that the involvement of the defence community in the development of a standard has on the subsequent adoption of a standard. The data revealed that developing ISO standards from within a predominately defence background had a direct negative impact on the subsequent adoption of those standards.
- The impact the research nature of standards development has on the development timescales of a standard.
- In the case of the adopter centric-approach, new perspectives were offered on the following:
- User attitudes towards standards. Some of these attitudes were tested using a questionnaire and the results were presented in Chapter 9.

Table 3. Summary of findings and novelty based on Objective 2

Objective 2				
Approach	Findings	Deliverables	Novelty	Chapter
Application of innovation-centric model to two SC4 standards, ISO 15926-2 and ISO 10303-224	Existence of eleven main innovation-centric factors that impact the adoption and diffusion of a standard.	- List of innovation-centric themes - Revised innovation-centric conceptual model	- Grounding of the factors in ISO/TC184/SC4 community - New perspectives on: The impact of defence involvement The impact of the research nature of standards development	Chapter 5

- The secondary adoption of standards within an organisation. What was particularly revealing was the importance of the standards community in supporting implementers to facilitate secondary adoption of the standards.

These findings and the novelty of approach are summarised in Table 3 and 4.

Test and Revise the Model and Apply the 'Adoption Checklists' to PLCS

The third objective was achieved in two steps. The first step was the development of the adoption checklists. The innovation- and adopter-centric models were used to develop questions around the main factors that emerged in the models. A majority of 'yes' responses would indicate a higher probability of the adoption of a data-exchange standard. The second step was to apply the 'checklists' to the adoption of

Table 4. Summary of findings and novelty based on Objective 2

Objective 2				
Approach	Findings	Deliverables	Novelty	Chapter
Application of adopter-centric model to UK MoD for three standards, ISO 10303-224, Def Stan 00-60 and NCS	Existence of primary and secondary adoption factors that impact the adoption and diffusion of a standard within an organisation.	- List of adopter-centric themes - Revised adopter-centric conceptual model	- Grounding of the factors in the defence community - New perspectives on: User attitudes towards standards The secondary adoption of standards within an organisation	Chapter 6

PLCS in order to assess the adoptability of the standard. From an innovation-centric viewpoint, adoptability was very positive but there were concerns with regards to not having an implementers forum and the setting up of a clear education and outreach programme. Some new perspectives were given in relation to how an organizations attitude towards information impacts the adoption of a standard. As a consequence, a new question was added to the adopter-centric checklist.

In the case of the adopter-centric application of the checklist, what emerged was that there was definitely primary adoption but there were clear issues that needed to be resolved for secondary adoption to take place through the MoD, such as having a central push, a strategic champion of the standard, funding and communication program and managing change.

In addition, in order to fully satisfy this objective, action research was carried out. In the innovation-centric analysis, investigations into the use of XML to implement PLCS were carried out and presented, and these results were used for the work done on the UMMS project. In the adopter-centric analysis, observations were made and a questionnaire administered during a workshop to establish some of the issues surrounding the secondary adoption of PLCS within the MoD. Novelty can be claimed by the development and application of the checklists, the assessment of XML for use with PLCS, and the questionnaire to assess user attitudes towards the standards. These findings and the novelty of approach are summarised in Table 5.

Limitations

Despite the findings and the novelty of this research, there are some limitations concerning the results. There are standards for virtually all the applications that can be enumerated, and the standards community knows that often, for the same application or function, there may be several applicable standards. There are approximately 175 organizations that are engaged in preparing standards at the international level. ISO and IEC (International Electrotechnical Commission) have contributed 85% of the international standards. A survey conducted by ANSI (American National Standards Institution) found that there are 89,000 standards in the U.S.A., 88,000 in the U.S.S.R., 18,300 in France, 8,800 in Japan, and 6,000 in Canada (Stevens 1993, cited in Deshpande & Nazemetz, 2003a). However, the scope of the author's research is limited to data-exchange standards such as STEP, which give common classifications and definitions of information about products and processes within industry. Therefore, due to the vast number of standards, a broader generalisation is beyond the scope of this research. However, novelty will be claimed from the drawing of parallels between the case study findings, which can be used to develop tools, such as conceptual models, themes and 'adoption checklists', to support the decision-making process.

Table 5. Summary of findings and novelty based on Objective 3

Objective 3				
Approach	**Findings**	**Deliverables**	**Novelty**	**Chapter**
Development of checklists based on the two conceptual models		Innovation- and adopter-centric checklists	The development of innovation- and adopter-centric checklists	Chapter 7
Application of innovation-centric adoption checklist	- Original factors confirmed with more insight. - Adoption of PLCS described as very positive with some concerns		- Use of the innovation-centric checklist. - Predictions about the adoption of PLCS - Insight on how organizations attitudes towards information impacts adoption	Chapter 8
Application of adopter-centric adoption checklist	- Original factors confirmed with more insight. - Primary adoption of PLCS not in question. However some concerns were raised regarding secondary adoption		- Use of the adopter-centric checklists - Predictions about the adoption of PLCS within the MoD	Chapter 9

RECOMMENDATIONS

Objectives four this research deals with the development of recommendations based on the findings of the research. The recommendations have been divided into the areas that they impact. The first outlines recommendations for the ISO/TC184/SC4 sub-committee responsible for the development of ISO data-exchange standards such as PLCS, and the second outlines recommendations for the MoD. Finally there are recommendations for future work.

ISO/TC184/SC4 Recommendations

ISO/TC184/SC4 sub-committee has many strengths. According to the SC4 Chairman, last year alone the sub-committee produced 13% of the total output of ISO standards. In addition, the committees' innovative approach to publishing standards using an HTML module repository garnered recognition and praise from the head of ISO. This research has looked at the factors that impact the adoption of these standards and, as a result, some recommendations based on the findings have emerged which are:

1. Continued development of ISO/TC184/SC4 standards using a combination of the benefits from consortium and ISO standards development processes.

In the research, what emerged was a discussion about the benefit of using both the traditional standards process and consortia to develop a standard. This approach proved fairly successful for ISO 15926-2 and more successful for PLCS, and more authors are calling for this dual approach. Therefore, the gains the committee has made with working with certain consortia such as PDES, inc and PLCS, inc should be nurtured and encouraged for the benefits of this collaborative environment to be realised.

2. Establishment of an implementers' forum that can be used to support implementers during adoption of the standards within organizations.

A number of implementers expressed a view that the standards committee often felt very remote. This then impacts the effectiveness with which they can implement the standards within an organization. Steps should be taken to get an implementers forum up and running. The forum could be run at two levels; firstly they could meet twice a year separate from the development meetings where real discussion and debate about the ongoing use of the standards can be facilitated. Secondly, online forums could be encouraged as well.

3. Strengthening of the Education and Outreach programme, and encouraging the publication of more success stories.

The importance of marketing the standards emerged very strongly in the innovation-centric analysis. Marketing and promoting the standards from a centralised team would help raise the profile of the standards. There is currently an education and outreach programme, however, priority needs to be given to resourcing the outreach program with people and finance.

4. Increasing the emphasis of the importance of implementing and linking the implementation of the standards with mainstream technologies such as XML, UML and future semantic web technologies such as OWL.

The profile of a number of mainstream technologies has increased within the SC4 community, and the importance of these technologies was made explicit in the innovation-centric analysis. These efforts need to be further championed and encouraged in order to exploit the benefits of SC4 standards in mainstream environments. With the increased emphasis on the semantic web, and the increase in the development of ontologies and taxonomies, SC4 has the opportunity to take a lead in the endeavours that are based around industrial data due to its over 20 years experience with the modelling of industrial data to support business processes

5.   Increased use of workflow and other business tools to facilitate greater end-user participation in standards setting.

The involvement of end-users is vital to the development process. However, not all end-users can attend development meetings - particularly SMEs. Therefore, participation can be encouraged through use of technologies and forums where end-user requirements and points of concern can be addressed.

6.   Increased collaboration with universities and research centres to support the development of the standards.

One of the main challenges facing standards like PLCS and ISO 15926-2 is completing all relevant sections of the standard. The delay in the completion of the DEXs and Reference Data is slowing the adoption process of these standards and may result in missed opportunities. One of the reasons for these delays is the voluntary nature with which people give their time to develop the standards. Working with universities and research groups could be an answer to this problem. For example a Masters research student could do some of the legwork involved with developing DEXs with help and support from experts, at a minimal cost.

MoD Recommendations

The MoD Coherence Project has shown that the MoD along with its industry partners are taking steps to successfully implement data-exchange standards that can facilitate information exchange within the MoD and defence supply chain. Analysis of the data in Chapter Six and Nine resulted in the following recommendations:

1.   Clear commitment from top-level management to take on board the recommendations laid out in the Coherence Project report, as was discussed in Chapter 9.
2.   Development of a clear funding directive with regards to who is funding the adoption of systems based on the data-exchange standards.

3.   Actioning and funding of some short-term wins, particularly a live IPT pilot that would keep the momentum gained from the Coherence Project.
4.   Increased use of workshops to facilitate adoption of the standards.

Recommendations for Future Work

This research sought to answer specific questions, but in doing so has created avenues for further research. These are:

1.   To further develop the adoption checklists presented in Chapter Seven to assess how they can be adjusted to meet the needs of specific stakeholders like, for example, software vendors.
2.   Apply the checklists to different IT standards to assess its applicability to a broader range of standards.
3.   Using the finalised models presented in Chapters Five and Six, questionnaires can be developed to establish if the identified factors are valid in a larger population of data-exchange standards.
4.   The findings presented in this research are limited to de-jure data-exchange standards. Therefore, research is required to establish if the findings of the research presented in this book are valid for other types of standards in order to assess if there are some basic ground rules that apply to ALL standards.
5.   Chapter Two gives an overview of Dreveremen's (2005) use of actor analysis to understand the motives, power and actions of various actors in the process industry, and how this impacts the adoption of standards in this industry. Further work can be done to apply actor analysis to the defence industry, to establish the how motives, power and actions of the actors in the defence industry impact the adoption of data-exchange standards within that industry.
6.   Chapter Five gives insight into how the development of standards within the defence community can negatively impact the subsequent adoption of the standards. There was disagreement about whether this sentiment is true. Therefore, further research can be done to establish the impact of the defence community on the standardization process.
7.   One of the major challenges facing ISO data-exchange standards is establishing business cases, as was detailed in Chapters Five and Six. Further research can be done to investigate methods that can be used to establish a business case for the use of data-exchange standards, particularly to establish the intangible benefits of using the standards. Having a more comprehensive business case may encourage some end-users and software vendors to take on the standard.
8.   Chapter Six discussed the involvement of consultants in the standards process, and the possible motivations of some consultants. Further work can be

      done to investigate the impact consultancies, such as LSC Group, have on the standardization process.

9.   Chapter Eight introduced the idea that the adoption of a standard within an organization can be impacted by the organizations attitude towards information. Further research can be done to establish if this correlation is true in a larger population of organisations.

10. Chapter Nine presents some initial investigations into how the terminology used to describe a standard may impact end-user attitudes towards standards. However, further research is required to establish a methodology to better verify and examine the issues surrounding the terminology used to describe a 'standard' and how that may impact on end-user attitudes towards standards.

REFLECTIONS ON RESEARCH METHODOLOGY AND APPROACH

The aim of this research was to establish the factors and barriers critical to the adoption of data-exchange standards such as STEP, and to establish ways to accelerate the adoption of these standards. In order to achieve this aim, an interpretivist research philosophy was adopted, based on a qualitative approach using a case study strategy during the first phase and the action research strategy in phase two, as detailed in Table 4 of Chapter 4. However, though the majority of data collected was qualitative, a quantitative element was included in both phases of the research. Miles and Huberman (1994) discuss at great length the benefits of linking qualitative and quantitative data. This linking of data can be carried out at three levels.

- The first level is called the 'quantizing level', where qualitative information can be either counted directly or converted into ranks or scales.
- The second level deals with linking distinct data types where qualitative information, for example from an interview, is compared to numerical data from a questionnaire filled in by the same person.
- The third level looks at a multimethod approach where researchers combine the collection of qualitative and quantitative data as they progress through their research study. An important aspect of this third level is to establish if the quantitative and qualitative sides are of equal status, are they interactive or separate, and how they will be sequenced (Miles and Huberamn 1994).

      In this research the second level linking was carried out during the first phase. Developers interviewed in the first phase were asked to rank the importance of different factors using a five-point importance scale. The results from this ranking were used to add validity to the factors that were identified as the key factors that impact the adoption of data-exchange standards during innovation-centric analysis.

Third level linking was used in the second phase of this research. At the start of this research, there was no intention to collect quantitative data during phase two. However, in late 2004 it emerged that the LLM POC workshop detailed in Chapter 9, was to take place in early 2005 (see Appendix C-2), and it was noted that this would provide an opportunity for issues identified in phase one of the research to be validated in a wider population using a questionnaire. Some of the issues identified in the workshop questionnaire were further verified in the interviews carried out during Phase two, giving a deeper understanding of some issues. Therefore, in this research, the qualitative and quantitative sides were of equal status, interrelated and sequenced using a qualitative→ quantitative→qualitative approach.

Both qualitative and quantitative research methods have particular strengths and weaknesses (Patton 2002), what this research has shown is that benefit can be derived from a combination of both approaches. This confirms the assertion made by Rossman and Wilson (1991) that, "there is growing acknowledgement that complex social phenomena can usefully be understood by looking at them both quantitatively and qualitatively" (p.315). Therefore, this research also contributes to the empirical research community by providing another example of where a using a combination of qualitative and quantitative approaches can be beneficial. In addition to that, this research has also demonstrated a practical example of using Eisenhardt's (1989a) 'Building theories from case study research' methodology, in Chapter Five and Six. Using this methodology, a series of theme were developed from the qualitative data gathered, and these themes were then critiqued against the existing literature. This methodology proved to be very helpful in analysing large quantities of qualitative data, and offers other researchers in the IS field an opportunity to see a practical application of this methodology.

CONCLUSION

Standards form an integral part of society, and many everyday activities are based around standards. The use of these standards brings benefits, and these benefits are only realised through the effective adoption and use of the standards. In particular, with the boom of technology and the explosion of e-business and Internet communities, IT standards are becoming more predominant and more work is going into the research of IT standards. One research field is focused on the adoption of IT standards. This research presented in this book has contributed to the field of IT standards adoption by grounding the research in two new contexts. The first context is the ISO/TC184/SC4 community, where only two previous items of research have been carried out into the 367 standards published by this committee. Secondly, this research has been grounded in the defence community, about which no peer-reviewed publication has been found in the literature regarding standards adoption. In addition, the dual approach of both an innovation- and adopter-centric combined analysis has offered an approach that limits the bias of each individual approach.

Various stakeholders can also use the three main deliverables of this research in different ways. The 'Adoption Checklists' that were developed are tools that can be used by researchers and IT departments working in the field of product data standards to assess the adoptability of data-exchange standards currently in use, and steps can be taken to facilitate adoptability where concerns may be raised. The checklists can also be used by standards developers to continually assess the state of a standard and its development/ adoption/ diffusion, with the intention of prioritising the areas that need to be addressed. Finally, the conceptual models and themes that were developed offer researchers the opportunity to test and validate these findings using different standards and contexts.

In conclusion, the research presented in this book sought to establish the factors and barriers critical to the adoption of data-exchange standards, and ways to accelerate the adoption of these standards. Using case studies and action research, this research project has successfully met all its objectives, the hope being that the findings presented in this book will result in more effective research, development and adoption of data-exchange standards.

REFRENCES

Deshpande, S., & Nazemetz, J. (2003a). *Global Harmonisation of Standards.* Oklahoma State University School of Industrial Engineering and Management, Computer Assisted Technology Transfer (Catt) Research Program. Oklahoma: Contract Number F34601-95-D-00376.

Dreverman, M. (2005). *Adoption of Product Model Data Standards In the Process Industry.* Eindhoven, The Netherlands: Eindhoven University of Technology.

Miles, M., & Huberman, A. (1994). *Qualitative Data Analysis.* Newbury Park, CA: Sage Publications.

Patton, M. Q. (2002). *Qualitative Evaluation and Research Methods.* Newbury Park, CA: Sage.

Rossman, G., & Wilson, B. (1991). Numbers and Words Revisited: Being 'Shamelessly Eclectic'. *Evaluation Review, 9*(5), 627–643. doi:10.1177/0193841X8500900505

Glossary of Abbreviations

AAM	Application Activity Model
ACM	Association for Computing Machinery
AIC	Application Interpreted Construct
AIM	Application Interpreted Model
AMS	Acquisition Management Systems
ANFOR	Association française de normalisation
ANSI	American National Standards Institute
AP	Application Protocol
ARM	Application Reference Model
BSI	British Standards Institute
CAD	Computer Aided Design
CAM	Computer Aided Manufacturing
CAQDAS	Computer-Assisted Qualitative Data Analysis Software
CAx	Generic term for Design, Engineering and Manufacturing
CDL	Chief of Defence Logistics
CDP	Chief of Defence Procurement
CEFACT	Centre for Trade Facilitation and Electronic Business
CEN	European Committee for Standardization
CENELEC	European Committee for Electrotechnical Standardization
CP	Coherence Project
CRP	Conference Room Pilot
CWE	Collaborative working Environment
DEX	Data EXchange set
DIN	Deutsches Institut für Normung e.V.
DLO	Defence Logistics Organization

DLogInfo	Director of Logistics Information
DoD	Department of Defence
DOI	Diffusion of Innovation
EAI	Enterprise Application Integration
EC	European Community
EDI	Electronic Data Interchange
EDIF	Electronic Design Interchange Format
EDIFACT	United Nations/Electronic Data Interchange For Administration Commerce, and Transport
EPISTLE	European Process Industries STEP Technical Liaison Executive
GDP	Gross Domestic Product
ICT	Information and Communication and Technology
IEC	International Electrotechnical Commission
IEEE	Institute of Electrical and Electronics Engineers
IGES	Initial Graphics Exchange Specification
ILS	Integrated Logistics Support
IPR	Intellectual Property Rights
IPT	Integrated Project Team
IRDS	Information Resource Dictionary System
IS	Information Systems
ISIS	Item of Supply Information System
ISO	International Standards Organization
IT	Information Technology
ITU	International Telecommunication Union
JIT	Just In Time
LLM	Lean Logistics Model
LLM POC	Lean Logistics Model Proof of Concept
MISQ	Management of Information Systems Quarterly
MoD	Ministry of Defence
NATO	North Atlantic Treaty Organization
NCB	NATO Codification Bureau
NCS	NATO Codification System
NIST	National Institute of Standards and Technology
NSN	NATO Stock Number
NSSF	National Standardization Strategic Framework
OASIS	Organization for the Advancement of Structured Information Standards
OEM	Original Equipment Manufacturer
PC	Personal Computer

PDM	Product Data Management
PLCS	Product Life Cycle Support
POC	Proof of Concept
RAMP	Rapid Acquisition of Manufactured Parts
ROI	Return on Investment
SC	Sub-Committee
SCRA	South Carolina Research Authority
SDAI	Standard Data Access Interface
SDO	Standards Development Organization
SET	Standard D'Exchange et de Transfert
SGML	Standard Generalized Markup Language
SME	Small to Medium Enterprise
SSE	Support Solutions Envelope
STEP	Standard for the Exchange of Product model data
TAM	Technology Acceptance Model
TC	Technical Committee
UK	United Kingdom
NCB	National Codification Bureau
UML	Unified Modeling Language
UN	United Nations
US	United States
USPI-NL	Uitgebreid Samenwerkingsverband Procesindustrie, Nederland
UTAUT	Unified Theory of Acceptance and Use of Technology
VDA-FS	Verband Der Automobilindustrie-Flachen-Schnittstella
W3C	World Wide Web Consortium
XML	Extensible Markup Language

Appendix A:
An Overview of Early Product Data–Exchange Standards

1. **IGES - Initial Graphics Exchange Specification:** IGES is the most widely used format for CAx data exchange and was developed by the IGES organization, which consisted of representatives of the CAD vendor and user communities. The development of IGES can be traced back to 1979, and several versions have been published since publication of the first draft in 1980. Most major CAD/CAM systems support IGES, and IGES has been accepted in many major companies and projects. However, over the years the shortcoming of IGES have emerged, and include issues such as large file sizes and processing times, and the lack of a rigorous technical architecture. Nonetheless, IGES provided a practical first solution for CAD data exchange. (Zhang and Warren 2003; Kemmerer 1999)

2. **SET - Standard d'Echange et de Transfert:** The French Standard d'Echange et de Transfert (SET) was a French effort to create a standard to exchange CAD data. The project was started at Aerospatiale in 1983, and initially they did a formal test of IGES. From this test, Aerospatiale concluded that it was the *IGES specification* that did not work. The result was a French effort to write a specification, standardize it, implement it, test it, and support its use in production. These efforts were driven by French industry, most notably the automotive and aerospace industries. SET, like IGES in the U.S. A., became a French national standard, and Association GOSET is an organization established by industry and government in France to support continued development, maintenance, and implementation testing of SET. GOSET representatives are also active

contributors to developing STEP and testing services to conformance test ISO 10303. (Zhang and Warren 2003; Kemmerer 1999)

3. **VDA-FS - Flachenschnittstelle des Verbandes der deutschen Automobil-industrie:** The Germans standardized Flachenschnittstelle des Verbandes der deutschen Automobilindustrie (VDA-FS) in response to the data-exchange requirements of their automobile industry in the 1980's. VDA-FS was based on IGES but offered a competing exchange file format to that of IGES. VDA is the German automotive industry trade association, and was the principle developer of the VDA-FS standard. The VDA was created in 1982 to increase the efficiency of the design process and usefulness of CAD/CAM systems. The Germans brought VDA-FS to the international table to contribute toward the international product model data standardization effort, and the Germans are now also directing their data exchange standards development efforts to STEP. (Zhang and Warren 2003; Kemmerer 1999)

4. **CAD*I - CAD Interfaces:** CAD*I standard emerged as a result of a European Commission funded ESPRIT project called CAD Interfaces (CAD*I), with twelve participating organizations from six European countries. The project began in 1984, and worked mainly in product model data exchange and on data exchange for finite element analysis. Kemmerer (1999) explains that as in STEP, the transfer of data was based on the use of schemas defined formally using a data modeling language. In 1987, the project achieved the first ever transfer of boundary-representation solid models between different CAD systems. CAD*I participants were involved in the development of STEP from the beginning of the work of ISO TC184/SC4, and much of the shape modeling capability of STEP is based on CAD*I work and the project also had a significant influence on STEP developments in the finite element area (Kemmerer 1999).

REFERENCES

Kemmerer, S. (1999). *STEP: The Grand Experience.* Gaithersburg, MD: National Institute of Standards and Technology.

Zhang, J., & Warren, T. (2003). *SMEs and STEP.* School of Industrial Engineering and Management: Computer Assisted Technology Transfer (Catt) Research Program, Contract Number F34601-95-D-00376 . Oklahoma State University.

Appendix B

APPENDIX B-1
Second-Tier Research Questions

The main research questions were:

- What are the factors and barriers critical to the adoption and diffusion of data-exchange standards across their target population?
- What can be done to facilitate and accelerate the adoption of data-exchange standards across their targeted population?

These questions laid the groundwork for the development of the conceptual frameworks/models. The formulation of the second-tier research questions emerges from the conceptual frameworks/models. These questions make theoretical assumptions more explicit and can inform a researcher about what they want to know most or first. These second-tier research questions can also point towards data gathering devices and can feed directly into data collection (Miles & Huberman 1994, pp. 22). For example, in this research, the second-tier questions acted as a starting point for the interview agenda questions.

The second-tier questions based on the innovation-centric model included:

- What impact do the motivations for development of a standard have on the adoption and diffusion of a standard?
- What impact does the nature of the development process have on the adoption and diffusion of a standard?
- What impact does the diversity and balance of development participant have

on the adoption and diffusion of a standard?

- What impact does involvement of tool providers (software vendors) during the development process have on the adoption and diffusion of a standard?
- What impact do revisions and the time taken for the approval and publication process have on the adoption and diffusion of a standard?
- What impact do the costs, benefits and level of support have on the adoption and diffusion of a standard?
- How is the ROI of a standard established?
- What impact does carrying out a ROI analysis on a standard have on the adoption and diffusion of a standard?
- What are the barriers to the adoption and diffusion of a standard?
- What impact do standardization issues have on the adoption and diffusion of a standard?
- What impact do the standards characteristics have on the adoption and diffusion of a standard?
- What impact do the characteristics of the adopting community/organizations have on the adoption and diffusion of a standard?

The second-tier questions based on the adopter-centric model included:

- What impact does an organizations characteristics have on the decision to adopt a standard within an organization?
- What impact does a standards characteristics have on the decision to adopt a standard within an organization?
- What impact do environmental characteristics have on the decision to adopt a standard within an organization?
- What is the decision criterion for adopting a standard within an organization?
- Who was the final decision maker?
- What impact does pre or post implementation investment appraisal (ROI analysis) have on the decision to adopt a standard within an organization?
- What are the outcomes of the decision on whether to adopt the standard or not?

Reference

Miles, M., & Huberman, A. (1994). *Qualitative Data Analysis.* Newbury Park, CA: Sage Publications.

APPENDIX B-2

Phase One Interview Agenda

This interview is divided into 5 sections based loosely on the lifecycle of a standard. The interview aims to address the following:

- The factors that influence the development of standards
- The factors that affect the adoption and diffusion of standards
- The factors that affect the adoption of a standard from an organizational decision making perspective.

Name:

Organization: _____

Position: _____

Email: _____

DEF STAN 00-60		NATO Codification System		ISO 15926		ISO 10303 -224	

Sections

Section A – Background

Section B – Conception and Development

Section C – Adoption and Diffusion

Section D – Organizational adoption and implementation

Section E – Tool Provider Involvement

Section A: Background

A.1 Which of these titles best describes you or your organizations' involvement with the standard?

Standard developer Section B & C	Adopter / User of the standard (Customer) Section D	Implementer Section D (Possibly E)	Tool Provider Section E (Possibly D)
Other:			

A.2 Which stage of the standardization process best describes the current status of the standard? Conception, Proposal, Drafting, Approval, Publication, Implementation and use

A.3 At what stage in the standardization process did you or your organization start to involve with the standard?
-   Why at that time?
-   How was that decision reached? Probe- any cost/benefit analysis done

Section B: Conception and Development

B.1 Who would you say were the main individual(s) or organization(s) that initiated the idea for the development of the standard?
-   What is their role in relation to the standard? (Probe - Owner, potential user, funder, tool provider)
-   Probe impact on development (IMPACT – positive, negative, both or none at all.)

B.2 What were the main drivers/motivations behind the development of the standard? (Probe – market driven, government driven)
-   Probe impact on development

B.3 What is/was the makeup of the development participants? (SDO's, the adopter and user community/organizations, government, tool providers (certification and accreditation bodies, software vendor, trainers), consultants, researchers, etc)
-   Do you perceive a balance of participation by the stakeholder groups affected by the standard?
-   Probe impact on development

B.4   Is there a formal or informal alliance between the development
participants?
-   Probe impact on development

B.5   What type of development process was followed? (Structured or
unstructured)
-   Probe impact on development

B.6   How long has the development process from conception to
publication taken or expected to take?
-   Were/have there been any hindrances or barriers to the
development of the standard? (Delays, competing standards)
-   If yes, why and how were these overcome?

B.7   Was the standard developed from any existing standards? If Yes,
Please state what they are.
-   Probe impact on development

B.8   Have there been any reviews or revisions of the standard? If yes,
when and why?
-   Probe impact on development

B.9   What are the main funding sources for this standard?
-   Probe impact on development

B.10   What were the main costs of developing the standard? Were there any
unexpected costs?

B.11   What are the expected benefits of the standard?
-   Have these been established or evaluated or established in
any form of Investment appraisal techniques?
-   If yes, How? (e.g, ROI, CBA, TCO)
-   If no, why not. (Probe – would you like to have some sort of
indication in the future, would you do it in the future)

B.12   Were any tools required for the development and/or implementation
of the standard? If Yes, what were they? (e.g certification, software,
training)

B.13   Were you or your organization involved in development of any specific tools for the standard? (If No, go to B.17 if yes, continue below)
- What were they and what were your considerations for going into the development of tools for this standard?
- What trade-offs were involved? (costs/benefits)

B.14   Have any activities been carried to encourage/support uptake of the standard?
- If yes, what are they? (promotion and awareness, Information and communication channels, pilots or demonstrations)
- Do you think this has been beneficial to the adoption and diffusion of the standard?
- Have they been beneficial to any adopting organizations?
- Do you think it is worth investing time and money to ensure the development and adoption of the standard

B.15   Has there been any form of support from other parties during the development and adoption of the standard? (e.g Government, NSB) How?
- Probe impact on development

B.16   Did the development of the standard meet your expectations?

B.17   What in your opinion are the main barriers to the development of a standard?

B.18   What in your opinion are the main factors that facilitate the development of a standard?

Section C: Adoption and Diffusion (Rate of Uptake)

This section seeks to determine the impact (positive, negative, both or none at all) of the following factors on the effective adoption and diffusion of the standard, and the relative importance of these different factors. The importance will be determined by using a five-point Importance scale. (Hand importance scale sheet to the interviewee).

Very Important	Quite Important	Fairly Important	Slightly Important	Not Important at all
1	2	3	4	5

C.1 Has there ever been any concern that there might not be uptake or adoption of the standard? If no, why?

- If yes, what were your concerns and how were they overcome/ avoided?

C.2 Have there been any hindrances to the successful uptake of the standard?

- If yes, what were they and how were they overcome?
- Could more have been done to overcome them

C.3 What impact do the following factors have on the adoption and diffusion of a standard, and how important do you think the following factors are in impacting the adoption and diffusion of the standard?

3.1   Role(s) of the initiator(s) of the development of the standard

3.2   Drivers for development of the standard

3.3   Type of development process

3.4   Revisions

3.5   Funding Agreements

3.6   Costs

3.7   Time taken for the development of the standard

3.8   Stakeholder participation (balance and diversity)

3.9   Type of alliance

3.10 Involvement of tool providers / vendors

3.11 Focus of the standard

3.12 Brand identification

3.14 Pilots or demonstrations

3.15 Promotion and awareness e.g launch days, seminars, workshops

3.16 Information and Communication Channels

3.17 Support – e.g govt or NSB's

3.18 Pre or Post investment appraisal (ROI, CBA, TCO Business case, real world examples)

3.19 Intellectual property agreements

C.4 How important do you think the following standard characteristics factors are in impacting the adoption and diffusion of the standard?

4.1   Relative advantage

4.2   Compatibility

4.3   Complexity

4.4   Stability

4.5   Developed from any existing standards

C.5 Were any specific technologies used to develop or implement the standard?

- Did any characteristics of these technologies impact the adoption and diffusion of the standard?
- How important were these characteristics in facilitating the adoption and diffusion of the standard?

Compatibility
Security
Scalability
Reliability
Maturity
A standard in its own right

C.6 Did any characteristics of the adopting community/organization impact the adoption and diffusion of the standard?
- How important were these characteristics of the adopting community/organization in facilitating the adoption and diffusion of the standard?
Size and type
Community / Organizational culture

C.7 How would you best describe the current adoption and rate of uptake (diffusion) of this standard as a whole? *(very good, good, fair, poor, very poor)* Why?

C.8 What in your opinion are the main barriers to the adoption and diffusion of standards?

C.9 What in your opinion are the most important factor(s) in the adoption and diffusion of standards?

C.10 Do you have any other general perspectives or comments on the effective adoption, diffusion and evaluation of [Military] [ISO] standards?

Section D: Organizational Adoption and Implementation

D.1 Have you or your organization been involved in the implementation of this standard within an organization? Which organization?
- What was your role?
- Why did you or your organization get involved?
  OR
Have you been involved with implementing the standard within your own organization?

D.2 Who initiated the idea to adopt the standard within the organization?

D.3 What were the motivations or drivers for adopting the standard?
- Probe impact on adoption decision

D.4 Were there any other external pressures or drivers for adopting the standard?
- What were they?
- Probe impact on adoption decision

D.5   What was the size and type of organization?
- Probe impact on adoption decision

D.6   Was the organization involved in the conception or development of the standard?
- Probe impact on adoption decision

D.7   Did the organization have a history or record of adopting standards?
- Probe impact on adoption decision

D.8   Which of these adopter terminologies do you think best describes the organizations attitude towards adopting this standard? (Innovator, early adopter, early majority, late majority, laggard) Why?
- Is this indicative of the organizations general culture towards adopting standards?
- Probe impact on adoption decision

D.9   Was there availability of resources to implement the standard? (Skills, support, training)
- Probe impact on adoption decision

D.10   Did the organization have standards with similar functions already implemented and being used? (installed base, sunk costs)
- Probe impact on adoption decision

D.11   Were any other competing standards considered during the adoption decision-making process?
- If yes, why was this standard in adopted in preference to any competing standard?

D.12   What were the main costs associated with the adoption of the standard? (Implementation costs-hardware, software, maintenance costs, Consultancy fees, Employee training, Organizational restructuring, Standard body membership fees..e.t.c)
- Were they expected, or were there hidden costs?
- Would prior knowledge of these costs have helped/hindered the adoption process in the organization

D.13 What were the benefits associated with the standard? (Improved business operations, development of new material and future sales, cost optimisation, influence on regional and international bodies, safety, increased commercial viability, legal compliance, improved data exchange...e.t.c)
- What were the most important benefits?
- Were they realised in the expected time frame.
- Did the benefits outweigh the costs?

D.14 Was any pre or post-implementation evaluation carried out?
- If yes, how was this carried out? (e.g ROI, CBA, TCO)
- If no, would this have helped the adoption process

D.15 Were there any barriers to the adoption of the standard within the organization? If no, why?
- If Yes, what were the barriers to the adoption of the standard within the organization? (Resistance to change, cultural issues, organizational politics, resource scarcity, user buy-in, difficulty in identifying costs and benefits, poor planning, reliability of the technology, security concerns, loss of intellectual property.)
- What were the most significant barriers
- How were these barriers overcome? (Securing support, conducting a value assessment e.g. business case, pilot project, joining standard development committees, training e.t.c)

D.16 Were any pilots or demonstrations carried out during the adoption and implementation phase?
- Probe impact on adoption decision

D.17 Was there a point person or project manager who championed the adoption of the standard within the organization?
- Probe impact on adoption decision

D.18 Were any of these characteristics of the standard an important factor in the adoption decision-making process within the organization? (Maturity, relative advantage, compatibility, complexity, trialability, observability, characteristics of the related technology - recommendation of the standard, security, scalability, reliability, maintainability, maturity, flexibility)

D.19 Was the current level of adoption and diffusion within the stakeholder community taken into account (Network effects)?
  - Probe impact on adoption decision

D.20 Was support for the standard available? (Sponsorship/funding, promotion and awareness, software, information channels & communication, other resources)
  - Probe impact on adoption decision

D.21 Who was the final decision maker(s) with regards to adopting the standard?
  - Are you aware of what the decision criteria was? Strategic, financial, technical, policy.

D.22 Is the standard still being actively used in the organization as specified/ agreed?
  - Is it regarded as being a success? How (cost savings, wider potential market, improved technological image, e.t.c...)

D.23 What in your opinion are the most important barriers to the decision to adopt a standard within an organization?

D.24 What in your opinion are the most important factor(s) in the decision to adopt a standard within an organization?

D.25 Do you have any other general perspectives or comments on the effective adoption, implementation and evaluation of standards within an organization?

D.26 Were you or your organization involved in the development of any tools/software fro the standard?
If yes, include section E

Section E: Tool Provider Involvement

E.1 What stage in the standardization process did you decide to get involved in the development of tools for the standard?
  - Why did you get involved at that time?

E.2 What were your considerations for going into the development of tools for this standard?
  - Was this established in any formal Investment appraisal? How?

E.3   Were there any challenges in being involved with the development of tools for the standard?
-   What were they and how were they overcome?

E.4   Were there any benefits in being involved in the development of tools for the standard?
-   Were they expected?

E.5   What were the main costs in being involved in the development of tools for the standard?

E.6   Are you or your organization committed to the continued uptake of the standard? Why

E.7   Do you believe there will be successful adoption and diffusion of the standard across its targeted stakeholder group? Why?

E.8   Do you have any concerns that there may not be uptake of the standard? Why?

E.9   What in your opinion are the main barriers to the effective adoption and diffusion of standards?

E.10   What in your opinion are the most important factor(s) in the effective adoption and diffusion of standards?

E.11   Have you or your organization been involved in the implementation of the standard within an organisation?
If yes see section D

Do you have any final comments or questions?

Thank you for your time.

END OF INTERVIEW

APPENDIX B-3

Phase Two Interview Agenda

Building on the results of the first case studies, this interview aims to identify the following:

- The factors that impact the adoption and diffusion of PLCS
- The factors that affect the adoption of PLCS within an organisation
- The factors that impact the general adoption of STEP (ISO 10303)

This interview is divided into 5 sections based on the roles of the interviewees.

Sections

Section A – Background

Section B – Developer questions

Section C – Software vendor questions

Section D – Implementer questions

Section E – End-user questions

Section A: Background

A.1   **Name:**

   Organization:

   Position:

   Email:

A.2 Which of these titles best describes you or your organizations' involvement with the standard?

Standard developer

Section B

Software Vendor

Section C

Implementer
(Involved in implementing the standard within an organisation)

Section D

End-User

Section E

A.3 If you have more than one role which would you say is your main role? *(Go to relevant section first, and do no more than two sections for each interviewee)*

Section B: Developer Questions

Development initiators and drivers

B.1 When did development of PLCS begin?

B.2   Who would you say were the main individual(s) or organization(s) that initiated the idea for the development of PLCS?
- Did they have a history of involvement in the STEP community
- What is their role in relation to the standard? (Probe - Owner, potential user, funder, software vendor)
- *Did this have an impact on the adoption of PLCS? If yes, is it positive, negative or both. Why?*

B.3   What were the main drivers/motivations behind the development of PLCS? - *Probe impact on adoption*

Development process

B.4   Which stage of the ISO development process best describes the current status of PLCS? (Proposal; preparatory; committee; enquiry; approval; publication, review, or implementation and use)

B.5   How long has the development process from conception to publication taken or expected to take?
- Had work been done on PLCS before it became part of the ISO process?
- Was the standard developed from any existing standards? If Yes, Please state what they are.
- Were there any delays in the development of PLCS?
- If yes, what caused these delays and how were they overcome
- *Probe impact on adoption*

B.6   Was there a high degree of learning during the early stages of development? If yes, what were the main learning areas?

B.7   Have there been any reviews or revisions of PLCS? If yes, when and why? - *Probe impact on adoption*

B.8   What were the main funding sources for the development of PLCS?
- Was the funding consistent
- *Probe impact on adoption*

Dynamics of the development team

B.9   What is/was the makeup of the development participants? (the adopter and user community/organizations, government, tool providers (certification and accreditation bodies, software vendor, trainers, consultants, researchers, etc)
- Did you perceive a balance of participation by the stakeholder groups affected by PLCS?
- Did you perceive a balance between academics and strategic business owners?
- Was there a full time dedicated developers or were they part time?
- Was attendance consistent?
- Was there a clear lead of the development teams?
- Was there a final decision maker? Who?
- In your view, was there any dominant stakeholder group?
- *Probe impact on adoption*

B.10   Were Small to Medium Enterprises involved in the development of PLCS? - *Probe impact on adoption*
- If yes, how did you engage the SME's?
- If no, why not?

B.11   Were software vendors involved in the development process? - *Probe impact on adoption*

B.12   Were subscription fees paid by the different stakeholder groups involved in the development of PLCS? If yes, were equal fees paid? - *Probe impact on adoption*

B.13   Were there any Intellectual Property Agreements? - *Probe impact on adoption*

Standard characteristics

B.14   Does PLCS have any competing standards?
- If yes, has PLCS got clear advantages over its competing standards?
- Has this been proven?
- *Probe impact on adoption*

B.15   Do you have an understanding of the ARM, AIM and MIM structure of PLCS? - *Probe impact on adoption*

B.16   Have you done any PLCS mapping? - *Probe impact on adoption*

B.17   Has the reference data library for PLCS been developed? - *Probe impact on adoption*

B.18   Some implementers and end-users of STEP think application protocols like PLCS are complex. Do you agree or disagree with this view? Why? - *Probe impact on adoption*

B.19   Are you aware of the cost of purchasing PLCS from ISO? - *Probe impact on adoption*

B.20   What are the expected benefits of PLCS?
-     Have these been established or evaluated or captured in any form of Investment appraisal techniques?
-     If yes, How? (e.g, ROI, CBA, TCO)
-     If no, why not?
-     *Probe impact on adoption*

B.22   Are you aware what the main implementing technologies of PLCS are?
-     Do you think the use of EXPRESS has an impact on the adoption of STEP application protocols like PLCS?
-     Do you think the use of Part 28 (XML) has an impact on the adoption of STEP application protocols like PLCS?
-     What technology characteristics are important to encourage adoption of standards like PLCS? (Security, scalability, reliability, maintainability, maturity, flexibility)

B.23   Are there software tools available to implement PLCS? - *Probe impact on adoption*

Communication Channels and Marketing

B.24   Have any activities been carried to encourage uptake of PLCS?
- If yes, what are they? (e.g. Launch days, pilots or demonstrations)
- Do you think this has been beneficial to the adoption and diffusion of PLCS?
- Have they been beneficial to any adopting organizations?

B.25   IS there a website devoted to the development and progress of PLCS?
- Probe impact on adoption

B.26   Do you think it is worth investing time and money in these activities to ensure the development and adoption of PLCS?

STEP community

B.27   Do you think there politics within the STEP community? *- Probe impact on adoption*

B.28   How is STEP marketed? *- Probe impact on adoption*

B.29   Is there an impartial body able to test and verify whether software vendor's products are compliant with STEP? *- Probe impact on adoption*
- If no, do you think this would be of benefit?

B.30   How does the STEP community keep up with new and emerging technologies? *- Probe impact on adoption*

B.31   Are there any success stories on the general adoption of STEP?
- If yes, how can these stories be accessed?
- *Probe impact on adoption*

ISO

B.32   Do you think the brand identification of ISO standards has an impact on adoption?

B.33   Do you think end-user perceptions of ISO have had an impact on adoption PLCS?

B.34   Do you think there is bureaucracy within the ISO? - *Probe impact on adoption*

General

B.35   Has there ever been any concern that there might not be uptake or adoption of PLCS? If no, why?
-   If yes, what were your concerns and how were they overcome/ avoided?

B.36   Have there been any hindrances or barriers to the successful uptake of PLCS?
-   If yes, what were they and how were they overcome?

B.37   What in your opinion are the main barriers to the uptake of STEP?

B.38   What in your opinion are the main factors that facilitate the uptake STEP?

B.39   Do you have any other general perspectives or comments on the effective adoption, diffusion and evaluation of STEP?

Section C: Software Vendor Questions

C.1   At what stage in the ISO standardization process did you decide to get involved in the development of tools for PLCS?
- Why did you get involved at that time?

C.2   What were your considerations for going into the development of tools for this standard?
-   Was this established in any formal Investment appraisal? How?

C.3   Is there an impartial body able to test and verify whether your products are compliant with STEP? - *Probe impact on adoption*
-   If no, do you think this would be of benefit?

C.4 Some implementers and end-users of STEP think application protocols like PLCS are complex. Do you agree or disagree with this view? Why? - *Probe impact on adoption*

C.5 What are the main implementing technologies of PLCS?
- Do you think the use of EXPRESS has an impact on the adoption of STEP application protocols like PLCS?
- Do you think the use of Part 28 (XML) has an impact on the adoption of STEP application protocols like PLCS?
- What technology characteristics are important to encourage adoption of standards like PLCS? (Security, scalability, reliability, maintainability, maturity, flexibility)

C.6 Were there any challenges in being involved with the development of tools for PLCS?
- What were they and how were they overcome?

C.7 Were there any benefits in being involved in the development of tools for PLCS?
- Have these benefits been verified?

C.8 Are you or your organization committed to the continued uptake of PLCS?

C.9 Do you believe there will be successful adoption and diffusion of PLCS across its targeted stakeholder group? Why?

C.10 Has there ever been any concern that there might not be uptake or adoption of PLCS? If no, why?
- If yes, what were your concerns and how were they overcome/ avoided?

C.11 Have there been any hindrances or barriers to the successful uptake of PLCS?
- If yes, what were they and how were they overcome?

C.12 What in your opinion are the main barriers to the uptake of STEP?

C.13   What in your opinion are the main factors that facilitate the uptake STEP?

C.14   Do you have any other general perspectives or comments on the effective adoption, diffusion and evaluation of STEP?

Section D: Implementer Questions

These questions relate to the adoption of PLCS within an organisation.

D.1   Have you or your organization been involved in the implementation of this standard within an organization? Which organization?
-   Why did you or your organization get involved?
OR
Have you been involved with implementing the standard within your own organization?

D.2   Who initiated the idea to adopt PLCS within the organization? - *Probe impact on adoption*

D.3   What are the motivations or drivers for adopting PLCS within the organisation?
-   Do you think the need to use standards for data integration is generally understood throughout your organisation? - *Probe impact on adoption*

D.4   IS there any external pressures or drivers for adopting PLCS? What are they? - *Probe impact on adoption*

D.5   Were you or your organization involved in the conception or development of PLCS? - *Probe impact on adoption*

D.6   Does the organization have a history or record of adopting STEP standards? - *Probe impact on adoption*

D.7   Is there an availability of resources to implement PLCS? (Skills, support, training) - *Probe impact on adoption*

D.8   Does the organization have standards with similar functions already implemented and being used? - *Probe impact on adoption*

D.9   Were any other competing standards considered during the adoption decision-making process?
- If yes, why was PLCS adopted in preference to other competing standard?

D.10   What were/are the main costs associated with the adoption of PLCS? (Implementation costs-hardware, software, maintenance costs, Consultancy fees, Employee training, Organizational restructuring, Standard body membership fees..e.t.c)
- Were they expected, or were there hidden costs?
- Would prior knowledge of these costs have helped/hindered the adoption process in the organization

D.11   What are the benefits associated with PLCS?
- Has a value assessment of any sort been carried out?
- If yes, how was this carried out? (e.g ROI, CBA, TCO, business case)
- If no, would this have helped the adoption process

D.12   Are any pilots or demonstrations carried out within the organisation? - *Probe impact on adoption*

D.13   Is PLCS being marketed within the organisation?
- If yes, how is it being done?
- Has the standard been marketed at all levels? - *Probe impact on adoption*

D.14   Is there a point person or project manager championing the adoption of PLCS within the organization? - *Probe impact on adoption*

D.15   Are you aware of the current level of adoption of PLCS across its stakeholder community been taken into account?
- Has this had an impact on the adoption decision within this organisation?

D.16   Is there support from the wider STEP community during the adoption of PLCS within this organisation?

D.17   Who is the final decision maker(s) with regards to adopting the standard?
- Are you aware of what the decision criteria was? Strategic, financial, technical, policy.

D.18   Are there any barriers to the adoption of PLCS within the organization? If no, why?
- If yes, have any of the following barriers emerged within this organisation?

(Resistance to change, "not invented here syndrome", end-user attitudes towards STEP and ISO standards in general, Initiative overload, funding for change, organizational politics, resource scarcity, difficulty in identifying costs and benefits, poor planning of the project, reliability of the implementing technologies, security concerns, industry dictating what the MoD do, identifying the business processes that are impacted by the standard based system)
- Are there any other barriers?
- What are the main barriers?
- Have any barriers been overcome? If yes, how?

D.19   What in your opinion are the main factors that could facilitate the uptake of a standard like PLCS within the organisation?

D.20   Do you have any other general perspectives or comments on the effective adoption, diffusion and evaluation of standards like STEP?

Section E: End-User Questions

These questions relate to the adoption of PLCS within an organisation.

E.1   How did you hear about PLCS?

E.2   Have you had previous exposure to PLCS? When and How?

E.3   Some implementers and end-users of STEP think application protocols like PLCS are difficult. Do you agree or disagree with this view? Why?

E.4   Are you aware of the benefits of PLCS?
-   Is it important for you to see the benefits quantified in a compelling business case?

E.5   Do you think there is a need for standards like PLCS in your work area?

E.6   Do you think there is a need for standards like PLCS in your organisation as a whole?

E.7   Do you think the need to use standards for data integration is generally understood throughout your organisation?

E.8   Do you think standards like PLCS should be mandated? Why?

E.9   Have you had to use other ISO standards? – *Probe impact on adoption and use*

E.10   Have you been to any pilots and demonstrations? Were they of any benefit?

E.11   Which is more important to you, understanding the standard, or having a system that works? Why?

E.12   Are there any barriers to the adoption of PLCS within your organization? If no, why?
-   If yes, have any of the following barriers emerged within this organisation?

    (Resistance to change, "not invented here syndrome", end-user attitudes towards STEP and ISO standards in general, Initiative overload, funding for change, organizational politics, resource scarcity, difficulty in identifying costs and benefits, poor planning of the project, reliability of the implementing technologies, security concerns, industry dictating what the MoD do, identifying the business processes that are impacted by the standard based system)
-   Are there any other barriers?
-   What are the main barriers?
-   Are you aware if any barriers have been overcome? If yes, how?

E.13 What in your opinion are the main factors that could facilitate the uptake of a standard like PLCS within the organisation?

E.14 Do you have any other general perspectives or comments on the effective adoption, diffusion and evaluation of standards like STEP?

Do you have any final comments or questions?

Thank you for your time.

END OF INTERVIEW

APPENDIX B-4
Letter Sent To Research Interviewees

Dear [name],

My name is Josephine Wapakabulo, and I am a PhD student from Loughborough University currently based at LSC Group in Tamworth, working alongside Dr. Tim King and his STEP/PLCS team. I have been carrying out research into the development of standards such as PLCS, and am now undertaking a series of case studies to further my research into the adoption, diffusion and evaluation of ISO data-exchange standards and military standards.

Ultimately, by means of this case study approach, I hope to identify and document answers to questions such as: What are the motivations or drivers behind the development of these standards? Who are the stakeholders involved in the development and adoption of these standards, what form of alliances do they have, and why did they come on board? What are the factors that influence the rate of adoption (uptake) of these standard? What are the main costs, benefits and barriers associated with the development and adoption of these standard? What tools are used to support the adoption and implementation of these standards? What methods are used to evaluate the return of investment of these standard? and, is it worth investing time and money into the development of a standard to guarantee adoption?

On the advice of Tim, you have been identified as someone who would be able to offer insight into this research area, specifically with regards to [ISO15926 / NCS / DEFSTAN 0060 / ISO 10303-224 / PLCS]. This email is therefore being sent to you to request your time, experience and patience for an approximately 1-hour interview at a time and place that is amenable with your schedule between [date] and [date]. In addition, I would like to tape record the interview only to facilitate transcription in the interest of research analysis. I will be interviewing about five different experts for each of four different standards and complete anonymity as regards to sources of information will be upheld. Once I have compiled the results, I will send you a summary of the complete research findings.

Thank you for your time, and I look forward to your response.

Kind Regards,
Josephine Wapakabulo Thomas

APPENDIX B-5
Research Code List

Original list of codes based on the conceptual models:

Code Description	Code
BACKGROUND	BG
BG.Interviwee role	BG.INTROLE
BG.standard current status	BG.STACURSTA
BG.interviewee involvement motivation	BG.INTINVOL.MOT
BG.interviewee involvement evaluation	BG.INTINVOL.EVA
BG.standards current status	BG.STACURSTA
CONCEPTION	CON
CON.initiators	CON.INI
CON.initiators role	CON.INI.ROLE
CON.initiators role impact (development) +	CON.INI.ROLE.IMPDEV+
CON.initiators role impact (development) -	CON.INI.ROLE.IMPDEV-
CON.initiators role impact (adoption) +	CON.INI.ROLE.IMPADP+
CON.initiators role impact (adoption) -	CON.INI.ROLE.IMPADP-
DEVELOPMENT	DEV

DEV.motivations	DEV.MOT
DEV.motivations impact (development)+	DEV.MOT.IMPDEV+
DEV.motivations impact (development)-	DEV.MOT.IMPDEV-
DEV.motivations impact (adoption)+	DEV.MOT.IMPADP+
DEV.motivations impact (adoption)-	DEV.MOT.IMPADP-
DEV.participants	DEV.PART
DEV.participants motivations	DEV.PART.MOT
DEV.participants balance	DEV.PART.BAL
DEV.participants balance impact (development)+	DEV.PART.BAL.IMPDEV+
DEV.participants balance impact (development)-	DEV.PART.BAL.IMPDEV-
DEV.participants balance impact (adoption)+	DEV.PART.BAL.IMPADP+
DEV.participants balance impact (adoption)-	DEV.PART.BAL.IMPADP-
DEV.alliance type	DEV.ALITYPE
DEV.alliance type impact (development)+	DEV.ALITYPE.IMPDEV+
DEV.alliance type impact (development)-	DEV.ALITYPE.IMPDEV-
DEV.alliance type impact (adoption)+	DEV.ALITYPE.IMPADP+
DEV.alliance type impact (adoption)-	DEV.ALITYPE.IMPADP-
DEV.process type	DEV.PRO.TYPE
DEV.process type impact (development)+	DEV.PRO.TYPE.IMPDEV+
DEV.process type impact (development)-	DEV.PRO.TYPE.IMPDEV-
DEV.process type impact (adoption)+	DEV.PRO.TYPE.IMPADP+
DEV.process type impact (adoption)-	DEV.PRO.TYPE.IMPADP-
DEV.process timescale	DEV.PRO.TIMESC
DEV.process timescale impact (adoption)+	DEV.PRO.TIMESE.ADP+
DEV.process timescale impact (adoption)-	DEV.PRO.TIMESE.ADP-
DEV.process barriers	DEV.PRO.BARR
DEV.process overcoming barriers	DEV.PRO.OVERBAR
DEV.existing standards	DEV.EXSTAN
DEV.existing standards impact (development)+	DEV.EXSTAN.IMPDEV+
DEV.existing standards impact (development)-	DEV.EXSTAN.IMPDEV-
DEV.existing standards impact (adoption)+	DEV.EXSTAN.IMPADP+
DEV.existing standards impact (adoption)-	DEV.EXSTAN.IMPADP-
DEV.costs	DEV.COSTS
DEV.costs expected	DEV.COSTS.EXP
DEV.costs unexpected	DEV.COSTS.UNEXP
DEV.costs impact (adoption)+	DEV.COSTS.IMPADP+
DEV.costs impact (adoption)-	DEV.COSTS.IMPADP-
DEV.expectations	DEV.EXPEC

DEV.facilitators	DEV.FACIL
DEV.intellectual property rights	DEV.IPR
REVISIONS	REVS
REVS.impact (development)+	REVS.IMPDEV+
REVS.impact (development)-	REVS.IMPDEV-
REVS.impact (adoption)+	REVS.IMPADP+
REVS.impact (adoption)-	REVS.IMPADP-
FUNDING SOURCE	FUNDSOR
FUNDSOR.impact (development)+	FUNDSOR.IMPDEV+
FUNDSOR.impact (development)-	FUNDSOR.IMPDEV-
FUNDSOR.impact (adoption)+	FUNDSOR.IMPADP+
FUNDSOR.impact (adoption)-	FUNDSOR.IMPADP-
BENEFITS	BENE
Benefits expected	BENE.EXP
Benefits tangible	BENE.TAN
Benefits intangible	BENE.INTAN
RETURN ON INVESTEMENT	ROI
ROI approach	ROI.APP
ROI impact (adoption)+	ROI.IMPADP+
ROI impact (adoption)-	ROI.IMPADP-
TOOL PROVIDER (Software vendors)	TP
TP.involvement motivations	TP.INVOL.MOT
TP.involvement evaluation	TP.INVOL.EVAL
TP.involvement impact (development)+	TP.INVOL.IMPDEV+
TP.involvement impact (development)-	TP.INVOL.IMPDEV-
TP.involvement impact (adoption)+	TP.INVOL.IMPADP+
TP.involvement impact (adoption)-	TP.INVOL.IMPADP-
TP.involvement benefits	TP.INVOL.BENE
TP.involvement challenges	TP.INVOL.CHALL
TP.adoption concerns	TP.ADPCONS
SUPPORT ACTIVITIES	SUPPACT
SUPPACT.impact (adoption)+	SUPPACT.IMPADP+
SUPPACT.impact (adoption)-	SUPPACT.IMPADP-

SUPPACT.impact (adoption decision)+	SUPPACT.IMPADPDEC+
SUPPACT.impact (adoption decision)-	SUPPACT.IMPADPDEC-
SUPPORT FROM FUNDING	SUPPFUND
SUPPFUND.impact (development)+	SUPPFUND.IMPDEV+
SUPPFUND.impact (development)-	SUPPFUND.IMPDEV-
SUPPFUND.impact (adoption)+	SUPPFUND.IMPADP+
SUPPFUND.impact (adoption)-	SUPPFUND.IMPADP-
BRAND IDENTIFICATION	BRANDID
BRANDID.impact (adoption)+	BRANDID.IMPADP+
BRANDID.impact (adoption)-	BRANDID.IMPADP-
STANDARD CHARCATERISTICS	STANCHAR
STANCHAR.relative advantage	STANCHAR.RELADV
STANCHAR.compatablity	STANCHAR.COMP
STANCHAR.complexity	STANCHAR.COMPLEX
STANCHAR.stability	STANCHAR.STAB
STANCHAR.maturity	STANCHAR.MAT
STANCHAR.impact (adoption)+	STANCHAR.IMPADP+
STANCHAR.impact (adoption)-	STANCHAR.IMPADP-
STANCHAR.impact (adoption decision)+	STANCHAR.IMPADPDEC+
STANCHAR.impact (adoption decision)-	STANCHAR.IMPADPDEC-
ORGANISATION CHRACTERISTICS	ORGCHAR
ORGCHAR.size and type	ORGCHAR.SZTY
ORGCHAR.existing infrustructure	ORGCHAR.EXINF
ORGCHAR.resource availablity	ORGCHAR.RESAVIL
ORGCHAR.organizational culture	ORGCHAR.ORGCUL
ORGCHAR.internal pressure	ORGCHAR.INTPRESS
ORGCHAR.external pressure	ORGCHAR.EXTPRESS
ORGCHAR.impact (adoption)+	ORGCHAR.IMPADP+
ORGCHAR.impact (adoption)-	ORGCHAR.IMPADP-
ORGCHAR.impact (adoption decision)+	ORGCHAR.IMPADPDECISION+
ORGCHAR.impact (adoption decision)-	ORGCHAR.IMPADPDECISION-
ORAGANIZATIONAL ADOPTION	ORGADOP
ORGADOP.motivation	ORGADOP.MOT

ORGADOP.costs	ORGADOP.COSTS
ORGADOP.costs expected	ORGADOP.COSTSEXP
ORGADOP.costs unexpected	ORGADOP.COSTSUNEXP
ORGADOP.benefits	ORGADOP.BENE
ORGADOP.barriers	ORGADOP.BARR
ORGADOP.how to overcome barriers	ORGADOP.BARROVER
ORGADOP.facilitating factors	ORGADOP.FACILFAC
ORGADOP.ROI approach	ORGADOP.ROIAPR
ORGADOP.network effects	ORGADOP.NETWORKEFFECTS
ORGADOP.ROI impact (adoption decision)+	ORGADOP.ROI.IMPADPDEC+
ORGADOP.ROI impact (adoption decision)-	ORGADOP.ROI.IMPADPDEC-
GENERAL ADOPTION	ADOP
ADOP impact+	ADOPIMP+
ADOP impact-	ADOPIMP-
Adoption concerns	ADPCONCERNS
Adoption barriers	ADPBARRIERS
Adoption facilitators	ADPFACILITATORS
Current adoption rate of the standard	CURRADOPRATE

Appendix C
Standards Questionnaire

Please answer all questions as accurately as possible by ticking the relevant box.

1. Have you been involved in the development of PLCS?

    Yes ☐   No ☐

2. Have you been involved in the implementation of PLCS?

    Yes ☐   No ☐

3. Have you been involved in the development and/or implementation of **other** data exchange standards similar to PLCS?

    Yes ☐   No ☐

4. Have you been to any pilots or launch days for **other** data exchange standards similar to PLCS?

    Yes ☐   No ☐

		Strongly Disagree	Disagree	Neither Disagree or Agree	Agree	Strongly Agree
5.	I think there are benefits in using data exchange standards like PLCS when integrating different systems	☐	☐	☐	☐	☐

		Strongly Disagree	Disagree	Neither Disagree or Agree	Agree	Strongly Agree
6.	I think there is no significant difference between the benefits of standards-based and non standards-based systems integration	☐	☐	☐	☐	☐
7.	I think it is important that systems integration is based on commonly agreed data meanings	☐	☐	☐	☐	☐
8.	I believe using standards like PLCS will limit the way I do my work	☐	☐	☐	☐	☐
9.	I think it is important to know the financial benefits of using standards like PLCS before implementing them	☐	☐	☐	☐	☐
10.	I think it is important that systems integration is based on a data exchange standard	☐	☐	☐	☐	☐
11.	I believe using standards like PLCS in systems integration is an unnecessary expense	☐	☐	☐	☐	☐
12.	I think it is important that systems integration is based on an *ISO* data exchange standard like PLCS	☐	☐	☐	☐	☐

		Strongly Disagree	Disagree	Neither Disagree or Agree	Agree	Strongly Agree
13.	I think standards like PLCS are only worth using when they are implemented using XML	☐	☐	☐	☐	☐
14.	I believe there are clear financial benefits from using data exchange standards like PLCS	☐	☐	☐	☐	☐
15.	I think standards like PLCS are not expensive to implement	☐	☐	☐	☐	☐
16.	I think it is hard to understand the benefits of data exchange standards like PLCS	☐	☐	☐	☐	☐
17.	I think data exchange standards like PLCS are complex	☐	☐	☐	☐	☐

18.   Please tick the box that best describes your managerial responsibility.

Senior/Board-level management   ☐   Other-level management   ☐   Non-managerial   ☐

19.   Please tick the box that best describes the nature of your job.

Mostly Technical   ☐   Mostly Non-technical   ☐

20.   Has your attitude towards using data exchange standards, like PLCS, been influenced by today's conference room pilot?

Yes   ☐   No   ☐

If *Yes*, are you:

More favourable   ☐   Less favourable   ☐

This is the end of the questionnaire.
Thank you for your time.

If you're interested in receiving a summary of the results please see Jo Wapakabulo.

About the Author

Josephine Wapakabulo Thomas was born in Tanzania and lived in Papua New Guinea before moving back to her home country of Uganda in 1987. In 1996, she relocated in England to attend Loughborough University where she obtained a Bachelors degree in Electronic and Electrical Engineering and Masters in IT before completing her PhD in Information Science in 2006. Since completing her PhD she has been working for Rolls-Royce in Derby, UK. She started her career in the Strategic Research Centre as a Technologist in Information Engineering, and is currently working as a Process Specialist in Information Management and Decision Support. In addition to her work at Rolls-Royce, she is a Director and Company Secretary of the Natural Computing Applications Forum.

Index